Cover:
Upper photo: Ch. Tyba Ron-Nie (reclining), owned by Mrs. Paula Lieberman and the late Mrs. Dorothy Cohen, and Karma Rus-Tilomar, owned by Paula Lieberman. Photo by Miceli Studios, Ltd. *Lower photo:* Karma Rus-Tilomar, owned by Mrs. Paula Lieberman. Photo by Miceli Studios, Ltd.

Back cover:
Three lovely Lhasas representing the Bella-Mu, Potala and Joi-San Kennels. Complete captions appear on page 96.

Frontispiece:
Ch. Tabu's King of Hearts, a magnificent Lhasa and a multiple Group winner and Register of Merit dog. He was Top Producing Stud Dog Lhasa in the *Kennel Review* magazine system for 1975, and he repeated this honor in the *Lhasa Reporter* magazine awards. He was among the Top Ten Lhasa winners in all systems for 1974, and he has sired seven champion offspring, including a Group winner. Owned and shown by Stephen G.C. Campbell, Rimar Lhasa Apso, West Trenton, New Jersey.

ISBN 0-87666-663-2

© 1977 by T.F.H. Publications, Inc. Ltd.

Distributed in the U.S.A. by T.F.H. Publications, Inc., 211 West Sylvania Avenue, P.O. Box 27, Neptune City, N.J. 07753; in England by T.F.H. (Gt. Britain) Ltd., 13 Nutley Lane, Reigate, Surrey; in Canada to the book store and library trade by Clarke, Irwin & Company, Clarwin House, 791 St. Clair Avenue West, Toronto 10, Ontario; in Canada to the pet trade by Rolf C. Hagen Ltd., 3225 Sartelon Street, Montreal 382, Quebec; in Southeast Asia by Y.W. Ong, 9 Lorong 36 Geylang, Singapore 14; in Australia and the south Pacific by Pet Imports Pty. Ltd., P.O. Box 149, Brookvale 2100, N.S.W., Australia. Published by T.F.H. Publications Inc., Ltd., The British Crown Colony of Hong Kong.

this is the
LHASA APSO

t.f.h.

joan mcdonald brearley

Table of Contents

ACKNOWLEDGMENTS
ABOUT THE AUTHOR
1. ORIGIN OF THE BREED 7
2. HISTORY OF THE BREED 15
   The First Registrations...First Lhasa at Westminster...Standard for the Breed...An Early Set-Back...Oriental Imports...End of an Era...Ming Kennels...Americal...Karma...Top Dogs in the 1950's...Top Dogs in the 1960's...The Breed's Top Brood Bitch...Lhasa in the Seventies
3. THE LHASA APSO ARRIVES IN GREAT BRITAIN........49
   Effects of World War I...New Popularity...The First Breed Club...Early Lhasa Apsos in Great Britain...The Lhasa and World War II...Championship Status Once Again...Prominent Kennels in Great Britain Today...Verles...Ramblersholt..British Champions
4. THE LHASA APSO AROUND THE WORLD.............67
   The Lhasa Apso in Australia...The Lhasa Apso in New Zealand...The Lhasa Apso in Canada...Lhasa Apsos in Other Countries...The Lhasa Apso in France...The Lhasa in Ireland...The Lhasa Apso in Germany...German Dog Shows...European Titles...The Lhasa Apso in Denmark
5. STANDARD FOR THE BREED......................102
   The United Kingdom's Description and Standard of Points...The First Standard for the Breed...A Change in Name...The European Standard...The Standard for India
6. BREED TEMPERAMENT AND CHARACTERISTICS....111
   Lhasa Coats...Lhasa Colors...Lhasa Movement...Lhasa Size...Lhasa Longevity...Muggs: The Cinderella Dog
7. THE AMERICAN LHASA APSO CLUB 127
   Lhasa Apso Specialty Clubs...Award Dinners...Club Bulletins...Lhasa Apso Publications...The United Kingdom Lhasa Apso Club
8. SOME OF THE TOP KENNELS TODAY 135
   Anbara...Barcon...Chen...Joi-San...Magestic...Nhamrhet...Norbulingka...Orlane...Potala...Rimar...Rimmon...Sheng-La...Tabu...Taglha...Tal-Hi...Tsan...Xanadu
9. GROOMING THE LHASA APSO 168
   Shedding...Bathing...Dirty Ends...Ear Care...Top Knot...
10. BUYING YOUR LHASA APSO PUPPY 175
    The Puppy You Buy...Male or Female?...The Planned Parent-

hood Behind Your Puppy...Puppies and Worms...Veterinary Inspection...The Conditions of Sale...Buying a Show Puppy...The Purchase Price...The Cost of Buying Adult Stock

11. BREEDING YOUR LHASA APSO 191
The Health of the Breeding Stock...The Day of the Mating...How Much Does the Stud Fee Cost?...The Actual Mating...Artificial Insemination...The Gestation Period...Probing for Puppies...Alerting Your Veterinarian...Labor...Arrival of the Puppies...Feeding the Bitch Between Births...Breech Birth...Dry Birth...False Pregnancy...Caesarean Section...Episiotomy...Socializing Your Puppy...Rearing the Family...Evaluating the Litter...Spaying and Castrating...Sterilizing for Health

12. TRAINING YOUR LHASA APSO 223
When to Start Training...The Reward Method...How Long Should the Lessons Be?...What You Need to Start Training...What to Teach First...The "Down" Command...The "Stay" Command...The Stand for Examination...Formal School Training...Advanced Training and Obedience Trials...Companion Dog Degree...Utility Dog Degree...Tracking Dog Degree

13. SHOWING YOUR LHASA APSO.......................235
Match Shows...Point Shows...Point Show Classes...The Prize Ribbons...Qualifying for Championship...Obedience Trials...Junior Showmanship Competition...Types of Dog Shows...Professional Handlers...The Cost of Campaigning

14. GENERAL CARE AND MANAGEMENT 253
Tattooing...Outdoor Housebreaking...Outdoor Manners...Geriatrics...Dog Insurance...Keeping Records

15. YOUR DOG, YOUR VETERINARIAN AND YOU 261
Aspirin: A Danger...What the Thermometer Can Tell You...Coprophagy...Masturbation...Rabies...Vaccinations...Snakebite...Emergencies...The First Aid Kit...How Not To Poison Your Dog...Symptoms of Poisoning...Allergies...Chewing...Bones...Hip Dysplasia

16. THE BLIGHT OF PARASITES 293
Fleas...Internal Parasites...How to Test for Worms

17. FEEDING AND NUTRITION 301
Feeding Puppies...Weaning Puppies...Feeding the Adult Dog ...The All-Meat Diet Controversy...Obesity...Orphaned Puppies...Feeding Newborn Puppies...Gastric Torsion

INDEX 318

Dedication

to

Marjorie Hackmann Blauvelt

the cousin with whom I have shared many a shaggy dog during all our childhood adventures.

Acknowledgments

The author wishes to acknowledge her sincere appreciation to those who contributed so greatly to this book. First and foremost, to Dorothy Cohen, who gave so generously of her photographs and information regarding the breed in this country; to Andre Cuny, who supplied me with so much material and so many photographs of the dogs not only in his country but also for all of Europe; to Mrs. D.M. Hesketh-Williams for her generous contribution of material and information regarding Lhasa Apsos in Britain; to Beverly Stanyon for her assistance with the Canadian fancy and for the charming story of Muggs—and most especially to Frances Sefton, who offered all the information and photographs available from her many successful years in the breed. As is their custom, the staffs of the libraries of the American Kennel Club, the American Museum of Natural History, and the 42nd Street (NYC) Library gave willingly of their time and efforts in my quest for research, Robert R. Shomer, D.V.M. gave his expert counsel and Stephen McDonald offered other special material. I would also like to thank each and every proud owner of an Apso Seng Kye for wanting to have their photographs included in this book dedicated to the glorification of this marvelous breed.

Joan Brearley
New York City, 1977

ABOUT THE AUTHOR

Joan Brearley has loved animals ever since she was old enough to know what they were. Over the years there has been a constant succession of dogs, cats, birds, fish, rabbits, snakes, turtles, alligators, squirrels, lizards, etc., for her own personal menagerie. Through these same years she has owned over thirty different breeds of purebred dogs, as well as countless mixtures, since the door was never closed to a needy or homeless animal.

A graduate of the American Academy of Dramatic Arts, Joan started her career as a writer for movie magazines, and as an actress and dancer. She also studied journalism at Columbia University and has been a radio, television and magazine writer, writing for some of the major New York City agencies.

Her accomplishments in the dog fancy include being an American Kennel Club approved judge, breeder-exhibitor of top show dogs, writer for various dog magazines, author or co-author of over a dozen breed books including *This is the Afghan Hound, This is the Shih Tzu, This is the Chow Chow, This is the Saint Bernard, This is the Bichon Frise, This is the Old English Sheepdog, This is the Siberian Husky, This is the Alaskan Malamute, This is the Irish Setter, The Wonderful World of Beagles and Beagling, The Book of the Pekingese,* as well as many others. For five years she was Executive Vice-President of the Popular Dogs Publishing Company and editor of *Popular Dogs* magazine, the national prestige publication for the dog fancy.

1: ORIGIN OF THE BREED

The Lhasa Apso as we have come to know it today traces its origin back to the land of Tibet on the Asian continent, along the northern border of India, near Mount Everest. History relates the presence as early as 800 B.C. of shaggy little dogs which were found in great numbers around the palaces and monasteries in this ancient country, referred to as "the roof of the world." This early, though vague, identification has earned our Apso the honor of being one of the oldest breeds of dog in the world.

While a prisoner in Genoa, Italy, Marco Polo dictated to Rusticiano, another prisoner, an account of his travels through the Orient. The stories of his journey constituted between eighty and ninety manuscripts, the most important of them being in the possession of the Bibliotheque Nationale in Paris; in it Marco Polo glorifies the life and times of Kublai Khan, grandson of Ghengis Khan.

It was on his return to Venice in 1294 after years of service in the court of Kublai Khan at Shangtu, not far from Peking, that he encountered the largest of the Tibetan breeds. . .the mighty Mastiffs. It is written that he obtained a couple of them for the Khan while on his travels. He claimed that they were as large as donkeys, serving as guard dogs chained outside the houses of their masters, and that he believed any two of them could finish off a lion that might invade their territory.

There were, of course, other Tibetan breeds during this early period. The medium-sized dogs of the same type were the Chow Chows, raised primarily for food; like the Lhasa Apso, the Chow Chow also carries its tail over its back and has a short snout. The toy varieties consisted of the long-haired Apsos, which were the favorite pets of the nobility and more than one Dalai Lama through the years.

As early as 1583, during the time of the Manchu Dynasty, it became the custom for the Dalai Lamas to give pairs of them to departing royalty, since it was believed that they brought all the benefits of prosperity and good luck by their mere presence. It was in this way that the Tibetan breeds found their way into China and other countries around the world. As the trade routes opened up and began to

Ch. Hamilton Chensezi (left) and Hamilton Tiny Tim, owned by Elizabeth P. Finn. The exotic aspect of the Lhasa Apso has been an important factor in bringing him to a secure place in the hearts of dog lovers.

Chs. Le and Phema, two of the earliest Apsos imported to the United States. This pair was sent to Hamilton Farms as a gift from the Dalai Lama to the Suydam Cuttings.

criss-cross the globe, the sailors and the early adventurers travelling from country to country took with them these little dogs, eventually breeding them to dogs in other lands as well.

This did not always please the Tibetans, and there are sad stories regarding the misfortunes which befell the little dogs when foreigners coerced the Tibetan natives into "giving" them dogs to take with them. The dogs were fed ground glass so that they would die enroute. Therefore it can be said that all of the Apso dogs which have survived down through the ages in places other than Tibet can be assumed to have ancestry stemming from the original Tibetan palace dogs that were given in friendship by the high potentates and were allowed to survive.

This photograph taken in the 1920's pictures an Apso Seng Kyi with a Tibetan Mastiff. Both dogs were owned by the Hon. Mrs. Bailey. Photograph courtesy of Frances Sefton.

Not all of the dogs were fortunate enough to live within the traditional home grounds of the Dalai Lama at his Potala Palace in Lhasa, the capital of Tibet, however. Many of them were destined to roam free on the streets of the small cities and villages. There were actually towns in which these dogs were bred by the residents for the specific purpose of being the indoor guard dogs for the royal palaces.

Ch. Hamilton Namsa, owned by Dorothy Benitez and bred by Mr. and Mrs. C. Suydam Cutting. Sire: Ch. Hamilton Sandupa; dam: Hamilton Dong. Namsa is another of the fine dogs bred at the Cuttings' famous Hamilton Farms. Photo by Douglas Meaney Studios.

It was from these special breeding places that not only the Dalai Lama but other wealthy Tibetans went to obtain their stock.

It must also be remembered that in those early days the term Apso was only one name which applied to these dogs. In the Tibetan language the word *Apso* means "wholly covered with hair." It is a corruption of the word "rapso," which means goat-like, thus associating the appearance of the dog with the small, long-haired Tibetan goat which it was said to resemble. The name Apso applied to all of the Tibetan breeds; Tibetan Terriers, Tibetan Spaniels, Tibetan Apsos, Lhasas, Golden Lion Dogs and Tibetan Lion Dogs. Names given to them by their owners usually included words such as *"singhi,"* which means lion, and *"singtuk,"* the Tibetan word for lion cub. Other names included Shen Trou and Talismen dogs.

This confusion was a result of the constant cross-breeding of different types and is documented in an article in the February, 1933 issue of the *American Kennel Gazette* by Margaret Hayes. She writes that she lived on the border of Tibet and became interested in all the many types, colors, sizes and the various names given to the Apso in that area. Today we have come to know each of the breeds individually, and all have very definite and distinct differences which must be adhered to according to precise Standards.

The Pekingese and the Shih Tzu have also been referred to as "lion dogs" in their native China. The Pekingese was said to have come into prominence in China only after an Apso-type dog had been around for quite some time. There are those who claim that the Chinese emperors actually used long-haired Tibetan dogs in their breeding programs to improve the coats of the Chinese breeds during the 19th Century.

Part of the visual similarity which has led to the constant and lasting comparisons between lions and Lhasas stems from the rich golden color of many Lhasas and the "mane" of thick hair around their necks, which give them their decided "lion" look. The dogs are also said to paw the ground in much the same manner as horses and lions do when they are restless or agitated. It certainly can NOT be said that the dogs ran wild with the lions down through the ages for there have never been any lions as we know them in Tibet! But it certainly can be acknowledged that these spunky, assertive little dogs have the courage of lions; their temperament and their resemblance to the king of the jungle have earned their title of Apso Seng Kye, which translated means "Bark Sentinel Lion Dog." This is their most popular name in their native land. The words *Apso Seng Kye* have

Ch. Hamilton Katha, owned by Mr. and Mrs. Tom Chenoweth and bred by Mr. and Mrs. C. Suydam Cutting. A true honey-gold, Katha has a distinguished record as a winner, which includes best of breed at the Westminster Kennel Club.

also been written *Abso Seng Kye* in modern times. Since the word for the dog in Tibet was Apso, it can be assumed that somewhere it was misspelled Abso and picked up incorrectly by others.

It is strange that since there were never any lions in Tibet, lions should be portrayed so extensively in the culture of that country. The sacred lion is found throughout much of Tibetan history and art, and lion likenesses are found on rare porcelains, friezes, murals, paintings and statuary. A pair of green lions adorns the traditional flag of Tibet. The lions appear with a yellow sun and snow-capped mountain against a field of red and blue rays.

The palace of the Dalai Lama...where it all began!

When we delve even deeper into the ancient history of Tibet we discover that the Dalai Lama's official "seat," or ceremonial chair, is referred to as "Sengti, the Lion throne." It features two lions on all of the four corners and was built according to specifications taken directly from the ancient Tibetan scriptures.

We learn further of the part the lion plays in Tibetan culture when we observe the little dog sitting at the feet of the ancient God of Learning in Ancient reproductions. The dog bears an undeniable resemblance to the Apso, and history tells us that it was believed the little dog could transform itself into a lion upon command from this God of Learning (named Manjuri Buddha) to enable him to escape in the face of any danger which might befall him in his travels.

Champion Ming Toy Nola, owned and campaigned by Anne Griffing of Mountainside, New Jersey. Nola was one of the early champions that helped to endear the breed to the fancy.

    It is also a matter of record that one of the Lama Gospels reveals in part: "The Lion is the King of Beasts. Its power of increase is without limit. Similarly it may diminish (at will) and become like unto a dog..." This would certainly complement the tale told about Manjuri Buddha and the power his little dog possessed!
    At one time it was traditional in some circles for the little dogs to have an ear pierced and a silk thread run through it and tied. Sometimes other silk thread was used, and the colors varied. More than likely the practice was the prelude to the hair on the head being tied up or pulled back while eating.
    Since the invasion of Tibet by the Communist forces in 1950, no dogs have been permitted to leave the country. The history of those which may remain, if indeed there are any at all being bred true, must remain a mystery.

In 1928 these six Lhasa Apsos, photographed in Tibet, became the property of Lt. Col. and the Hon. Mrs. Bailey. Left to right, Lhasa (a gray and white), and the golds Taktru, Droma, Tsitru, Pema and Litsi. Photo courtesy of Frances Sefton.

We can take some comfort in the thought, however, that the tradition of the Lhasa as a companion dog to priests in the monasteries is not completely lost. In Scotland two exiled Lamas and three monks maintain a small temple in the hills where they continue to follow the teachings of their Lord Buddha...but sharing their exile are no fewer than five Lhasa Apsos helping them to preserve an old tradition.

We must recognize that with the exile of the Dalai Lama into neighboring India the best of the breed went with him and that for now and on into the future, the foundation of the Lhasa Apso breed centers around his temporary base in that country. And due to the precarious world situation we must also realize that the future of the breed actually lies outside its native land; we must all rely on the ancient stock and current winners stemming from the original palace dogs to carry on the breed.

2: HISTORY OF THE BREED

Mr. and Mrs. C. Suydam Cutting of Gladstone, New Jersey, were responsible for the arrival of the Lhasa Apso in the United States, for which all of us who love the breed shall be eternally grateful!

Born in 1889, Mr. Cutting was a naturalist and friend of Colonel Theodore Roosevelt and his brother Kermit, sons of the famous United States President and big game hunter. It was in 1925 when Mr. Cutting first accompanied the two brothers on their expedition to Chinese Turkistan. The purpose of this expedition was to collect specimens of animal life for various museums here in the United States. Again in 1928 Mr. Cutting travelled along with the Roosevelt brothers to the Orient, this time in quest of the giant panda, in Chinese Tibet. In Ramona and Desmond Morris's book *Men and Pandas*, published by McGraw-Hill in 1966, there is a photograph of this 1928 expedition which includes Mr. Cutting along with the story of the intent and purpose of their search.

The Roosevelt brothers were convinced that with a pair of good bear hounds they could track down the elusive and rare panda and had agreed to shoot simultaneously in order to share the "unique honor of being the first white man to kill a giant panda." The local dogs provided by the natives were a disappointment since they were sadly lacking when it came to having a keen sense of smell. Unfortunately for pandas the expedition received help from the local Lolos (native people), and in their book titled *Trailing the Giant Panda* the Roosevelts wrote of their "triumph," since both of the shots fired by them on April 13, 1929 were effective. The skin of the giant male panda they killed was eventually stuffed and exhibited at Chicago's Field Museum.

It was on these two expeditions and subsequent trips to the Orient that Mr. Cutting's interest in Tibet was nurtured, and he made repeated attempts to visit that country, and the city of Lhasa in particular.

Not only is Tibet geographically difficult to visit, but the ever-present hostility of the natives and the rarity of audiences granted by their high chiefs were frustrating to Mr. Cutting. But after a 1930 trip Mr. Cutting managed to strike up a correspondence with His Holiness, the 13th Dalai Lama of Tibet.

Their written communications included several personal favors granted on an official government level and performed by Mr. Cutting, to the benefit of the Dalai Lama's country. Apparently all went well, for by 1931 their continued communication led to the eventual exchange of dogs that led to the establishment of the Lhasa Apso breed in this country. Mr. Cutting sent his friend, the Dalai Lama, a breeding pair of German Shepherds and a pair of Dalmations for his pleasure. In the spring of 1933 His Holiness returned the favor and sent the Cuttings a pair of Lhasa Apsos, about which he advised them to "take good care of when you receive them." To put it mildly, they were received and excellent care was given them! They were named Tarkee, a black and white, and Dinkie, a bitch "the color of raw silk," and they were to go down in history as the first Lhasa Apsos in the United States of America.

Mr. Cutting wrote a book some years later entitled *The Fire Ox and Other Years* in which this exchange of dog flesh is documented. It was fortunate timing of the royal gift, since the Dalai Lama died later that year on December 17, 1933.

Just how influential these two shaggy little dogs were in prompting the Cuttings' return to Tibet early in 1937 is open to discussion, but the Cuttings did accept an invitation to attend the 25th Jubilee of the King's Accession in Nepal extended by Lt. Colonel and Mrs. F.M. Bailey, the British Minister to Nepal and his wife. The Baileys were ardent dog lovers also and were later responsible for "launching" the breed in their native England when they returned to Great Britain. The Baileys were also the first people to register the breed by name outside of Tibet.

It was on their 1937 trip while riding along the route from India into Lhasa that Mrs. Cutting spied a very good black and white Apso. She was photographed on horseback with some of the native women, babies and Lhasas! While they were guests at the British fort in Gyantse, the Cuttings saw their first solid black Apso in the quarters of Rai Shahib Wangdi. It was during the summer when they eventually reached their destination that they met and had tea with the Regent Kashag, who was in residence at the summer palace at Norbu Linga. It was Kashag who had granted Mr. Cutting and Arthur Vernay, owner of an Apso named Lundu, permission to visit Shigatse in 1935 and at that time had extended the invitation to Mr. and Mrs. Cutting for this 1937 visit.

During their conversations the Cuttings told him that they had received some Apso dogs from the late Dalai Lama and that they were breeding them with great success at their kennel in New Jersey. As they were leaving their host promptly promised to give Mrs. Cutting

Mrs. C. Suydam Cutting and a Lhasa Apso ride horseback through a Tibetan village.

a pair of Apso dogs as a gift. The dogs of the rulers, we must remember, were never sold, only given as gifts to visiting royalty and important dignitaries. The Cuttings were delighted to be considered as such.

On the last day of their three-week visit, the Cuttings were presented with two gold-colored Apsos as promised! The little dogs and a quantity of milk to sustain them on their journey were provided and they rode out of Tibet on horseback toward a new life on another continent.

In his book Mr. Cutting described their homeward journey while documenting the remarkable aptitude of this sturdy breed. He wrote:

"...the dogs rode well, especially Tsing Tu, the female, who bounced miraculously on my wife's saddle, mile after mile. A mile and a half from every stop they would race ahead, chasing marmots."

It was these first little dogs running free in the palaces of the great dignitaries and also on the roads of old Tibet that endeared the breed to the Cuttings and formed the foundation of their Hamilton Farm Kennels line; the backbone of the breed in this country.

The Cuttings received their last Apso dogs from the 14th Dalai Lama after a visit to Kalimpong in 1950 just before the Communist invasion. Fortunately they had acquired Tundu, Tsing Tu, Le Pehma, Bidgy, Tsaring and Sarong before the Communist take-over when all communications ended, though not before the Cuttings had expressed

Hamilton Lama, owned by Mr. and Mrs. C.S. Cutting and photographed by William Brown. Circa 1940.

Ch. Hamilton Tatsienlu, sire of 11 champions and one of the original homebred stud dogs at the C.S. Cuttings' Hamilton Farms Kennels in Gladstone, New Jersey.

their gratitude by sending gifts of particular value from our Western civilization. These included a canopied chair, a set of sterling silver eating utensils, a cuckoo clock, a pair of lucite blocks with sea horses embedded in them and a horse and a pigeon made of Steuben glass. The latter two were particularly well received.

When Le and Pehma arrived in this country in 1950 they had not yet been given names. They arrived in excellent condition after having been transported first by yak from Tibet to Calcutta, India, before flying off to New York via London. They were believed to be about a year old and were introduced upon their arrival at the Hamilton Farms kennel to approximately thirty-five other Lhasas already in residence there and bringing fame to the Hamilton name and the breed.

Mr. Fred Huyler managed the kennels for the Cuttings along with an assistant, James Anderson. They, as well as the Cuttings, looked forward to the new blood which these two dogs, a male and a female, and both the desirable gold color, would introduce into the lines already established at the Hamilton kennels as well as the line they would produce when bred to each other.

THE FIRST REGISTRATIONS

The first Lhasa Apso registered with the American Kennel Club belonged to the Cuttings and was recorded in the 1935 American Kennel Club Stud Book in May of that year. Hamilton Bidgy, a bitch, and Hamilton Tsaring, a dog, were both imports. These were followed by their offspring, all bearing the Hamilton prefix, of course, and were named Tashi, whelped in 1933 and Drepung, Khampa, Lhun Po, Padmeh, Rimpochi and Sera, all from a 1935 litter. Rimpochi was the only bitch among them.

FIRST LHASA AT WESTMINSTER

During the early years in this country the Lhasa Apso was referred to as a Lhassa Terrier, and the first one was shown at the Westminster Kennel Club Show in New York City's Madison Square Garden under that name in 1934. The Cuttings were very active in the show ring and exhibited many dogs at the shows to help popularize the breed with the fancy and with the public. In 1952 at the Westminster Kennel Club show James Anderson and Ch. Hamilton Tatsienlu, one of the most famous winners during the early days, and Fred Huyler handling Ch. Pehma captured the breed wins for their owners. At the Morris and Essex Kennel Club show that same year the Cuttings' dogs accounted for eight of the nine entries. It was easy to see that their continued successes in the show ring indicated their support of the breed and as a tribute to the care and conditioning of the dogs by Fred Huyler and James Anderson.

The breed continued to attract attention and in a 1954 issue of the *New Yorker* magazine an erudite reporter made mention of the fact by writing: "Perhaps the catalogue of the Westminster show no longer bristles with as many distinguished owners' names as it once did, but recent editions of it have contained at least one name that is fully as eminent as any of its earlier entries. That is the name of the Dalai Lama of Tibet who is listed as a breeder of one of the Lhasa Apsos belonging to Mr. and Mrs. Charles Suydam Cutting. At last winter's Westminster show, the Cuttings owned twelve of the fifteen specimens of this breed that were exhibited. The Lhasa Apso, a long-haired terrier-like dog that is revered in Tibet and carried around there in the arms of noblemen to keep it from getting tired, was introduced into this country by Cutting, a wide-ranging naturalist, shortly after he visited Tibet in 1930 and became friendly with the then reign-

Two of the earliest Lhasas in America, Champion Ming Changnopa and Champion Ming Tongo, who belonged to one of the pioneers of the breed in this country. . .Judge Frank T. Lloyd, Jr., of Merchantville, New Jersey. These dogs figured prominently in the breed in the early days.

The last picture taken of Ch. Hamilton Tatsienlu who lived to be 17½ years old. He was never used at public stud but was the sire of 10 Hamilton Farm champions, the best known being Ch. Hamilton Torma, the first Best in Show Lhasa Apso in the United States. "Tats" was Best of Breed at Westminster in 1952, 1954, 1955 and 1956. Owned by Dorothy Cohen, Karma Kennels, Las Vegas, Nevada.

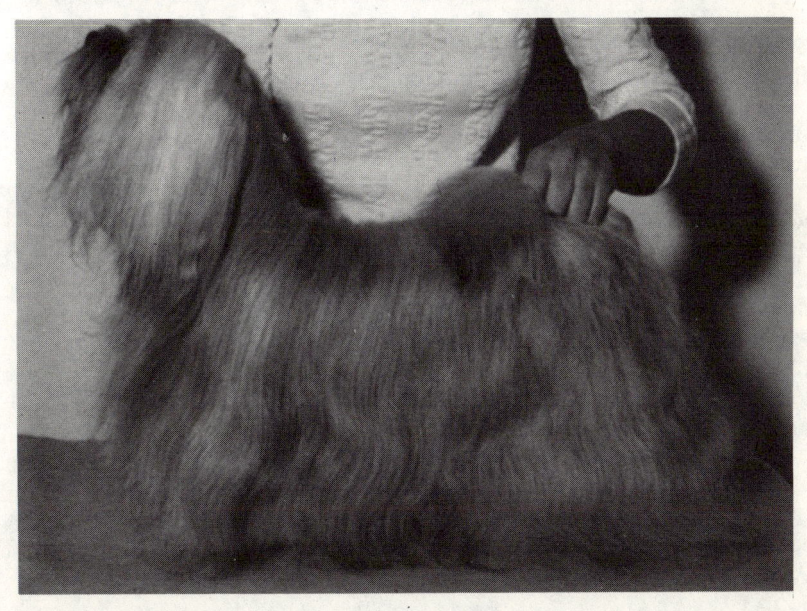

ing Dalai Lama. Cutting brought back a pair of the dogs from his trip and picked up another pair on a second jaunt, in 1935."

THE STANDARD FOR THE BREED

It was in May of 1935 that the American Kennel Club also approved the Standard for the breed. This Standard is still in effect and speaks well for the responsible breeders who adhere to it in order to preserve the original conformation and personality of the little lion dogs from Tibet.

AN EARLY SET-BACK

It was most unfortunate that in the late 1930's as the breed began to increase in popularity with imports coming in from England (where soldiers from India had introduced them) that a serious setback occurred. Six dogs imported to this country from England were registered and bred extensively here as Lhasa Apso; they were discovered to be actually Shih Tzu, and were registered as Shih Tzu in the country of their origin.

This discovery played havoc with the breeding programs in this country. However, it must be recalled that in their native land the Apso dogs were all under one classification. With this in mind, it becomes more apparent, though no less serious, how the misunderstanding between the Lhasa and Shih Tzu is one of the reasons why the Standard for these breeds are so precise today, since many of the newcomers to each breed can easily become confused.

The original confusion began in the late 1930's, before World War II, when Mr. William Patch, the son of a United Stated Commander at Pearl Harbor, purchased two long-haired dogs from the Holly Heath Kennels of Mrs. Harvey Hill in Shanghai. The dogs were represented as being two Lhasa Terriers. Named Ming Tai and Tai Ho, the two little dogs created much publicity and interest, and more dogs were imported from Mrs. Hill.

While negotiations for these imports were under way, Tai Ho whelped three bitch puppies (sired by a dog named Rags) while in quarantine in Hawaii. Rags happened to be Tai Ho's sire as well. Ming Tai and Tai Ho were litter mates sired by Rags out of a bitch named Peggy. Another of the imports, named Shanghai, was sired by Rags out of a bitch named Betty. Another imported bitch named Lhassa was by Monk and Prim, and she and Shanghai were both bred to Hamilton Sigme. The parents of these bitches is where the Shih Tzu breeding was introduced and created the problem.

It was also the breeding of Ming Tai and Tai Ho that produced the bitch, Ch. Ming Lu, which became the foundation bitch at Judge Lloyd's Ming Kennel. She was the grandmother of the celebrated early west coast winner and top producing sire, Ch. Ming Tali II, C.D. Once the mistake was discovered it was rectified in all future breed-

An important show photograph from yesteryear...judge Alfred LePine awarding Best of Breed at a Beverly Riviera Kennel Club show to Americal's Leng Kong (on the left) for a 4-point major. Kong is shown by his owner, Mrs. John Licos; on the right, the famous Hamilton Torma finishes for her championship with a 4-point major win, handled by her owner, Mrs. Marie Stillman.

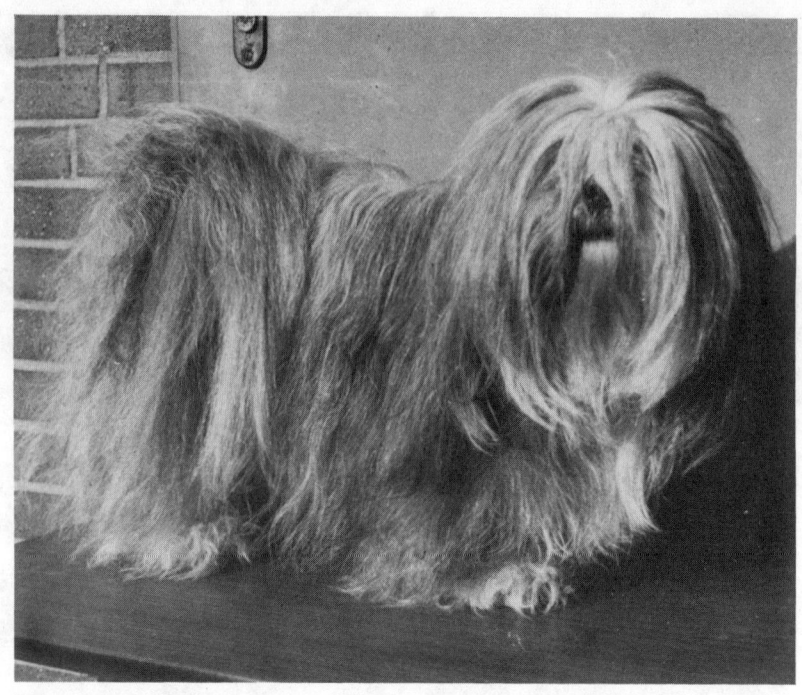

Dshomo vom Potala, bred and owned by Dr. Mary Tauber of Germany. She is a daughter of Ting-La v Boliba *ex* Krysants Lendzema.

ings, but nevertheless, the names of Shih Tzu can be found behind many of the early and best Lhasa Apso in this country. It has been a sore spot among breeders for years and no doubt will continue to be.

Many Orientals considered the controversy "much ado about nothing" since, as we have pointed out before, the Lhasa, Shih Tzu, Pekingese and all of the other Tibetan breeds were cross-bred down through the centuries in their countries, not only on the streets but among those belonging to royalty.

OTHER ORIENTAL IMPORTS

Let us not lose sight of the fact that during the 1930's and early 1940's not all of the imports came from the Dalai Lama's stock. There were some other imports from China which represented descendants of the breeding done in China within the Manchu Court with the dogs presented to them by the Dalai Lama. Others bred by the Tashi Lama, who chose to spend his exile in China, also found their way into the United States. And, of course, a few of them had been brought into the United States from Britain.

THE END OF AN ERA

After the death of his wife in 1961, Mr. Cutting decided to disperse the famous Hamilton Farm Kennels after so many years of dedication to the breed. But this was not before they had seen the breed "catch on" with the dog fancy, and had several important people attracted to them. In 1947 Hamilton Xanar was sold to a movie company and made several appearances in films. Perhaps it was these roles in the motion pictures that caught the attention of Errol Flynn, who bought Hamilton Towasg in 1950. One year later Lily Pons, the diminutive opera star, purchased Hamilton Asia. The breed continued to be adored by royalty, and also, in 1961, Mr. Cutting exported a pair of Lhasas to Mrs. Krisna Jutheesing in India. She is the younger sister of the former Indian Prime Minister Nehru.

By 1962, however, all of the Hamilton Lhasa Apso had gone to Dorothy Cohen in Las Vegas, Nevada, to carry on the Hamilton bloodlines under her famous Karma prefix.

Mr. Cutting died in 1972 still interested in the welfare and progress in the breed, and an honorary president of the American Lhasa Apso Club. Nevertheless, his demise must be acknowledged as the end of an era in the history of the breed.

THE MING KENNELS

The Ming Kennels in Merchantville, New Jersey, were owned by Judge Frank T. Lloyd, Jr. Frank Lloyd began raising Lhasas in 1943 after obtaining two from China. The first champion at the Ming Kennels was Ming Loo. She further distinguished herself by producing five champions out of two litters containing a total of five puppies.

Mr. Lloyd's Ch. Ming Chanopa was one of the first of the breed to win a Non-Sporting Group back in the early days of the breed and three of his Ming dogs won the breed at the Westminster show, Morris and Essex and Chicago International. He has produced many, many champions. Many puppies from his kennel were sold and shown all over the United States helping to establish the breed in the fancy.

There is a touching story to be told regarding Frank Lloyd's Ch. Ming Tongo. The day after Tongo finished for his championship he slipped a disc in his spine and lost the use of his back legs. Numerous veterinarians and experts gave the dog up as a hopeless cripple. But Mr. Lloyd's faithful kennel man asked if he could work with the dog to try to restore the power to the hind legs. Patiently he massaged and exercised the dog and encouraged it over many months of recovery. After two years the dog was able to reenter the show ring and was winning once again. This story not only illustrates what tender loving care can do for a dog, but makes it clear that the spirit and effort to please their owners can bring these fiesty little dogs through all sorts of adversities.

Ch. Hamilton Torma, pictured winning Best of Breed at the 1957 Westminster Kennel Club show; he went on to Group Second under judge Dr. Malcom Phelps. Torma's sire, Ch. Hamilton Tatsienlu, was Best of Opposite Sex. Torma's record for a total of 73 times shown was 60 Bests of Breed (including Westminster 1957 and 1958), 35 Group placements, nine Group Firsts, second in the Group at Westminster in 1957, and Best in Show under Maurice Baker in October, 1957. Torma was also Best Opposite Sex 12 times. Owned by the Alfred Stillmans of California.

Americal's Amo, owned by Mr. and Mrs. Sheldon Benston, pictured winning at a show.

AMERICAL

Marie Stillman became interested in the Lhasa Apso in the early 1950's. She purchased the famous Best in Show Champion Hamilton Torma from the Cuttings in 1953, shortly after she won Winners Bitch at the Westminster Kennel Club Show. Torma was just a little over one year of age at the time, having been whelped on February 6, 1952.

Torma was shown 73 times and won the breed 60 times with 35 Group Placings. But it was on October 26th, 1957 that she made breed history by becoming the first Lhasa Apso to win an all-breed Best in Show. This was at the Twin Cities Kennel Club Show in Yuba City, California under judge Maurice Baker. Handled by Mitch Wooten, this marvelous 16-pound red-gold bitch truly brought fame to the breed.

Torma was not only a marvelous show dog, but an excellent brood bitch as well. Her son, Ch. Americal's Torma Lu, owned by

Best of Breed at the 1958 Westminster Kennel Club show was Ch. Hamilton Torma, owned by Marie Stillman of Beverly Hills, California. Handled by Mitch Wooten.

Ch. Americal's Torma La, pictured winning Best of Breed at the 1962 Sacramento Kennel Club show. Frank Sabella handled for owner Marie Stillman.

Dorothy Benitez, won the Breed and Group Fourth at the 1965 Westminster Kennel Club Show. Torma had won the Breed and 2nd in the Group at the 1957 show. Torma's grandson, Ch. Licos Kulu La, owned and bred by Grace Licos and handled so beautifully by Maxine Beam, was the second Lhasa Apso to win a Best in Show. Kulu La was out of Ch. Americal's Rika, a bitch from Torma's first litter.

Marie Stillman's kennel was founded on the Hamilton stock and her name, as well as the name of her kennel, will always be remembered for the quality dogs they produced, and as an integral part of the history of this breed in America. Their contribution has been great and their name respected both then and now.

KARMA

The names of Dorothy and Sammy Cohen of Las Vegas, Nevada, were first known and associated with the Poodle breed. They had two poodles before their first Lhasa Apso, Mula, joined them and piqued their interest in this rare oriental breed.

It was Christmas Eve, 1956, when the Cohens met a plane from New York City bringing them the five-month-old Hamilton Karma, a bitch destined to bring fame to the Cohens and to the breed and that was Mrs. Cohen's Christmas present from her husband. Before they had left the airport carrying their newest treasure three servicemen had approached them and remarked about the dog, recognizing it after their tours of duty in the Far East.

Karma, the name they adopted as their official kennel prefix in honor of their new show girl, finished for her championship in four consecutive shows at the age of eight months. So enchanted were the Cohens with their latest acquisition that they made a special trip back east to Gladstone, New Jersey, to buy some more Lhasas from the Cuttings' Hamilton Farms Kennels. They returned with Hamilton Tan-La and Hamilton Garba, litter brother and sister out of a Ch. Hamilton Kalon and Hamilton Samada mating. Tang-La finished his championship at just over a year of age, and Garba finished not long after that under the ownership of Mrs. Isabelle Lloyd.

After a show career that was highly successful, Karma was taken back to be bred at Hamilton Farms during her third season. The stud chosen was Ch. Hamilton Kung. Their first litter produced Karma Getson who finished for his championship at 10 months of age. He was also a Group winner and top Apso in the country for 1959. Another puppy from this same litter, Karma Sangpo, had already won her Mexican championship and finished for her American title a day after Getson. Karma Lobsang finished at 13 months and Karma Gyapso, a fourth puppy in the first litter, went on to win four Groups in her brief ring career.

Another Lhasa, Licos Nimu-La finished for her championship also and Karma's Best of Opposite Sex win in 1959 at the Westminster Kennel show on their first trip to New York City was all they needed to encourage additional breeding at their fast-growing kennel. Yet another trip was made to the Hamilton Farms in Gladstone, just before the 1961 Westminster show. Dorothy Cohen returned to Nevada with Hamilton Shi-Pon, Hamilton Chang-Tru, and Hamilton Zig-Tru. A new larger house to accommodate more dogs, and an urge to breed these delightful dogs prevented Dorothy Cohen from doing too much showing, but the new owners of the Karma dogs carried on in the show ring successfully during this period.

Sam Cohen, an ardent baseball fan, travelled East for the World Series each year, and it became the custom for the Cohens to also pay a visit to Hamilton Farms. By 1962 they had 28 Lhasas in residence

Ch. Hamilton Sandupa, one of Hamilton Farm Kennels' top sires and later a top sire at Dorothy Cohen's Karma Kennels. Sandupa is photographed here at 12 years of age. His litter sister, Ch. Hamilton Katha, was a multiple Group winner. The sire was Ch. Hamilton Tatsienlu.

Two cute puppies from Dorothy Cohen's Karma Kennels: Ch. Karma Luntse, a Group Winner in Canada, with a litter sister named Ch. Karma Talung.

and after their visit to Hamilton Farms on this occasion they returned home with Mr. Cutting's entire kennel of 31 dogs. Mrs. Cutting had died and assistant kennel manager Fred Anderson had died also, and Mr. Cutting could think of no better hands in which to place their treasured stock than those of Dorothy Cohen. The Cohens purchased the entire stock of Apsos from the ages of three weeks to 13 years of age.

That year they saw only one game of the World Series; the rest of their 10-day vacation was spent making arrangements for the shipping of the dogs to Las Vegas. And upon their return—plans for a new and larger Karma Kennel! Sam Cohen, who was owner of the Santa Anita Race Book in Las Vegas, was quoted as saying, in the August 4, 1966 issue of the *New York Times*, that "My wife's Karma Kennels is probably the only one in the world in which horses support the dogs." It was the largest kennel in the world devoted to the breed. The kennel, also called Pet Town, U.S.A., contained air-conditioning as well as 42 runs, measuring 30 feet outdoors and 22 feet inside. There were play areas surrounding the 50-foot main building and a marvelous climate for the dogs' good health and well-being.

By this time Ch. Hamilton had been retired to rest on her laurels and watch all her offspring "do their thing" in the show ring. In 1966 the breeding at Karma was somewhat curtailed and the family moved to a private breeding site. However, serious and prolonged illness curtailed plans even further and once again the show honors must be won by those owning the Karma puppies. But we cannot speak of the fabulous Karma Kennels and their record number of champions without giving credit where credit is due. It was the dedication and high principles of Dorothy Cohen which made her kennel so successful and for which all of us who are interested in this breed will always owe a debt of gratitude. For it was Dorothy Cohen who wrote:

"Many are interested in breeding and exhibiting dogs. It is a very interesting hobby. I am interested in preserving from extinction possibly one of the oldest breeds to man; known a few years ago as Tibetan Lhassa Apso, rare then and rare now. Since the invasion of Tibet by the Chinese, the monasteries where these had been raised for centuries have been looted, many destroyed. The dogs cannot be duplicated or replaced from Lhasa or all of Tibet. What we have of Tibetan origin now is all we are destined to ever have. Breeders are needed that will continue and preserve this line for posterity. Another Karma? Impossible! But a reasonable facsimile if you're lucky!"

With this idyllic premise as a guide it is little wonder that Karma Kennels produced over 50 champions and on that fateful day in 1962 was entrusted with the heritage Hamilton Farms had produced and designated to carry it on in the many years to come...

The following names of magnificent Lhasa Apsos represent the names of the champions finished by the Karma Kennel or by the lucky owners who purchased one of Dorothy Cohen's dogs:

Ch. Hamilton Karma winning Best of Breed at the 1959 Westminster Kennel Club show. Handled by Frank Sabella for owner Mrs. Dorothy Cohen, Karma Kennels, Las Vegas, Nevada.

CH. HAMILTON KARMA
CH. HAMILTON TANG-LA
CH. KARMA GETSON (Group Winner)
CH. KARMA SANGPO (Amer. & Mex. Ch.)
CH. LICOS NIMU-LA
CH. KARMA LOBSANG
CH. KARMA GYAPSO (Group Winner)

CH. KARMA KUSHOG
CH. KARMA KANJUR
CH. HAMILTON TSO-TRU
CH. AMRICAL'S LHA LU
CH. HAMILTON DUL-TRU II
CH. MILBRYAN KARMA VEGAS
CH. KARMA NAROPA
CH. KARMA AMI-CHIRI
CH. KARMA DMAR-PO

CH. KARMA FROSTY KNIGHT
  (9 BIS)
CAN. CH. KARMA LUNTSE
CH. KARMA KANDO
CH. KARMA KARKA-TA
CH. KARMA BENES CHUNG
  KING
CH. KARMA SKAR-CEN
  (Group Winner)
CH. KARMA RUS-TI (Group
  Winner)
CH. KARMA CRICKET PUFF
CH. KARMA ZINGA
CH. KARMA TALUNG
CH. KARMA KAN SA
CH. KARMA ATISHA
CH. KARMA TAKALA
CH. KARMA LINGTAM (Group
  Winner)
CH. KARMA RUS-TI CAESAR
CH. KARMA JA-LU
CH. KARMA BIDANG
CH. KARMA RUB-TA-JAH OF
  GOLD
CH. KARMA CIU-RI
CH. KARMA GHIN-GER
CH. KARMA MUFFIN OF
  NORBULINKA
CH. KARMA KUBLA KHAN
CH. KARMA RUS-TIGU (Group
  Winner)

CH. KARMA RUS-TIMPA
CH. KARMA BYA NAG
CH. KARMA RUS-TILOTA
CH. KARMA RUS-TIKULI
CH. KARMA RUS-TILOPA
  (Group Winner)
CH. KARMA RUS-TIMAR BAR
CH. KARMA RUS-TIMALU
CH. KARMA RUS-TILOLO
CH. KARMA RUS-TIMANTRA
CH. KARMA RUS-TIMALA
CH. KARMA CHANG-TRU
CH. KARMA BANDIDO
CH. KARMA CHANG PO
CH. KARMA JO-BO
CH. KARMA TEN-ZING (Group
  Winner)
CAN. CH. KARMA DAWA
CH. KARMA SANPO
CH. KARMA TSUNG
CH. KARMA CHANGNOPA
CH. KARMA SAKYI
CH. KARMA CHA
CH. KARMA MA KILI
CH. KARMA KASHA
CH. KARMA FROSTINA
CH. KARMA RGYAL PO-CHAN
CH. KARMA RUMTEK
CH. KARMA LOLOKO

Opposite, upper photo:
A magnificent portrait of Dorothy Cohen's famous Ch. Karma Getson in full coat at the height of his show ring career. The Karma Kennels are in Las Vegas, Nevada.

Opposite, lower photo:
Ch. Karma Ka-Sha groomed and in full coat for the show ring. Bred by Dorothy Cohen and owned by Joan Pettit of Mio Lhasa Apso, Woodmere, Long Island, New York. Ka-Sha was photographed in November, 1974.

35

Champion Karma Rus-Timala, ROM, dam of six champions (including Ch. Rimmon Ripsnorter, a Best of Breed Specialty winner), is pictured winning at a recent show under judge Edd Bivin. Handled by Jeri Cates for owner Lois M. Magette, Long Beach, California.

Ch. Karma Lobsang, an early Lhasa Apso, bred and owned by Dorothy Cohen, Karma Kennels, Las Vegas, Nevada. Bennett photo.

Ch. Karma Rus-Ti pictured during his ring career on the East coast in the 1960's with handler Jane Kamp Forsyth. Owned and bred by Dorothy Cohen, Karma Kennels, Las Vegas, Nevada.

On the right, judge Louis Murr awards Best of Breed at the 1959 Harbor Cities Kennel Club show to Ch. Karma Getson, handled by George Payton, and Best of Opposite Sex to Getson's dam, handled by the owner of both dogs, Dorothy Cohen of Las Vegas, Nevada.

The Karma Lhasa Apso kennels are no longer actively breeding. After a 20-year period of producing quality dogs Dorothy Cohen is content to let others carry on with this end of the fancy while she graciously offers to support in any way possible those still carrying on in the breed.

TOP DOGS IN THE 1950'S

An indication of the progress being made within a breed can pretty much be determined by the number of entries which can be found in the catalogues of some of the major dog shows around the country. Morris and Essex, of course, was considered to be one of the biggest and one of the most prestigious, and the first appearance of the Lhasa Apso drew an entry of eight in 1936.

1939 and 1940 drew 18 for each year. Most of these represented dogs from the Cuttings' Hamilton Farms Kennels. It was only after 1952 that enough interest had been aroused to show the breed being campaigned by those fanciers that had either purchased dogs from the Cuttings to exhibit themselves, or purchased show dogs from those who had bought their stock from the Cuttings.

The 1951 Westminster Kennel Club catalogue had an entry of 17 Lhasas being listed in the Terrier Group. In addition to the 17 in the championship classes there was a brace and a team entered also. The Cuttings took a full page ad in the catalogue to further promote their dogs and to encourage new ownership.

Among the entries at this show was a dog named Thic Hai, which the catalogue revealed was whelped in 1949 and listed as being bred by the Thurbo Tea Estate in Darjeeling, India, owned by the Riberbend Kennels.

TOP DOGS DURING THE 1960'S

By the mid-1960's there were ten Lhasa Apsos represented in the Phillips System that were magnificent representatives of the breed. Number one on the list was Ch. Kham of Norbulingka, a beautiful dog that did a lot of winning and was highly thought of by all. Kham was retired in 1967.

The second ranking dog was Ch. Kyi Chu Shara, three was Ch. Drax Ni Ma Me, four, Ch. Tsans Drima, five, Ch. Karma Rus Ti, six was Ch. Sivas Vishnu, seven was Victor Cohen's Group-winning Ch. Cherryshores Bah Bieh Boy, eight, Ch. Teako of Abbotsford, nine, Ch. Gyal Kham Nag of San Jo, and ten was Ch. San Saba Singh Sabba.

Mrs. Josephine Johns of Lansing, Michigan owned Ch. Cherryshores Cha Cha Cha; Ann Hoffman came into the breed in the mid-60's, and Geraldine Baker of Eaton, Ohio, was also exhibiting the breed. Ann Hoffman and Marlene Annunziata co-owned Ch. Kasha's Tsonya of Tal-Hi, which Marlene bred.

Late in 1969 the American Lhasa Apso Club held a match show which drew an entry of 108! The judge was the noted Asian authority on Tibetan culture, Mr. George Montgomery. Mr. Montgomery, a poet, a former director of Asia House Museum in New York City and the Museum of American Folk Art, has traveled all through the Orient and was an excellent choice to pass judgement on the Asian dogs presented to him. This Match Show was dedicated to the memory of the late Robert B. Griffing.

Al Likewise, President of the Club, delivered a eulogy praising Mr. Griffing's pioneering in the breed and his constant devotion to Lhasas. It was a solemn and fitting tribute to both Bob and Anne who has carried on a more restricted basis since Bob's death. Mr. Montgomery's selection on this memorable occasion was the Stangs' golden puppy Chu-Shu's Dick Lionheart, winner of Best Puppy, Best Junior Puppy and Best in Match awards!

It was Bob and Anne Griffing who were two of the breed's earliest and greatest supporters. They bought their original stock from Judge

Lloyd back in 1950, and these dogs were bred to the Cuttings' Hamilton lines. It was Anne and Bob who were first to win two Non-Sporting Groups for the breed on the East Coast and did much to encourage newcomers in the breed.

The Griffings were among the first in the parent club, and while the first Match Show put on by the club was held at the Cuttings', the next nine were held on the grounds at the Griffings' home in Mountainside, New Jersey. After these first 10 matches, the entries became so large that public facilities had to be taken to accommodate the entries.

The Griffings had Boston Terriers before getting into Lhasas and Bob became a judge of Bostons and later many other breeds as well. He and Anne both have always been very active in the Stewards Club of America and the Lhasa Club, where Bob served as a past President and Anne as Secretary. Their knowledge and support added to the benefits offered by the breed club.

The top-producing bitch in the breed during her time... Berano's Nah-Ni-Soo, owned by the Berano Kennels in Hickory Hills, Illinois. Her sire was Cherryshores Nah Tsot *ex* Ch. Cherryshores Ting a Ling.

THE BREED'S TOP BROOD BITCH

By the end of the 1960's the breed had produced a bitch worthy and qualified to appear in the Phillips System Top Sires and Dams listings. Bitches in each breed must produce at least three or more champions during the preceding one year period in order to qualify. In Lhasas it was Berano's Nah-Ni-Soo, owned by Bea and Ralph Gutelius, Berano Kennels in Hickory Hills, Illinois.

The three champions, Ch. Berano's Moiki-Tsu, owned by Elsie Dunkle, and Ch. Bernano's Li-Tsu and Ch. Berano's Hop-Sun-Tsu, were all from her first litter. Another bitch from her second litter just needed a second major to finish or it would have been four champions for her in 1969! Not only did her three finish for their championships, but won many Bests of Breed and Group Placements as well.

Opposite:
Ch. Hamilton Jimpa and his daughter, Ch. Tsan's Datso. Ch. Jimpa started life as a personal favorite of Mrs. C.S. Cutting. Then he was sold to LaVerne Payton with the understanding that he be bred to all available quality bitches on the West Coast to help establish the true Lhasa type. Over a ten-year period Jimpa was to produce 12 champion sons and daughters, 43 champion descendants altogether, including five Group winners and three Best in Show winners, among whom Ch. Kyi Chu Friar Tuck won 15 Bests in Show during his ring career. LaVerne Payton's Tsan's Kennels are in Covington, California.

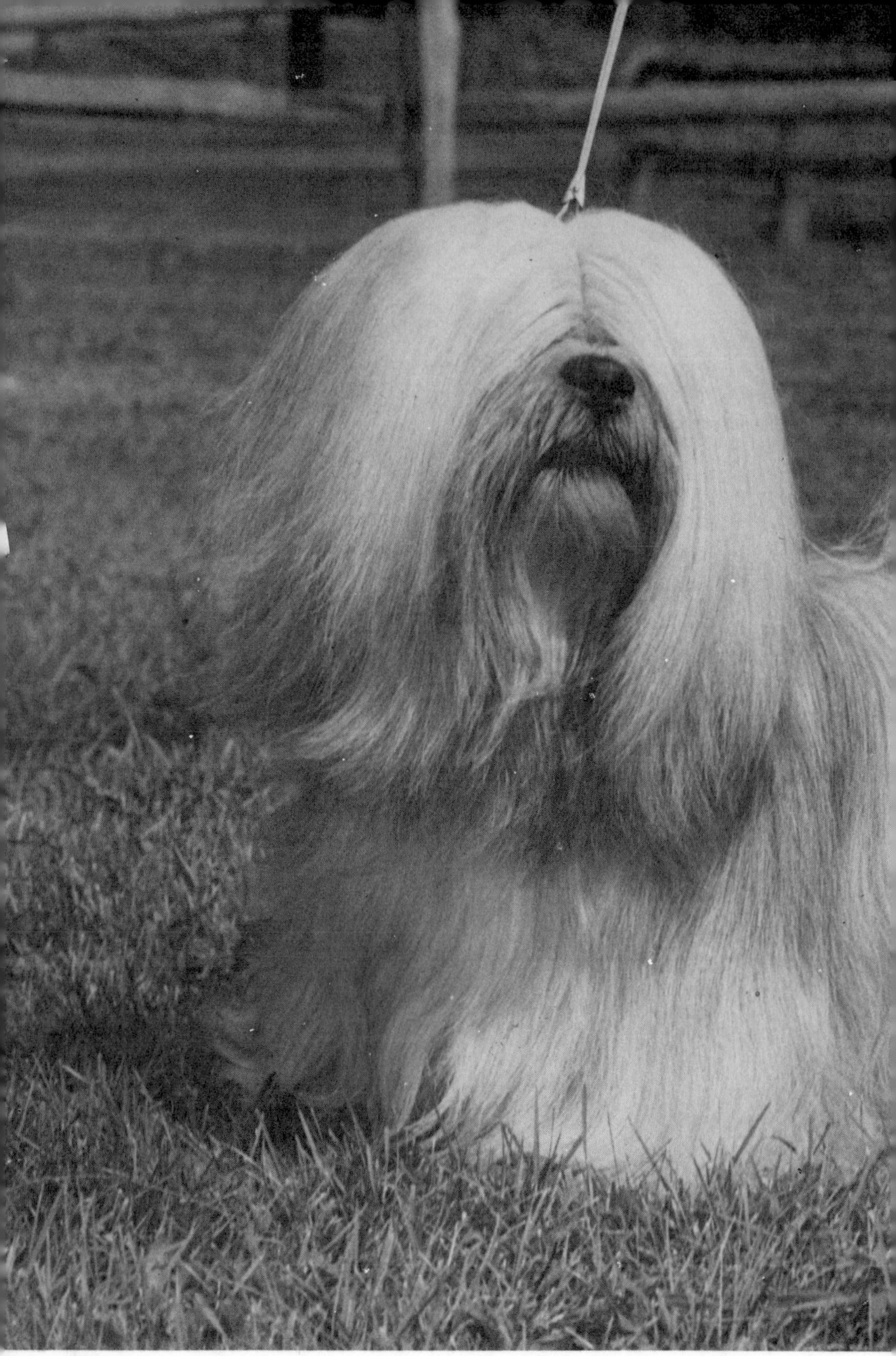

The famous Best in Show winner, Ch. Tibet of Cornwallis, ROM, whelped in March, 1966, and sire of 28 champions as of November, 1975. Among his get is the multiple Best in Show winner, American and Bermudian Ch. Kinderland's Tonka, the top-winning Lhasa bitch in the history of the breed. Tibet is owned by Norman and Carolyn Herbel, Tabu Kennels, Lucas, Kansas.

American, Canadian and Bermudian Ch. Ku Ka Boh of Pickwick, Best in Show-winning Lhasa, pictured winning the Breed at the 1970 Lehigh Valley Kennel Club show under judge Clark C. Thompson. He is the sire of Ch. Kinderland's Zimba, a Group winner from the classes. Owner-handled by Carolyn Herbel, Tabu Kennels, Lucas, Kansas.

LHASAS IN THE SEVENTIES

The Lhasa Apso is an oriental breed and 1970 was the Chinese Year of the dog!

By the beginning of 1970 Lhasa Apsos were not only a popular breed, but were holding their own in the Non-Sporting Group as winners in the show rings. Ch. Kyi Chu Friar Tuck, owned by Marvin Frank of Norwalk, Connecticut, and beautifully presented and handled in the ring by Robert Sharp, finished up the 1969 show season as #1 Lhasa Apso in the nation and #6 of all Non-Sporting dogs according to the Phillips System ratings in *Popular Dogs* magazine.

This win represented a total of 8,655 points garnered from the winning of four Bests in Show, 28 Fourth Firsts, 21 Group Seconds, 10 Group Thirds and five Group Fourths.

Carolyn Herbel was the proud owner of both the #2 and the #5 Lhasas in the Top Ten competition with her Ch. Ku Kah Boh of Pickwick which was handled by Jane Kay while she herself was campaigning Ch. Tibet of Cornwallis to his #5 position. While Ku Ka Boh did not win a Best in Show in 1969 he did win 11 Group Firsts and 27 other Group Placements for a total of 3,273 Phillips System points. Tibet captured a single Best in Show win with two Group Firsts and 12 Group Placements.

Other Top Show winners that were winning at the beginning of the 1970's were Ch. Karma Frosty Knight o'Everglow, owned by M. Aspurus and A. Rossie of Florida, and winner of two Bests in Show during 1969; Ch. Orlanes Good As Gold, owned by Mrs. W. Kendall; Ch. Karma Rus Tigu, owned by Mrs. Dorothy Cohen of Las Vegas; and Ch. Pan Chen Tonka, owned by Mrs. B. Finigan of San Francisco. Frosty came into the show ring in the 1970's as the #3 Lhasa the previous year, while Gold was #4, Rus Tigu #6, and Tonka #7. Ch. Kambu Kyimo Tessa, owned by M. Hagemeier of St. Louis, Ch. Teako of Abbotsford, owned by the J. Roberts of Canada, and Ch. Stonewalls Gung Ho, owned by C. Ellsworth of Oconomowoc, Wisconsin were numbers eight, nine and ten in the ratings for the top ten show dogs in the nation.

By the time of the American Lhasa Apso Club Specialty Show in May of 1970, Pat Chenoweth's Ch. Chen Korum Ti was the Best in Show winner at this important event. Pat had come East for the show and watched Bob Sharp pilot Kori to this coveted win under judge Cyril Bernfeld over an entry of 114. It was a good day for Pat in other categories as well. Her Chen Hapi Nu Yer, co-owned with Lila Kaiser, was Reserve Dog, and her Chen Tompar Nor, co-owned with her husband Tom, won the Futurity! It was also the occasion of the first presentation of the Robert Griffing Memorial Trophy for Best of Winners.

Trophy Chairman Allan Lieberman had a fabulous array of trophies for the winners, including a magnificent silver wine cooler for Best of Breed offered by none other than Mr. Charles Suydam Cutting. Ruth Deck was the President of the Club during this first year of the important decade of the 1970's, and Anne Griffing Corresponding Secretary, Cheryl Hueneke, Secretary, and Mrs. Dorothy Benitez, Treasurer. The day this Specialty was held was extremely cold, wet and windy, but the sun broke through for the Parade of Champions following the Best of Breed judging and it was a beautiful sight to see.

Parading around the ring were Ch. Ku Ka Boh of Pickwick, owned by Dorothy Herbel, Ch. Kyi Chu Inshallah, owned by Ruth Smith, Ch. Chin Chu of Emberheights, owned by Marieanne Decker, Ruth Fairfield's Ch. Kinderland's Nichola, the Sledziks' Ch. Pon Go's Chi Kha, Peg Chenoweth's Ch. Chen Nyun-Ti, and her Chen Krisna Nor, co-owned by her with Wendy Harper, Marvin Franks' Ch. Ky Chu Friar Tuck, Allan Lieberman's Ch. Tyba Le of Ebbtide, and Helen Werner's Ch. Fu Yan of Yoshi. Each and every one a beautiful representative of the breed and excellent example of what had been winning in the breed during the 1960's.

Proof of the exceptional quality in the breed by the beginning of the 1970's was borne out by no less an authority than judge Anna Katherine Nicholas. In her column in the special Non-Sporting issue of *Popular Dogs* in August, 1970, she wrote:

"Two of the breeds which I have found especially exciting during this past decade are the Lhasa Apsos and the Chows. My entries in them have invariably been filled with quality, and they have brought before me some of the most glorious dogs I've had the pleasure of judging.

"How well I recall the first time I saw Friar Tuck! It was, I believe, at the Bronx, and I know that it was one of my earliest Lhasa assignments. I simply could not take my eyes off this stunning little dog from the moment that he entered my ring! He was young and immature and not half the superb showman that he is today. But there he stood, just starting toward titular honors, and simply to LOOK at him made one's heart beat faster. His win that day was one of his earliest.

"Another dream of a Lhasa to which I awarded high placement in the 1963 Westminster Non-Sporting Group was Ch. Licos. Mrs. Grace Licos owned this gorgeous dog, which was sensationally beautiful in every feature. He was unforgettable, and his loss at an early age a tragic one, indeed, for the breed.

"Ch. Kham of Norbulingka I have admired from ringside on various occasions. What a dog! Ch. Tibet of Cornwallis I have judged with pleasure and think extremely handsome. Ch. Licos Namni La is a favorite bitch of mine, has been Best of Breed under me, and is a VERY worthy Lhasa.

"I have been thrilled at the number of truly splendid young class dogs and bitches which have gained points towards their titles under me during 1969 and early 1970!"

The first half of the 1970's saw several well-established Lhasa kennels doing well for the breed from coast-to-coast. Sharon Rouse's Sharbo Kennels were active in San Ramon, California. In Florida Winifred Drake was breeding and selling puppies at her Drax Kennels in Hialeah, and Mrs. Maise Boyer was breeding and offering stud service at her House-Boy's Kennels in Abilene, Kansas. The same

Ch. Chig Shatta, owned by Mrs. Anna Griffing of Mountainside, New Jersey, and dam of her famous show winner Ch. Chig-Jo-Mo. A William P. Gilbert photograph.

was true at the Ricefield Kennels in Westwood, Massachusetts. Phyllis Marcy and Norbulingka dogs were still winning handsomely, and the name of Dorothy Cohen and Karma Kennel dogs were frequently the center of conversation wherever and whenever Lhasa people congregated, just as the names of Rudy and Dorothy Benitez and Daisy Fraiser's Lost Horizon Kennels are mentioned.

In the New York-New Jersey metropolitan area there are several other active kennels producing quality contenders for the show ring, like the Griffings in Mountainside and Ruth Deck in Dover, New Jersey. In Pennsylvania, Keke Blumberg had established her Potala Kennels in Rydel, and Jim and Elsie Dunkle were celebrating the championship wins of their first Lhasa, Berano's Moki Tsu, which had also placed Second in a Group on the way to his championship.

Mr. Robert Griffing, one of the earliest pioneers in the breed on the East Coast. The highly respected Mr. Griffing was a former American Lhasa Apso Club president and prominent judge. Unfortunately, Mr. Griffing was killed in an automobile accident on the way home from a dog show where he had been judging Lhasa Apsos.

Early in the 1970's they were again campaigning their Dunklehaven Ama Lil Boi, Berano's Taji O'Dunlehaven and Dunklehaven Ama Guh Gurl.

Catalogues representing the hundreds of shows held each year present an amazing array of names of Lhasa Apsos that we can all be proud of. We have come a long way in less than half a century. As this book goes to press we are still several years away from the decade of the 1980's, but the future of the breed will depend on the quality of the dogs we are producing in this decade. In Chapter 8 I present an alphabetical listing of some of the more prominent and active kennels of today where the dedicated breeders are planning to carry on the breed to even greater heights of glory in the years to come.

3: THE LHASA APSO ARRIVES IN GREAT BRITAIN

As early as 1901 Miss Marjorie Wild owned a Lhasa Apso. It was a black and white dog, bred by the Hon. Mrs. McLaren Morrison and living to be 18 years, full proof of the reports of their sturdy constitutions. Additional Lhasa Apsos, originally known as Lhassa Terriers, were brought into England in 1904 by members of the Younghusband Exploratory Expedition. One of the members of this expedition was Lt. Colonel F.M. Bailey, who was in later years to become very influential in the breed.

During its earliest days in Great Britain around the turn of the century, efforts were being made to gain recognition for the Lhasa Terriers. In 1901 Lionel Jacob was writing a Standard for the breed and in 1902 the Rev. H.W. Bush was working toward Kennel Club acceptance as a separate classification for the Lhasa Terrier, while going on record as drawing a distinction between two sizes of the Lhasa Terrier; one averaging 14" inches in height and a smaller version of the same dog standing 10" at the withers.

Prior to World War I two classes were held at the Cheltenham-Gloucestershire Championship Show where the Lhasa Terriers actually competed for championships. A Tibetan import named Rupso was the most talked about dog of oriental heritage at that time and became the first Tibetan breed of dog to attain championship. He was imported from Shigatse in 1907 by Mrs. E.G. Webster. After his death in 1917 he was stuffed and is displayed at the British Museum in Tring, Hertfordshire. Rupso was a black dog, and won the breed honors for four consecutive years, 1908 through 1911, at the Ladies Kennel Association show.

THE EFFECTS OF WORLD WAR I

World War I took its toll on this relatively new breed to Britain and several years after the end of the war the Lhasa became almost extinct. The few imports, mostly from India, were not typical. They varied greatly in size and type and added little but new blood to the strains which had been on the way to an established breed prior to the war. It wasn't until 1928 when the Baileys returned to England from Tibet with six small dogs which could be called Lhasa Apso in the true sense of the word.

After the Younghusband expedition in 1904 Lt. Colonel and Mrs. F.M. Bailey had resided in Gyantse where he was a British Trade Agent from 1905 through 1909. In 1921 he took over the duties of Sir Charles Bell as British Political Officer for Sikkim, Tibet and Bhutan. It was during this period that he made many significant discoveries in the world of insects and plant life as well as becoming involved with the shaggy little dogs indigenous to that country.

It began when the Honorable Mrs. Bailey was presented with her first Apsos by Colonel R.S. Kennedy of the Indian Medical Service in 1922. Colonel Kennedy had been presented with the dogs by a patient, Tsarong Shope, the Commander-in-Chief of the Tibetan Army. These

In 1928 these two Lhasa Apsos were imported to England from Tibet by Mrs. Bailey. Their names are Taktru and Droma. Photo courtesy of Frances Sefton.

little dogs were named Sangtru and Apso. The Baileys also borrowed a bitch named Demon from a Tibetan Army officer and began breeding.

When Colonel Bailey visited Lhasa in 1924 they added to their stock and bred litters which consitituted the stock they brought home to Britain with them in 1928. In succeeding years others were brought back to England by other military men who had served in the Orient and by dog lovers and wealthy dignitaries who had seen them and had been presented with them during their travels.

The Lhassa Apso, as the name was spelled in Great Britain at one time, once again made its appearance in the show ring after World War I. It was at a member's show of the Ladies Kennel Association in November, 1929. In 1933 the first class for Apsos was held by the W.E.K.S. Championship Show. Listed under a "Tibetan Breeds" classification were dogs regarded as Lhassa Terriers, Tibetan Terriers and Lhassa Apsos. There was a time when the British referred to the Lhasa as a Tibetan Apso. Today they have at last settled the matter by narrowing down the varieties into three categories: Tibetan Terrier, Shih Tzu and Apso!

It is worth mentioning that the Tibetan breeds did cause great confusion in Britain. Edward C. Ash, a famous dog man, wrote in his book, *The Practical Dog Book*, published in 1930, about his own doubts on the proper category for them within the fancy. He stated: "It is difficult to know where to place these dogs. In type they resemble the Old English Sheepdog, so I am placing them here, merely on such superficial resemblance."

He also listed them in his book as Lhassa Terriers, and spelled Tibet "Thibet" when writing about their ancestry there. He further revealed their use in "Thibet" as guard dogs and wrote that they supplied the "Thibetans" with their clothing since during the hot weather the dogs were shorn just as the sheep were in England and their hair was woven into cloth.

When writing about the coloration he explained that the Tibetans preferred the pure white dog, or pure black, and the nearer the dog approached those colors the more valuable it was. Most of the dogs, he claimed, were red and white, black and white, gray and white, and great numbers of them were gray and "of a somewhat bluish shade."

NEW POPULARITY

Following their appearance in the show ring again their popularity began to rise once more. The fanciers began to show interest in importing and breeding. But it was a slow process since the dogs were still not for sale in their homeland as we mentioned before, and it was not feasible for devotees of the breed to travel to the orient in order to ingratiate themselves with the royalty in order to receive them as gifts!

THE FIRST BREED CLUB

Mrs. W.D.S. Brownrigg, who chose to refer to the dogs as Tibetan Lion Dogs, was one of the breed's first and staunchest supporters, and founded the specialist club for Apsos. The organization was registered with the Kennel Club on the 19th of December, 1933. A Tibetan breeds Association was formed in 1934 by Colonel and Mrs. Bailey and many of the same Apso owners, breeders and exhibitors, belonged to this club as well, in an effort to further advance the establishment of the breed in the British Isles. The club members, at the request of the Kennel Club, were to draw up descriptions of the breeds to clarify the differences between the various Tibetan dogs. As a result there were four distinct Tibetan breeds officially accepted: the Mastiff, the Lhasa Apso which was listed as being 10 inches high, the Tibetan Terrier listed as 14 to 16 inches high, and the Tibetan Spaniel. The Shih Tzu was classified as a Chinese dog and recognized as a separate breed entirely.

In January, 1957, the Lhasa Apso people left the organization and formed their own breed club.

THE EARLY APSOS IN GREAT BRITAIN

In the early days, as now, the breed was seen in many colors, shades and patterns, with personal preference or availability being the deciding factor in the acquisition of a Lhasa Apso. Many of Mrs. Brownrigg's dogs were parti-colored and two of them, named Hibon and Yantze were exhibited at the 1933 West of England Ladies Kennel Association Open Dog Show at Cheltenham.

A dog named Changru, owned by Lady Freda Valentine, caused a sensation in 1933 when he was exhibited at the English shows. He was said to have possessed an excellent head according to the Standard for the breed. A gold-colored bitch named Soma, bred by Mrs. A.C. Dudley and owned by Miss Marjorie Wild of Cheltenham, was said to be the best bitch yet seen in England. As was mentioned earlier, it was Miss Wild that owned a Lhasa as early as 1901 that was bred by the Hon. Mrs. McLaren Morrison, who brought several dogs back to England from Darjeeling, India. Miss Wild remained active and loyal to the breed until her death in 1971, showing under her Cotvale kennel name.

Mrs. Dudley was reputed to be a great Lhasa Apso authority and was also the owner of Taktru and Droma, prominent dogs in the early days of the breed in England, and especially lauded for their heavy

English Champion Cheska Endymion, bred by Frances Sefton and owned by Mrs. B. Allen of Staffordshire, England.

Miss Marjorie Wild's first Lhasa Apso, photographed in 1901. This black and white dog, which lived to be 18 years of age, was bred by the Hon. Mrs. McLaren Morrison. At the turn of the century the Lhasa Apso was known as a Lhasa Terrier.

coats. Even then heavy coats were desired and expected on show specimens.

Lhasas named Satru and Sona were owned by Mr. William Hally, another breed authority, and both dogs won Firsts in the Open Classes as well as Best of Breed and Opposite Sex at the 1934 L.K.A. Championship Show at the Crystal Palace in May of that year. They were also given the silver medal, awarded by Mr. Lapwood, for being the Best Apso in the show. Satru succeeded in beating his own sire, the imported dog, "Lhassa," which had never before been beaten. Colonel Bailey was the judge at this particular event.

Miss E.M. Hutchins was another prominent breeder in the 1930's. She owned a dog named Lung-Fu-Su and another Lhasa named Tang. A top dog in his time, Good Company, was the name of a dog bred by Mrs. A.C. Dudley and sired by her Lhasa-Litsi. Litsi later became the property of Mrs. May Ingmire. The decade of the thirties was also the time when Mrs. Geoffrey Hayes was showing Aislaby Chen-Joe Singhi, a parti-color. It is little wonder that the amount of winning these dogs did during this period was the biggest stir in the dog fancy and made the greatest advance of any of the Tibetan breeds introduced in Great Britain.

But then another crushing blow! World War II...

THE LHASA AND WORLD WAR II

Unfortunately for the breed which had endeared itself to the British during the decade of the thirties, World War II heralded the beginning of the nineteen forties and, as with every breed, the devastating war took its toll on the canine population.

Colonel Bailey's dogs, which had played an important part in the lines established in Great Britain, all but died out during the war years and any further development from these early dogs came to a resounding halt. Marjorie Wild, one of the earliest and hardiest pioneers in the breed, managed to survive the war only to be literally wiped out by a siege of hardpad and distemper in the late 1940's. Only a meager few line breedings managed to survive and those only through Dr. Greig's two Apsos, Ladkok and Lamleh, that went back to Colonel Bailey's imported Lhasa and Litsi.

Two other lines which had come down from the Bailey stock managed to carry on some of the bloodline. One was Mrs. Florence Dudman's Ramblersholt dogs, still active in the 1970's, and Miss Hervey-Cecil's Furzyhurt lines, though with very few specimens she had to actually "begin again" to preserve the breed, with various imports of questionable background necessary to increase their numbers.

Fortunately for the breed, Mrs. G. Henderson, the woman serving as the Honorable Secretary of the Himalayan Club in Darjeeling, fully recognized and was sympathetic to their plight and sent them some of the best dogs they had to offer for breeding purposes. One of them was a dog named Jigmey Tharkey of Rungit, who proved his worth by siring a great new specimen in the breed that was to be influential in the "new" resurrection of the Apso in England. Ch. Brackenbury Min-Nee, was to become what breed authority Frances Sefton refers to as "one of the most travelled of all Lhasas." Gunga Din not only became prominent in his native England, but lived for awhile in Peru and then moved on to South Africa where he died in May 1974 at the age of 15½ years after a well-fought, but losing battle with two guard dogs.

English Champion Verles Yangdup of Cheska, a smoke and black Lhasa, whelped August 16th, 1962. Bred by Mr. and Mrs. F.J. Hesketh-Williams and owned by Frances Sefton, this magnificent Lhasa is the sire of three champions. His sire was Ch. Brackenbury Gunga Din of Verles *ex* Brackenbury Kalu of Verles.

By 1947 Colonel R.C. Duncan, a member of the British Army returned to England with his Lhasa Apso named Tomu of Tibet. This shaggy little dog had been a gift to Colonel Duncan from a Lama he had met at Kathmandu, the capital of Nepal. The Lama had been accompanied on his journey by the little dog and he subsequently presented Tomu to the Colonel. Long after Colonel Duncan returned to England he and the Lama carried on a correspondence during which the Lama never failed to inquire about the health of his beloved little dog which he had so graciously given to his British friend.

There is no denying that the 1940's were a time of much hard work in the breed to get it back on its feet. But a small dedicated group of Lhasa Apso fanciers managed to do it and the breed did more than just survive; once again it began to thrive. By 1957 it had become so numerous and so well established as a breed of its own that the breeders and exhibitors decided to sever relations with the old Tibetan Breeds Association and formed a club of their own.

CHAMPIONSHIP STATUS ONCE AGAIN

During the early years of the 1960's the registrations for the breed in Great Britain totalled the required 150 and the breed was granted separate registration and championship status starting in 1965. Four champions were finished to help celebrate that inaugural year and the very first to claim the title of Champion was Ch. Brackenbury Gunga Din of Verles who had been winning at the shows for a period of five years. He was seven years old at the time of his championship and was even more in demand as a sire than ever before! This remarkable little dog was bred by Miss Beryl Harding and owned by Mr. and Mrs. F.J. Hesketh-Williams, prominent themselves in the world of dogs, as is their Verles kennel name.

One of the first and most important bitches in the history of the breed after it reached championship status was the sable, gold and white parti-color Champion Cheska Bobette. This lovely bitch was sired by Camvale Tomu Singtuk out of Cotsvale Chuni. She was bred and formerly owned by Frances Sefton in England, and is now owned by Mrs. Irene Plumstead, who handled her so successfully to her English title.

Bobette was whelped on January 19, 1967 and is considered not only to be a top show dog but a great and important brood bitch. She is the dam of several champions including the well-known Champion Cheska Alexander of Sternoc. She has champion offspring in Canada and also two in Australia.

Ch. Cheska Alexander of Sternoc was whelped in May, 1969 and bred by Mrs. Frances Sefton of the Cheska prefix. Alexander won his first Challenge Certificate at seven months of age and had earned his championship title by 17 months. To date Alexander holds the record for the greatest number of C.C.'s...36 by the end of 1975. He won several Groups including three times Best of Breed at Crufts, 1972, 1973 and 1974. He was also the first Lhasa Apso to win a Group in the United Kingdom and the only Lhasa as of 1975 to win Best Exhibit in Show at an English all-breed championship show. This was accomplished in 1973 at the Ladies Kennel Association Show with an entry of 8,000 dogs.

He is the sire of so many Championship and Challenge Certificate winners that his owners have lost count. This remarkable gray and white dog was handled for his co-owners by Mrs. Cross-Stern during his ring career. His sire was English Champion Tayung of Coburg and the dam was English Champion Cheska Bobette.

SOME PROMINENT KENNELS IN GREAT BRITAIN TODAY

The unfortunate passing of Marjorie Wild in 1971 was a sad note with which to begin the decade of the seventies in the Lhasa breed. But fortunately for the breed several of the "old guard" were still breeding and exhibiting and were welcoming many of the more recent newcomers to the breed destined to carry on at the present and in the future.

English Champion Cheska Alexander of Sternoc, the Best of Breed dog at Crufts in both 1972 and 1973. Other wins include Best in Show in 1973 at Olympia and Best in Group at Crufts in 1974. His dam was Eng. Ch. Cheska Bobette.

Miss B. Harding, famous for her Brackenbury line, judged at Crufts in 1972, calling upon her twenty years of experience in the breed to help her decide her placements. When Colonel and Mrs. Irwin went abroad in 1952 Miss Harding was asked to care for their two Lhasas, Dzongpen and Minaong of Madamswood. She agreed, since one of the conditions was that she could breed the pair if she wished and could keep for her trouble all of the litter except the pick of the males. Miss harding took the gamble and the litter of three produced two bitches and a dog that went to the Irwins. Miss Harding kept the bitch she named Brackenbury Lhotse and the rest is Lhasa history, for it is from Lhotse that a large portion of the present day Lhasas in England descend, and not the least of them is her famous grandson, Ch. Gunga Din of Verles.

Mrs. Anne Matthews' Hardacre Kennels in Sussex are most active in the breed. Just 10 years old in 1975, Hardacre has fashioned their breeding plan to combine both show quality dogs with the soundness and desirable temperament. It was Mrs. Hesketh-Williams who found their foundation bitch for them and got them off to a good start. Her name was Ch. Tungwei of Coburg. As of 1975 she was the dam of three champions and a very special personality at Hardacre.

Other Lhasas that reside at Hardacre are the 11-year-old Ch. Verles of Puti of Lymparton, Ch. Hardacre Ang Tharkay, Ch. Hardacre Hedda and her daughter Hardacre Happiness, Hardacre Hartley, Hardacre Sinful Skinful, Hardacre Preston and two imports, American and Canadian Ch. Hardacre Kinderlands Bhu-Sun and Royal Ambassador to Hardacre. Gone but not forgotten is Ch. Willowcroft Kala from Hardacre, killed by a hit and run driver in 1974.

Mr. and Mrs. R.G. Richardson are known for the Belazieth Lhasa Apsos. Their gold and white Ch. Hardacre Hitchcock, known as "George," has a record of 27 Bests in Show all-breeds and five Reserve Bests in Show. He was second top winning dog in the United Kingdom all-breeds for the St. Aubrey Dog World competition in 1971, the Best of Breed winner at the 1971 Crufts show and top stud dog for 1972. These are just a few of his wins which led up to his being named top-winning Lhasa in the United Kingdom for 1970, 1971 and 1972, and winning for him the coveted Brackenbury Lhotse cup.

The Richardsons also own Hardacre Gloria of Belazieth. Sired by Ch. Brackenbury Gunga Din of Verles out of Hardacre Ang Lahmu, Gloria was Best Puppy in Show at the Lhasa Apso Club's First Open Show. She has won three Best Puppy in Show awards, all-breeds, and has won many firsts at Championship and Open shows. Some other of the Richardsons' Lhasas include Verles Jogmaya of Belazieth, a lovely gold bitch and dam of their Ch. Belazieth's Honey Amber, Ch. Belazieth's Saucy, Malcolm, Soot-N-Snow (a black and white, naturally!) Gold Sensation, Birdson, Miss Clare, and William, all bearing the Belazieth's kennel prefix. Their Gay Daniel of Belazieth is also at stud, and Mrs. Hesketh-Williams owns their Belazieth's Ja of Verles.

VERLES

Mrs. D.M. Hesketh-Williams is the owner of the famous Verles House from which so many great Lhasas have emerged. Ch. Brackenbury Gunga Din of Verles who lived from December 1958 until May 1974, was the first British postwar champion and was Best of Breed at Cruft's in 1963, 1965 and 1967. Together with Brackenbury Kalu of Verles he was the foundation stud at Verles and well-known as a show winner. Mrs. Hesketh-Williams' Ch. Verles Tom-tru was another great dog, and the 1968 Best of Breed winner at Crufts. He had a Best In Show win to his credit, along with 10 Challenge Certificates and 15 Bests of Breed.

Ch. Verles Tom-tru, bred and owned by Mrs. D.M. Hesketh-Williams of Kent, England.

English Ch. Willowcroft Kala, sired by the great Ch. Brackenbury Gunga Din of Verles. Owned by Mrs. A. Matthews, Hardacre Kennels, Sussex, England.

Other Lhasas bred and exhibited by Verles were Ch. Verles Nying-Chem-Po and Ch. Verles Keepa. Other Verles dogs are owned by exhibitors in other countries. Dutch Ch. Verles Nang-was is owned by Mrs. Schneider-Louter in Holland, Ch. Verles Ka-U is a Nordic Champion and owned by Mrs. Paasio in Finland and Ch. Verles Jigme-Tru is owned by Mrs. Gray in the United States and is now an American and Canadian Champion.

RAMBLERSHOLT

Mrs. F. Dudman owned the Ramblersholt Lhasas, another of the more prominent dogs in Britain. Her Soraya and Kikuli were descendants of two of the original Apsos imported by Mrs. Bailey in 1928. They were named Lhasa and Litsi. Soraya was the dam of American Ch. Ramblersholt Shah-Naz that produced four American Champions.

Ramblersholt is one of the oldest established Apso kennels in Britain, and Mrs. Dudman's love for the breed dates all the way back to the days when she first saw them in their native land. Another of her foundation bitches was Conquistador Golden Glow and later Brackenbury Nupso, a litter sister of Brackenbury Lhotse, bred by the Irwins.

In Australia, Mrs. Beard was owner of Aus. Ch. Ramblersholt Da Norbu. While in England, Ramblersholt Chumba, Ramblersholt Rham and Sam-A-Da are doing their share of winning. Rham won the club stud dog trophy in 1967. Overseas, in addition to Mrs. Beard's Da Norbu there is Australian Ch. Ramblersholt Sonam, sire of 11 champions and owned by Mrs. Michaelis. A granddaughter of Chumba is a champion in New Zealand and her name is Surabay Maha Kala.

Other active kennels in the breed by the mid-seventies are Mrs. Irene Ashfield's Kobe dogs, Paul Stanton and Terry Young's Tintavon line, Mrs. W.G. Smith's Sauchrie Lhasas, H.C. Tillier's Zungeru line, Mrs. K. Brownlie's Scarba Apsos, Sheila Charlton's Charlton kennel, Stanley and Miriam Chamdler's Burdyck prefix, Mrs. Doreen E. Martin's Aladean Lhasas, Vicky Mann's Kingshill breeding, Lynda Gaches and the Tersos Lhasas, Mrs. Thelma Morgan and the Frith dogs, Jon Ford and his Jonters kennel, Mrs. J. Brackenridge with the Kayinim title, Mr. and Mrs. Moore and their Trician line, and Mr. and Mrs. Allen with their Wyrley dogs.

Others include: D.F. Goode's Camvale prefix, Eileen T. Stephen's Applelake Apsos, Mrs. Jean Blyth known for her Saxonsprings dogs, Sue and Dick Chalk and the Sunluck Lhasas, Miss H. Cooper and Mrs. A. Robertson and the Starmyre dogs, Mrs. I. Plumstead and her Showa Lhasas, Mrs. P. Cook and Coomar, Mrs. S. Linge and the Lingstoc Lhasas, the F.E. Wallis and the Viento lines, Miss J.M. Davies and her Sigroc line, and the E.K. Powells, and Mrs. P. Tierney that exhibit but do not use a kennel name.

Ch. Licos La, R.O.M., whelped in August, 1963 and owned by Reana Wilks of New York City. Bred by Mrs. John Licos, the sire was Ch. Licos Chapila La *ex* Ch. Licos Nyapso La. Namni La is a glorious red-gold.

With this impressive roster of active and devoted fanciers the breed can be said to be in good hands with an even more active future.

THE LHASA IN ENGLAND IN THE 1970'S

In the years immediately following the championship status of the Lhasa Apso in Great Britain registrations were up substantially and Britain boasted 45 champions by the end of 1974. From these 13 males and 12 bitches which had earned their titles, all but one traced its ancestery back to Miss Harding's Brackenbury lines. During 1970 over 400 registrations had been made with the Kennel Club.

Oddly enough, by the end of 1975, no Lhasa Apso had yet achieved a Best of Show at an all-breed championship show in Great Britain. Quite a contrast to the ever-increasing number managing to capture this coveted top award in the United States. However, we are certain that as the breed gains in popularity in that country and with the truly magnificent specimens being exhibited there, the top award is not too far off in the future! With more and more of them managing to win Group awards, a Best in Show seems imminent.

BRITISH CHAMPIONS

The following is a list of the names of Lhasa Apso in Great Britain which have finished their titles since the breed once again gained championship status in that country in 1965.

Jonters Benito, whelped January 10, 1973, has one Championship Certificate and three Reserve C.C.'s. Sired by Saluq Annapurna Quapito, an import from France, *ex* Torrens Eva; he was bred, owned and shown by John Ford, Jonters Lhasa Apso, Warks, England. Active as a top stud in England, he and his progeny are winning at the top shows. His pedigree goes back to the Hamilton (U.S.A.) breeding, with a touch of French on the dam's side.

1965
Ch. Brackenbury Gunga Din of Verles
Ch. Princess Potala (bitch)
Ch. Brackenbury Chigi-Gyemo (bitch)
Ch. Namista Yarsi

1966
Ch. Veles Ton-Tru
Ch. Pontac Adham Tarhib

1967
Ch. Brackenbury Tongi-Gyemo (bitch)
Ch. Verles Yangdup of Cheska
Ch. Verles of Lymbarton (bitch)
Ch. Cotsvale Brackenbury Kan-Ri (bitch)
Ch. Brackenbury Nantle

1968
Ch. Verles Nying-Chem-Po
Ch. Tungwei of Coburg (bitch)
Ch. Cheska Jesta (bitch)
Ch. Rampa of Scarba
Ch. Hardacre Ang Tharkay
Ch. Beautybox Gunga-Din

1969
Ch. Johara Beautybox Perkyi (bitch)
Ch. Tayung of Coburg

1970
Ch. Cotsvale Meeru
Ch. Hera of Torrens (bitch)
Ch. Cheska Alexander of Sternoc
Ch. Cheska Endymion
Ch. Cheska Bobette (bitch)

1971
Ch. Hardacre Hitchcock of Belazieth
Ch. Verles Keepa (bitch)
Ch. Cheska Gregor
Ch. Sauchrie Mingmatsering
Ch. Camvale Sunlight (bitch)
Ch. Belazieth's Honey Amber (bitch)

1972
Ch. Hardacre Hedda (bitch)
Ch. Starmyre Kyong-Pa (bitch)
Ch. Wicherty Thea of Tintavon (bitch)

1973
Ch. Cotsvale Anna (bitch)
Ch. Haylemill Katuscha (bitch)
Ch. Willowcroft Kala from Hardacre (bitch)
Ch. Belazieth's Saucy (bitch)

1974
Ch. Sidewater Becki-La (bitch)
Ch. Wyrley Hermes
Ch. Isa-Joy of Piplaurie (bitch)
Ch. Silver Hebe (bitch)
Ch. Annakapelli of Saxonsprings (bitch)
Ch. Saxonsprings Lobsang
Ch. Belazieth's Malcolm

Best in Show at the 1969 Suffolk County Kennel Club show was Marvin Frank's Ch. Kyi-Chu Friar Tuck. Tuck was handled to this win by Robert Sharp under judge James A. Cowie. Club President Gerald Winus presents the trophy.

Ch. Belazieths Saucy, bred, owned and shown by Rob and Doreen Richardson of Essex, England. Saucy has five Challenge Certificates and was the youngest Lhasa bitch to attain championship status (at 14 months of age). Another Hitchcock daughter, she won her first C.C. at 10 months, when this photo was taken, and has also won two Best Puppy in Show awards at all-breed events. A Diane Pearce photograph.

Georgina of Witneylea, sired by Witneylea Scruffy *ex* Ramblersholt Goron Zola, is a gold with black fringes and an important foundation bitch at Mrs. A.L. Weller's Witneylea Kennels in Oxon, England.

English Ch. Hardacre Ang Tharkey, sired by the American import Hamilton Dewatas *ex* Ch. Tungwei of Coburg. Owned and bred by Mrs. A. Matthews, Hardacre Kennels, Sussex, England.

Ch. Hardacre Hedda, beautiful homebred champion owned by Mrs. A. Matthews, Hardacre Kennels, Sussex, England.

4: THE LHASA APSO AROUND THE WORLD

THE LHASA APSO IN AUSTRALIA

It was in the early 1960's when the Lhasa made its presence known in Australia. Apart from the few which had come into Australia as pets, the first registered stock imported to Australia for breeding and exhibiting arrived there in 1961 and 1962. These were imported by Mrs. Joan Beard of Sydney, New South Wales, and were purchased from the English Ramblersholt Kennels. They were Ch. Ramblersholt Trag-Pon, Ch. Ramblersholt Dzom Tru and Ch. Ramblersholt Da Norbu.

However, it was difficult for Mrs. Beard to establish the breed all by herself, and consequently the breed did not take root there for several years. An English couple, Mr. and Mrs. John Mason, arrived in Australia in the late 1960's and, upon their settling in at their new home in Victoria, became active in the breed. They had brought with them their three Lhasa Apso which were related to the well-known English Champion Brackenbury Gunga Din of Verles. These three little newcomers created some new interest in the breed, especially around the Victoria area.

Their Tsangpo of Coburg became an Australian champion and was used extensively as a stud. One of Mason's bitches, Jordonian Droma did her part, after having left some excellent puppies back in England. Her son, a gold dog named Tasam Ten Tru Tao, became an Australian Champion when campaigned by Mr. and Mrs. Alan Day of Victoria. He won several Royal Challenge Certificates and also won a Best Exhibit award six times in a row at the semi-specialty club show. At the time, this was the only club which held a show catering to the Lhasa, though sharing the honor with two other Asian breeds, the Chow Chow and the Shih Tzu.

Although better known in the fancy by the end of the 1960's due to the exposure and exhibiting by these few dedicated people, the breed suffered a great setback in late 1969 when Australia enforced a ban on the importing of dogs when Britain reported a couple of cases of rabies. While in the past Australia permitted the importation of animals

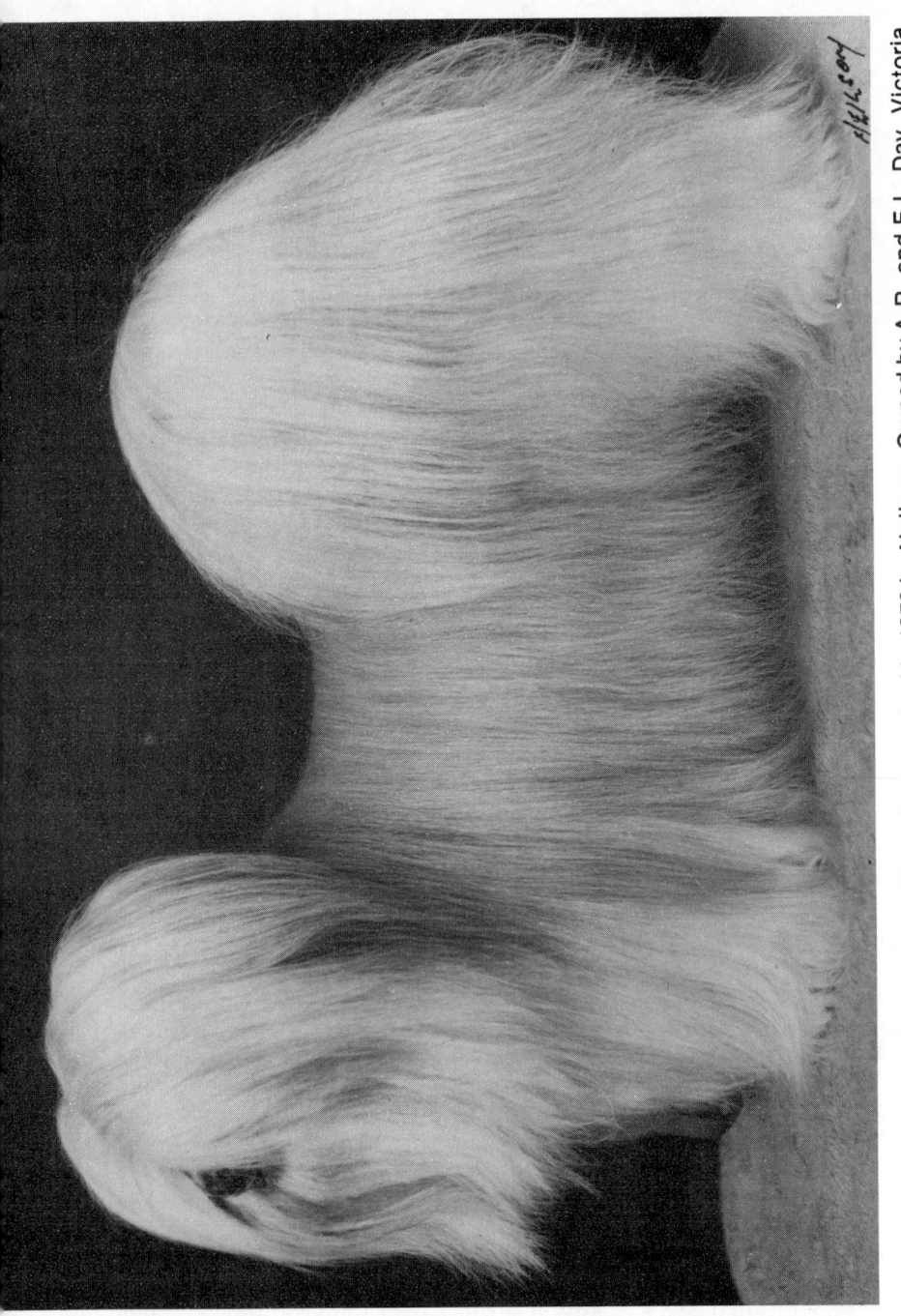

Australian Champion Tasam Ten True Tao, photographed in 1973 by Neilson. Owned by A.R. and E.L. Day, Victoria, Australia.

only by sea and only from the United Kingdom or New Zealand, with a lengthy quarantine period as well, this complete and total ban of imports naturally effected the breeding by cutting of new bloodlines.

The ban was finally lifted in 1971 and one of the first imports after that was a bitch which had already made history in the English showring. She was Mrs. Frances Sefton's English Ch. Cheska Jesta, winner of ten Challenge Certificates. She was imported in whelp to her half-brother, English Best in Show winner and champion Cheska Gregor. This litter was born on the ship as it steamed into Sydney Harbour, and was reared to eight weeks of age in the quarantine kennel.

The lovely Jesta went on to further show honors in a career of less than a year in Australia, her new homeland. She won her Australian title in record time and created history for the breed by winning a Best in Show at an all-breed championship show, with several Groups along the way and a Best of Opposite Sex in Show at the prestigous Sydney Royal Show in 1973, under Finnish judge Mr. Hans Lehtinen.

The Sydney Royal show can be compared to our Westminster Kennel Club show or the British "Crufts." This important Sydney event draws between 3,000 and 5,000 entries from all over Australia and lasts for ten days.

Jesta was retired from the showring, and her outstanding record was not matched until 1975, when a puppy from the litter she whelped on the boat topped it. He became Australian Ch. Cheska Archee, owner-handled by Miss Helen Jardine of Sydney. Archee achieved two Bests in Show awards at all-breed championship shows and was also Best Opposite Sex in Show at the Adelaide Royal Show, another major event in the dog world.

There was one other Best in Show winning Lhasa by the end of 1975 and he was Australian Champion Showa Dynamatic, an English import and a parti-colored dog co-owned and handled by Mrs. Jenny Longmire of the Amesen Kennels in Sydney.

While these are the Best in Show Lhasas, there were several group winners, referred to in that country as "Class in Group" and "Class in Show" winners. They also did a great deal to get the breed before the public and increase its popularity in Australia, so that by the end of 1975 the Lhasa Apso had taken a firm hold in the dog fancy. The breed is strongly entrenched in New South Wales where the competition is unusually keen, and the breeding is coming up close behind in Queensland. The few dedicated breeders and exhibitors in Victoria maintain the breed in the showring there. Elsewhere, while the breed's presence is felt, progress is still slow in the remaining states on that continent.

A strong influence on the breed were the imports which arrived from the time of the lifting of the ban in 1971. They were all from important kennels with winning bloodlines and did much to improve the quality of the dogs which were already in Australia. A good many imports were brought in in 1974 and 1975 whén Mrs. Ann Michaelis and

Australian Champion Cheska Archee with owner Helen Jardine winning a Best in Show in Australia. Photograph by Michael Trafford.

Miss Angela of Sydney added further bloodlines to their Singtuk Kennel stock from American as well as British kennels. Miss Diane Lemaire of Melbourne brought in a French-bred dog, which also carried American bloodlines, which further strengthened the French stock already in Australia. While admittedly the majority of imports to Australia were from important British kennels, there was a smattering of French, American, and some Indian lines.

The fear of the dreaded rabies, which imposed the strict quarantine laws, definitely had an effect on the breed in the past. However, there is now enough stock in Australia to prevent any threat of a serious consequence should another ban be put on the importation of animals. However, such a thing is still dreaded since every responsible breeder wishes the choice to go outside when he feels it to the advantage of his breeding program. This is one of the reasons why the

The 1973 Sydney Royal Show in Australia. Mrs. Frances Sefton on the right with Ch. Cheska Jesta (winner of the Best Opposite Sex in Show award), congratulates Mrs. Pat Connors with her Australian Terrier, winner of Best in Show.

breeders in Australia are keeping a watchful eye on the progress being made in the use of frozen semen.

Another great step forward was accomplished in 1975 with the formation of a specialty club for the breed. The Lhasa Apso Club was formed in New South Wales, though membership includes breeders and exhibitors from all over Australia and also New Zealand. Mrs. Frances Sefton, who was so prominent and influential in the breed in England before moving to New South Wales, was made one of the patrons of the new club; an honor owing to her contribution to the breed in both countries. The club's first show, an open parade and a non-championship event, was planned for May 1976. With this club and its intention of looking after the interests of the breed, Lhasas should make even further progress in the coming years.

While the important dogs and the progress of the breed in Australia have been touched upon, it is important to go a little further into their backgrounds. One of the major influences was Australian and

English Ch. Cheska Jesta. Jesta was bred, owned and always handled by Mrs. Frances Sefton. Jesta was whelped in April 1967 and won her first C.C. at seven months. By the time she had reached three and a half years of age she had won 10 Challenge Certificates in England, a record which had not been surpassed by the end of 1975, although one other English bitch also has ten. When the Seftons moved to Australia in 1970 it became necessary for them to leave Jesta behind for almost two years until the ban on the importation of dogs was lifted. It was during this time that she whelped her litter by half-brother Gregor, now deceased. Jesta's show record has been mentioned earlier and suffice it to say that she is now a beloved housepet which Mrs. Sefton brings out occasionally for the veteran classes, since her true beauty and value is still much in evidence.

Australian Ch. Mangalam Tensing, photographed in January, 1969; owned by E.L. Day of Melbourne.

Australian Ch. Belazieth's Birdsong, imported from the United Kingdom and photographed at 20 months of age with her daughter, now Australian Ch. Singtuk Mandapanda Tru. Birdsong's spectacular show career has included Best of Breed wins at Brisbane and Melbourne Royals. At the Melbourne show she defeated 17 champions. Both Lhasas are owned by Angie Michaelis, Singtuk Kennels, New South Wales, Australia.

While Frances Sefton is unable to show as much as she would like to because of pressing business committments, her Cheska dogs continue to be seen in the ring mostly campaigned by friends. Cheska He's A Hobo, for instance, was whelped in 1973 and is campaigned by his co-owner Peter Warby; while others are seen with Ian Murray in Sydney and Mrs. June Hopkins in Victoria.

I have also mentioned Australian Ch. Cheska Archee. He was whelped in December, 1971, and was sired by English Ch. Cheska Gregor out of English and Australian Ch. Cheska Jesta. He was a highly successful showdog and winner of many Best in Group awards and twice Best in Show at all-breed championship shows. He and his litter sister, Australian Ch. Cheska Anthea, won the dog and bitch Challenge Certificates while Archee was also Best of Breed at the 1975 Royal Melbourne show under American judge Mrs. Winifred Heckmann.

Another show star was Australian Ch. Showa Dynamatic. An import from England, Dynamatic's sire was from Belgium and, through his son, brought the "best of Belgian bloodlines" to Austra-

Australian Champion Show Dynamatic, imported from the United Kingdom and bred by Mrs. I. Plumstead; Dynamatic's owners in Australia are Mrs. Frances Sefton and Mrs. J. Longmire.

lia! Bred by Mrs. I. Plumstead of the English Showa prefix, Dynamatic is co-owned by Frances Sefton and Mrs. Jenny Longmire, who also handles him in the ring. He is another of the few Best in Show all-breed championship show winners in Australia. By the end of 1975 he had sired two champions. His dam was the well-known and excellent English Ch. Cheska Bobette, and as we said, his sire was the Belgian dog Saluq Shaggy Wonder Ulan.

We must also include Australian Champion Tasam Ten Tru Tao when listing signifigant dogs in the breed history in Australia. Born in 1969, Tao was well-known showdog during the early 1970's and won several Royal Challenges. He was also Best Exhibit in Show on six consecutive occasions at the semi-specialty shows for the Asian Breeds Club. He is sire of several Australian Champions as well. This lovely gold dog is owned by Mr. and Mrs. Day and bred by the J. Masons. His sire was Australian Ch. Mangalem Tensing ex Jordanian Droma, an import from the United Kingdom.

By the end of 1975 other show dogs were appearing on the scene to carry on. Mr. and Mrs. Richardson's Australian Champion Belazieths Birdsong, Mrs. Shirley Forbes's Australian Champion Showa Kyi, Mr. Perk's Ch. Karwa Kyasma and Bovais Apollo (sired by Rufus of Cheska).

While these mentioned are considered the foremost breed progenitors in Australia, there are many others coming up from the ranks which will make themselves heard in the present and future. The breed is now well-established "down under" and in good hands. They are more than holding their own in the showrings and account for many of the top wins.

Dog shows in Australia are quite different from those in Britain. All breeds, even if there is only one dog of that breed in the country, are entitled to be awarded Challenges. That is, if they are deemed worthy by the judge. Championships are earned by winning 100 points. A Challenge rates five points plus one point for every animal of the same sex competing. Winning a Challenge on one's own rates six points. The maximum number of points permitted at any one show is 25. It is obvious that it is very difficult to make a championship in a breed where there are large entries, but easy at the country shows where sometimes a winner never has competed against another of the same breed.

However, entries at the Australia shows vary. At the large shows with total entries of 1,500 to 1,800, the average Lhasa entry is around ten or twelve. At other shows, such as the Sydney Royal, the entries can go as high as 40 or 50.

THE LHASA APSO IN NEW ZEALAND

The New Zealand Kennel Club is affiliated with the Kennel Club in England and follows their Standards for the breed. The Lhasa Apso, therefore, falls into the Non-Sporting Group in New Zealand as it does in England. By 1975 it was the 54th ranking breed, according to the number of individual registrations. In 1974 registrations in all breeds totalled 16,602, with the Lhasa Apso accounting for only 31 of these.

Most of the dog shows held in New Zealand carry championship status and average 500 to 700 entries, but while the quality of the dogs is high, the number of shows and number of entries is quite small. In New Zealand, as in Australia, the strict and lengthy quarantine laws play a part in holding down the number of imports each year. However, it also means that the imports which do reach their shores are of the highest quality, or the New Zealanders simply do not bother to import.

While local dog registration fees are high, show entry fees are low. No professional handlers are allowed in this country, and most of the exhibitors enter either one, or just a few dogs in their particular breed, so the Lhasa entries represent only one or two of the entries. The Lhasa still is one of the minority breeds, but interest is strong and closely related to the activities of the breed in Australia.

The first imports to New Zealand were brought in by Miss Jean Marlow of the Surabaya Kennels located on the North Island of New Zealand. She imported two Lhasas in 1963; they were Australian Champion Lelo Tehran and Australian and New Zealand Champion Soemirah Pon Dzara. Both of these dogs were of the Ramblersholt breeding and were 14 years of age in 1975. Mrs. Elizabeth Luck of the Fortstone's Kennels on the South Island has imported stock from both Britain and Australia and works together with her mother, Mrs. Wearmouth of England.

Mrs. Luck also owned the first Best in Show Lhasa Apso in New Zealand.

New Zealand considers dogs as working animals. This is partly due to the fact that the sheep far outnumber the three million people, and herding and working dogs are of prime importance. But more and more the "sporting" aspect of owning and breeding dogs is be-

A trio of winners at the Nonsuch Kennels of Ann-Marie Adderly in Montreal West, Quebec, Canada. On the left is Canadian and American Ch. Crestwood's Babycham; Champion Nonsuch Ashanda Devi is in the middle, and on the right is Canadian and American Champion Nonsuch Amne Machin.

New Zealand Champion Hardacre Holdfast of Fortstones, bred by Mrs. A. Matthews and owned by Mrs. Elizabeth Luck, South Canterbury, New Zealand.

coming appreciated and will undoubtedly have its effect on the number of dog shows as well as the number of entries at these shows.

THE LHASA APSO IN CANADA

One of the earliest breeders of the Lhasa Apso in Canada was Mrs. Roberts of Abbotsford, British Columbia, Canada. Mrs. Roberts adopted the name of her town as a kennel suffix and has bred and sold these little dogs both in Canada and the United States. Her top-winning dogs did much to establish the breed in both countries and are still found in many of the pedigrees of top-winning show dogs today.

Among the most remembered are her dogs: Teako of Abbotsford, Sumchen of Abbotsford and Kyma of Abbotsford.

Starting in 1962 with foundation stock from Mrs. Grace Lico's Hamilton stock, Dr. Ellen Brown of Willowdale, Ontario, Canada, established her Balrene Kennels with the Hamilton bitch Lico's Yarto Lu, and a male, Ch. Carroll Panda, purchased from Mrs. Margerie Carroll of the English Ramblersholt line. It was from this combination of two excellent bloodlines that produced Dr. Brown's famous Canadian and American Champion Balrene Chia Pao.

Augie, as he was called around the Balrene Kennels, has won 13 Bests in Show including the 1971 American Lhasa Apso Club Specialty show held in conjunction with the Trenton Kennel Club show in New Jersey each year. He has sired over 20 champions to date and has over a hundered Group Placements on his show record.

This Balrene line was the foundation behind several eastern Canadian kennels as well. Notable is the Treepine Kennels of Mr. and Mrs. E.G. Carpenter of Bolton, Ontario, whose recent Ch. Treepine Chumbi had over 30 Group Placements before he was one year of age. Chumbi is a grandson of Chia Pao, and was seven times Best Puppy in Show.

Balrene and the influence of good breeding on the part of Dr. Brown is also behind the Nonsuch Kennels of Mrs. Ann-Marie Adderley of Montreal West, P.Q., Canada. Mrs. Adderly has been exhibiting and breeding seriously since 1968, though she had purchased her first Lhasa as early as 1960.

Nonsuch's top-winning dog is Canadian and American Ch. Nonsuch Amne Machin. Sired by Dr. Brown's Canadian and American

Canadian and American Champion Crestwood's Babycham, owned by Ann-Marie Adderly of Montreal West, Quebec, Canada. This Group-winning bitch was among the Top Ten Lhasas in Canada for 1972. Bred by Mrs. Lise Halvorsen, Babycham is a top bitch at the Adderley Nonsuch Kennels.

Canadian and American Champion Balrene Chia Pao, a Best in Show winner and sire of over 20 champions. Pictured here with little Lorna Scobie, "Augie" has 13 Bests in Show to his credit, including the Lhasa Apso Club of America Specialty in 1971 held in conjunction with the Trenton Kennel Club event. Augie's sire was Ch. Carroll Panda *ex* Ch. Licos Yarta La. Bred, owned and handled by Dr. Ellen Brown of Willowdale, Ontario, Canada. Pao's record was second-ranking dog all-breeds in Canada in 1970 after 82 times in the ring. In 1971 he won the American Specialty over an entry of 116.

Canadian and American Ch. Nonsuch Amne Machin, top-winning Lhasa at Ann-Marie Adderley's Nonsuch Kennels in Canada, pictured winning at a recent show under judge Mildred Heald. The sire was Can. and Am. Ch. Balrene Chia Pao, the dam was Can. and Am. Ch. Crestwood's Babycham. On the left is 10-month-old Ch. Balrene Nicola, bred by Dr. Ellen Brown and owned by Ann-Marie Adderley. Nicola's sire was Dunklehaven Nicky *ex* Kokonor Kala. Handling are Ann-Marie Adderley (with Machin) and Magdalen Adderley with Nicola. Machin was third-ranking Lhasa in Canada for 1974 and was in the Top Ten for 1973 through 1975; he has 10 Group Firsts to his credit and 39 Group Placements.

Ch. Blarene Chia Pao out of Canadian and American Ch. Crestwood's Babycham, Machin was third-ranking Lhasa in Canada for 1974. He placed in the Top Ten Lhasa Apsos in Canada from 1973 through 1975. Shown on a rather limited basis, Machin has 39 Group Placements to his credit including 10 Group Firsts.

This solidly built red-gold dog has always been owner-handled in Canada and the United States. He has placed well in both countries in the Groups and has won under respected judges from Canada, the United States and Australia. He has many sons and daughters with points toward championship.

The top-winning bitch at Nonsuch is Canadian and American Champion Crestwood's Babycham. Bred by Mrs. Lise Halvorsen, this solid gold-colored bitch placed among the Top Ten Lhasas in Canada in 1972. She had 10 Group Placings, including a First. She is the foundation bitch of the Nonsuch Kennels and to date is the dam of one American and three Canadian champions.

American and Canadian Champion Tal-Hi Kori Ti-Ko, pictured winning the Group at the 1972 Mexican Kennel Club show in Mexico City under English judge Joe Braddon. Black, with red feet and tail, Ti-Ko won over 26 contenders in the Group and 10 in the Best in Show competition. He was one of four left in contention after six others had been excused. Owner Ann Hoffman of Waverly, New York, tells us he didn't win Best in Show but was a wonderful representative of the breed in the show ring! Beverly Reed handled for the owner in the Group.

American, Canadian and Mexican Champion Magestic Gyad-Po handled by Evonne Chashoudian for owner Miss Pamela L. Magette of Long Beach, California.

LHASA APSOS IN OTHER COUNTRIES

From the early days, Lhasa Apsos had been seen in most all of the European countries, including Finland, Italy, Sweden, Denmark, Holland, Germany and, of course, Belgium. The breed was also found in New Zealand and Australia. Today it is safe to say that in each of these countries the breed is "well established." Especially in France.

THE LHASA APSO IN FRANCE

Madamoiselle Violette Dupont introduced the first Lhasa Apso to French dog shows. It was a Belgian import named Xeres which she obtained in 1949. It was a golden dog and caused quite a stir in the fancy in that country.

However, it was a bitch, Hamilton Kangmar, which she purchased and imported from the Cuttings in America which became the first officially registered Lhasa in France in 1950. It not only became the first officially registered Lhasa at the French Kennel Club, but went on to become the first French, Swiss and International Champion. Kangmar became the foundation bitch for Mlle. Dupont's Annapurna Kennels and produced many top-winning Lhasas including a very prominent stud, Ch. Fo de l'Annapurna. It was one of Fo's daughters

Sol-Wa of Ro Nang, a real Tibetan black, with eight Tibetan imports in six generations of his pedigree. Owned by Mrs. U.M. Collins, Ro Nang Kennel, Fife, Scotland. This charming photograph was taken in October, 1973.

which earned the first Group Award as Best Toy. Her name was Ch. Jo Wa de l'Annapurna and was owned by Dr. F.P. Clement. Her total Toy Group wins numbered 16!

Dr. F.P. Clement is one of today's most prominent breeders and exhibitors of the Lhasa Apso in France. In 1968 one of his American imports, Ch. Licos Djesi La, bred by Grace Licos of Beverly Hills, California, and one of his home-breds, Ch. Mani de Gangamak, who was shown at 11 shows under 11 different judges in four different countries, won all of the CC and CACIB awards for their sex. Djesi was Best of Breed, and Mani Best of Opposite Sex. Djesi has won a total of nine Best Toy awards as well.

Dr. Clements and his kennel manager, Mr. Andre Cuny, have produced and presented many quality dogs over the years and are truly dedicated to the breed. Mr. Cuny has judged in England and was most helpful to this author in the presentation of the breed in Europe. Their successes in the show ring and their show records prove their success and great admiration for the breed.

THE LHASA IN IRELAND

Breeding of the Lhasa Apso on the Emerald Isle is quite limited. However, the Saluq Kennels, owned by Mrs. V.L. Stringer of County Antrim in Northern Ireland have made quite an impressive entry into the show ring in England. Saluq Shaggy Wonder Ulan is a stud at the Kayinim Kennels of Mrs. J. Brackenridge and is the sire of Showa Dainty of Sunluck.

THE LHASA APSO IN GERMANY

The Lhasa Apso is a comparatively new breed in Germany, but one that has taken tremendous hold on those who are responsible for its appearance in the show rings in that country. The first dog was imported in 1966 from England, and was named Verles Norbu. He was bred by Mrs. Mason at her Verles Kennel in England.

Once imported to Germany, he was mated to Ting Ambrosia of Cheska, a daughter of Licos Ting La, an important export from the United States by Mrs. Frances Sefton. He became the sire of Ting La von Boliba, the first Lhasa of German breeding to earn the title of champion—or German Bundesieger, as the title is called there. This title was earned under English judge Lady Freda Valentine. Along with Krysants Lendzema, a bitch imported to Germany from Sweden, Boliba became the foundation of Dr. Mary Tauber's Vom Potala Kennels in Germany.

As the breed caught on and increased in popularity other kennels began to spring up: Ch. Brackenbury Nanttle brought fame to the newly formed Brackenbury Kennels; Lucy of Torrens established the Torrens Kennels; and Ramblersholt Tsake La, while of English origin, started the German kennels off to a good beginning. There were

Beautiful head study of Jo Wa de l'Annapurna, bred by Miss Dupont and owned by Dr. F.P. Clement, France. Jo Wa was the foundation bitch of "de Gandamak" Lhasa kennels and later the dam of International Champion Mani de Gandamak, the top-winning European Lhasa Apso of all time.

Gautama de l'Annapurna, bred and owned by Miss V. Dupont of France. The sire was Gourou *ex* International Champion Hamilton Kangmar. Kangmar, an American import, was the very valuable foundation bitch of Miss Dupont's Annapurna Kennels.

Opposite: American and Bermudian Ch. Chen Korum Ti, one of the all-time great Lhasa Apsos owned by Mrs. Patricia Chenoweth of Saratoga, California. Kori is being shown here at a Bermuda Kennel Club show by his handler, Robert Sharp.

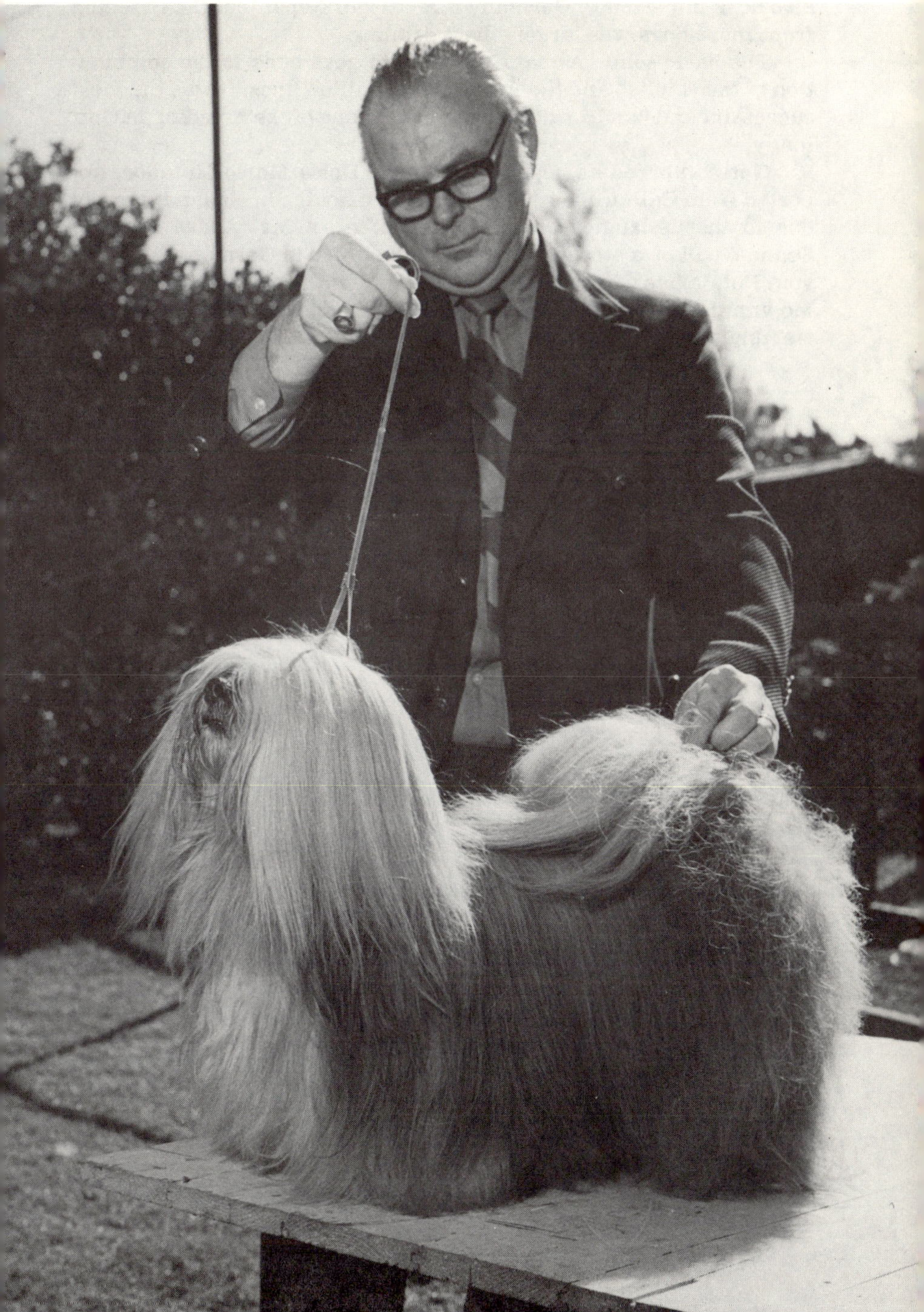

also dogs imported to Germany direct from Nepal, but the breeding from these dogs was largely disappointing.

The basic solid foundation stock still goes back to the combination of the English and the American Hamilton lines. It was the most successful and can be said to be the backbone of the breeding in Germany.

German breeders hope the beautiful Dolsa Marlo Matador, imported from California by Mrs. Schneider-Louter in Holland, largely due to the assistance and encouragement of Mr. Andre Cuny of France, will be a strong influence on the breed in Germany. Dshomo vom Potala has whelped a litter by Matador and a Matador son, Pag Mo van de Warwinckel, owned by Mrs. Bracksieck, who is already starting a successful show ring career for her kennel Trashi Deleg.

German Bundessieger Ting-La v Boliba, owned by Dr. Mary Tauber of Germany. Boliba was bred by F. Allefheuser; the sire was Verles Norbu *ex* Tong Ambrosia of Chesra, a daughter of Licos Tong-La.

Kyamo vom Potala, bred by Dr. Mary Tauber of Germany. The sire was a dog named Lucky, imported directly from Lhasa, and the dam was the Swedish bred bitch Krysant's Lendzema. Kyamo is owned by Mrs. Bracksieck.

By 1975 there were still not too many Lhasas in Germany and no specialty club. Those interested in club activities belonged to the Internationale Klub for Tibetische Hunderassen, or translated, International Club for Tibetan Breeds. The club has about 200 members, and in Germany between 80 and 100 Lhasas represented. Entries at the German shows are usually between four and six, with the 1975 show at Stuttgart featuring an entry of eight and the European Show in Essen with 11.

GERMAN DOG SHOWS

Classes at the German dog shows include the Jungestklasse for Lhasas six to nine months of age, Jungendklasse for nine months to 24 months, Offenklasse for dogs 15 months and older, and Championklassee for those which have obviously attained championship, and a class called Out of Competitionklassee. There are about six shows a year in Germany, but we must remember the small countries enable traveling to adjacent countries not only to earn championships in neighboring countries but to achieve International championships.

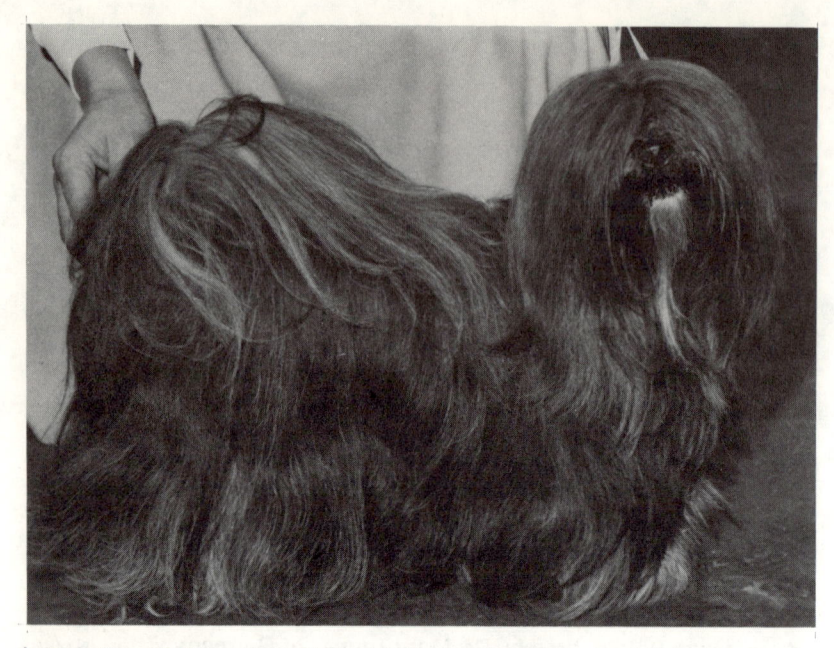

International Champion Shaggy Wonder V'Thanka, bred by Mrs. Mewis de Ryck in Belgium and owned by Mrs. Busser of Holland. Thanka, pictured here at two years of age, is a champion in Holland, Belgium and Germany.

EUROPEAN TITLES

The various European titles really do accumulate for the dedicated exhibitors in Europe. Charles Patronas, a German Lhasa fancier and exhibitor cites the perfect example of this. The sire of one of his dogs is entitled to precede his name with International-French-Dutch-German-Belgian-Hungarian-Czechoslovakian-European and World Champion as well as International Champion of Beauty! It is understandable in the light of succession of achievements that most Europeans only use the words "Champion" or "International Champion" for their dogs!

THE LHASA APSO IN DENMARK

According to Ann Dilso, owner of the Nordhoj Kennels in Denmark, interest in the lovely little Lhasa Apso began in 1970.

The breed was established in the early days by the wonderful imported dogs from the Shaggy Wonder Kennels in Belgium. Namely, Belgian and International Champion Shaggy Wonder U'Tou Fou, who quickly became a Danish champion as well. Tou Fou was bred by

Two Lhasa Apsos photographed on the dog show grounds in Italy in 1971; the Lhasa was a rather rare breed in Italy at that time. The photo illustrates the "natural" condition of the coat (grooming was a rarity). However, the breed was important enough to be featured on the front cover of the September 1971 issue of *I Nostri Cani,* an Italian dog magazine.

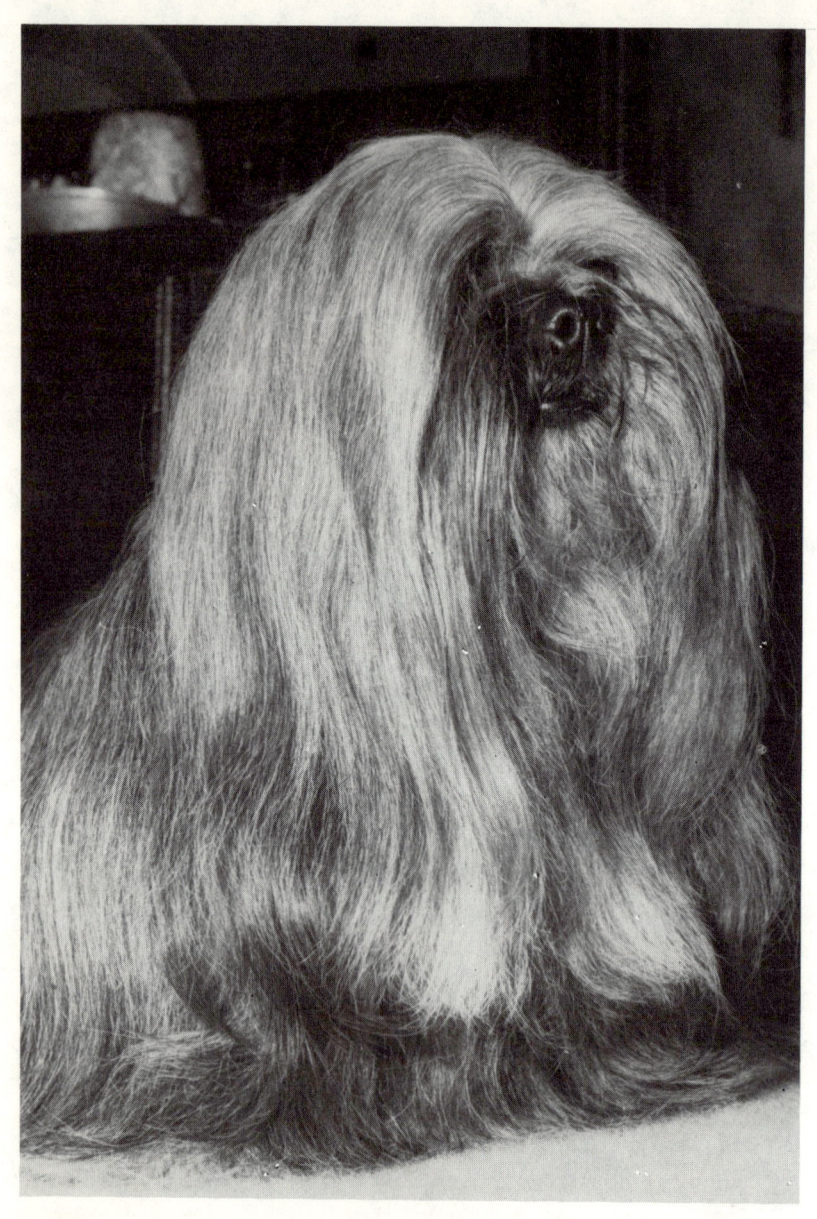

The top-winning European Lhasa Apso of all time. . .International Champion Mani de Gandamak, bred and owned by Dr. F.P. Clement, Loire, France.

Mrs. Mewis de Ryck at her Shaggy Wonder Kennels and was imported to Denmark by Ann Dilso.

Another Shaggy Wonder dog imported to Denmark was the black Lhasa Holland and International Champion Shaggy Wonder V'Opa Mes, who also became a Danish Champion for owner Lizzie Peterson of the Lizette Kennels in Jyderur, Denmark.

The influence of these Shaggy Wonder dogs was apparent as the breed began to attract attention and two more kennels were added to the rostrum. New bloodlines were imported from Sweden, Holland and Switzerland. With the new and widespread importations came the inevitable spectrum of colors and color combinations. In just a few short years the Danes had their Lhasas in all different hues.

Danish, Dutch and International Champion Shaggy Wonder V'Opa Mes, bred by Mrs. Mewis de Ryck and owned by Lizzie Petersen, Lizette Kennels, Jyderur, Denmark.

There are four major kennels in Denmark that are prominent in perpetuating the breed...the aforementioned Nordjof Kennels of Ann Dilso, the Lizette Kennels of Lizzi Peterson, El Gunga Din Kennels owned by Lis Davidsen and the Banzi Kennels owned by Asta and Jorgen Hinlev. It is through their intensive dedication and cooperation that there is much serious breeding being conducted in Denmark. Even in this short period of time, they have dogs of such quality that they can compete and win on an international level at dog shows in other countries as well as their own. They do not hesitate to import without regard to distance or expense and their selectiveness in breeding stock is getting them off to a marvelous start.

Finishing for her American Championship under judge Mildred Heald is American, French and International Champion SharBo Tsan Chu, bred by Sharon Rouse and handled during her American show ring career by Rosemarie and Joe Crandah. Chu was later exported to France, where she became an integral part of the kennel of Dr. F.P. Clement of Loire, France.

THE LHASA APSO IN INDIA

The Lhasa Apso breed has been a favorite in India for many years, and especially after the exiled Dalai Lama crossed the border into that country after the Communist invasion of Tibet. Today the dogs serve primarily as pets and companions and in some cases they are exhibited as show dogs.

One of the most famous of the kennels in India, which has bred and exhibited in the recent past, belonged to Mr. Tenzing Norkey of Darjeeling, whose stock was bred from a dog given him from the Ghangar monastery lines. However, Mr. Norkey has received much more publicity and fame from his reputation as a famous sherpa and one of the conquerors of Mount Everest. In his autobiography, *Man of Everest,* there are several photographs and references to this original little dog which was the foundation of his kennel.

In 1964 Colonel Donald McClain, United States Army, was a consulting engineer stationed in India and involved in the building of a canal for the government of Pakistan. Colonel and Mrs. McClain were dog lovers and it became their aim to locate two Lhasa Apsos which they could register with the Kennel Club of India and also breed. Their efforts took them from the priory at Nainital, Calcutta, to Mr. Tenzing Norkey at Darjeeling, to His Highness, the Maharaja Adheraj of Charkheriin, India, and finally to the Buddhist priest at the Temple of the Eyes of the World in Nepal.

The McClains had become interested in the breed while still in the United States and contacted the AKC for names of those to contact in India upon their arrival. Through the cooperation of the American Kennel Club and the Kennel Club of India, they met Dr. M.R. Sharma, a famous veterinary surgeon, Honorary General Secretary to the Delhi Kennel Club, Honorary Veterinary Advisor to the Delhi Zoo and a man very interested in promoting seeing-eye dogs for India.

Many frustrating events occurred before they were finally presented with the white scarf of welcome at the inner sanctum at the Temple of the Eyes of the World and were allowed to see the sacred dogs. They were told that the Lhasas were the constant companions of the priests and that they were considered good luck talismans. They also revealed that their stock was rapidly becoming depleted because of distemper!

Depletion was also due to the fact that so many were given to royalty and American doctors and missionaries and people like Tim Mendies, owner of the Snowview Hotel in Kathmandu, Nepal, by way of thanks for his help with the Tibetan refugees. The Mendies had been given three Lhasa Apso for their kindness in adopting as their own some Tibetan children whose parents had died on their flight from Lhasa. It was from these dogs that the McClain's dogs were bred. They chose two females and a male, and with the help of the Kennel Club of India, and Dr. Sharma, the parents were eventually registered. Beyond that the pedigree was lost!

Later the McClains bred their little red-gold female to a male from Tenzing Norkey's kennels but the pedigree could go back just so far since Mr. Norkey had stopped breeding and registering dogs after the death of his wife. During their stay in India, the McClains also met a girl working with the Peace Corps who owned a Lhasa Apso which had been a gift from the royal family in Nepal, but whose pedigree could not be traced.

In 1967 the McClains entered two of their dogs in the largest dog show in the country at Lahore, Pakistan. One of the bitches, Ranie of Chaksam, went Second Best Dog in Show, and in 1968, her sister won Best in Show! They were particularly pleased since the dogs had to go under five different judges to attain the title. The McClains tell us it was thrilling to see the sheiks ride up to the ringside on their beautiful Arabian horses to cheer for the "smallest dog in the show!"

Only the third generation of the McClain's breeding was brought back with them when they returned to the U.S.A. and settled in Lake George, Colorado. Their original stock was placed with friends. Before leaving the McClains observed a beautiful golden Lhasa following along behind a camel train through the Khyber pass.

Opposite:
Top left: A bevy of little beauties make ready for the Christmas season at their kennel in Saratoga, California. Owned by Pat Chenoweth.
Top right: Mohican's Tigress of Bella-Mu, pictured winning Best of Breed at 9 weeks of age at a Lhasa Match Show under judge Eileen Nelson. Owner-handler by Ann Sergio, Bella-Mu Kennels, Woodbury, Long Island, New York.
Center left: Ch. Potala Keke's Tomba Tu, pictured winning under judge Henry Stoecker at the 1975 Hatboro Dog Club Show. Tomba has over 100 Bests of Breed and 9 Group Firsts. Owned, bred and handled by Keke Blumberg, Potala Lhasa Apsos, Rydal, Pennsylvania.
Center right: Ch. Potala Keke's Golden Gatsby wins a major on the way to his championship under judge Dr. Samuel Draper at the 1975 Monmouth County Kennel Club show. He is handled here by breeder-owner Mrs. Keke Blumberg.
Bottom left: Ch. Taglha Sinsa of Kinderland, pictured winning Group Second at a 1975 show in Easton, Maryland. Sinsa is owned by Mr. and Mrs. Wilson Browning, Jr., Taglha Kennels, Norfolk, Virginia.
Bottom right: Ch. Joi-San's Happieh-Go-Luckieh wins the Kentuckiana Lhasa Apso Club Specialty Show in August, 1975! The judge was Dr. Robert J. Berndt and the handler Annette Lurton for breeder-owner Joyce Stambaugh. Co-owned by Jim Stambaugh of New Providence, New Jersey. The sire was Ch. Arborhill's Bhran-Dieh; the dam was Chu Shu's Kiri. This lovely red-gold dog is also a multiple Group winner.

BEST OF
BREED
ANDERSON PHOTO

BEST OF BREE
OR VARIE
HATBORO
DOG CLUB, INC
OCT.3,1975

WINNERS
DOG

BEST OF BREED
KENTUCKIANA
LHASA APSO CLUB
AUG. 29, 1975
PHOTO BY THACKER
KLAC

Back in the states the McClains began looking for a male for the two bitches they brought back with them while waiting for their registrations to come through. Meanwhile they will be breeding and showing from American stock to establish their Chaksam Lhasa Apso strain in this country.

A spring highlight in India each year is the Tibetan Dog Show held in New Delhi at a place called Tibet House. A panel of Tibetan judges officiate; silver trophies and brocade dog collars with bells are awarded as prizes for dogs that win according to a Standard calling for "the smaller the better" in the size category; long, thick, soft straight hair preferred; large eyes, short, strong and hairy tails and "a tail curled tightly over the back" is preferred.

The show is not only an exhibition of the Tibetan dogs, but is the meeting place for those looking for stud dogs and, in general, is considered a social event. The show was originally organized by an American photographer named Marilyn Silverstone. Each year she has watched the entry grow to the point where now not only American dog lovers living in India participate, but more and more dogs owned by the Indian Army men enter, bringing their dogs down from the mountains for the show.

At the 1973 show 48 dogs competed and Princess Sodeum Yapshi Pheunkhang of Sikkim showed her dog Layzom, a four-month-old puppy. Layzom won the Best Puppy in Show award that year. Mrs. George Tobias, whose husband is with the Ford Foundation in that country, showed her dog, Whiskey, to winner of the "over four years old" class.

This show has been held each year since April 11, 1970, to raise money for the emergency fund for Tibetans in India that have been living there since the exile of the Dalai Lama when he fled from the Chinese and relocated high on a mountain top in Upper Dharmsala on land granted to him by the Indian government. This is currently the home of the 14th Dalai Lama and the more than 85,000 Tibetans who now live in Dharmsala; it is the center of activity for all Tibetans who wish to carry on the traditions and customs observed by the devoted Lamaists while they are forced to dwell on foreign soil.

Many Lhasa Apsos are seen in Dharmsala and there is no attempt whatsoever to control the breeding of them. They breed freely with the Tibetan Spaniels and that country makes no recognition of them as separate breeds. While in India the favorite color seems to be the whites, the indiscriminate breeding leads to a complete array of colors. Veterinary services are not available and the extreme weather conditions make it next to impossible to keep coats in good condition, except by those who either dote on them as treasured family pets or by those who intend to exhibit their dogs at the shows.

American Lhasa fancier Joan Beard, who acquired her first Lhasa in 1961, was so intrigued by both the breed and its illustrious

A handsome trio of lovely Lhasas owned by Mrs. Paula Lieberman, Tyba kennels, Baldwin Harbor, Long Island, New York. From left to right: Ch. Hamilton Sha-Tru, Ch. Tyba Le of Ebbtide, Karma Tsa Tsa. Sha Tru is the dam of Ch. Karma Frosty Knight of Everglo.

history that she made a trip to Dharmsala and was granted an audience with the Dalai Lama. She reported seeing both Lhasa Apso and Tibetan Spanials everywhere, and that only a few of them were groomed.

Captions for pages 100 and 101:
Page 100, top: Ch. Potala Keke's Yum Yum wins Best of Breed at the August, 1975 Penn Ridge Kennel Club show under judge Dr. Samuel Draper. Yum Yum is handled by Carolyn Herbel for breeder-owner Keke Blumberg.
Page 100, bottom: Ch. Rimar's Rumpelstiltskin is shown winning a Winners Dog decision under Dr. Samuel Draper at the 1974 North Country Kennel Club Show. Handled by Stephen Campbell for owner Richard Hoyt of Trenton, New Jersey.
Page 101, top: Ch. Karma Frostina, a white Lhasa bitch bred by Mrs. Dorothy Cohen and owned by Mrs. Paula Lieberman, is shown by handler Allan Lieberman to a Best of Opposite Sex title under Mary Nelson Stephenson.
Page 101, bottom: Ch. Rimar J.G. King Richard, the multi-group winning Lhasa bred by Stephen Campbell and owned by Susan C. Hutchins, is shown winning Best of Breed at the 1975 Ox Ridge Kennel Club Show under judge Samuel Draper. "Dickie" was sired by Ch. Tabu's King of Hearts ex Ch. Rimar's Tipit, whelped in September, 1973. Handled here by Robert Sharp.

BEST OF BREED

ASHBEY PHOTO

WINNERS

NORTH COUNTRY
KENNEL CLUB, INC.
AUG. 16, 1975   KLEIN

BEST OF
OPPOSITE
ASHBEY PHOTO

BEST OF BREED
OR VARIETY

OX RIDGE
KENNEL CLUB, INC.
SEPT. 20, 1975

5: STANDARD FOR THE BREED

CHARACTER: Gay and assertive but chary of strangers.

SIZE: Variable, but about 10 inches to 11 inches at the shoulder for dogs, bitches slightly smaller.

COLOR: Golden, sandy, honey, dark grizzle, slate, smoke, particolor, black, white or brown. This being the true Tibetan Lion Dog, golden or lion-like colors are preferred. Other colors in order as above. Dark tips to ears and beard are an asset.

BODY SHAPE: The length from point of shoulders to point of buttocks longer than height at withers, well-ribbed up, strong loin, well developed quarters and thighs.

COAT: Heavy, straight, hard not wooly nor silky, of good length and very dense.

MOUTH AND MUZZLE: Mouth level, otherwise slightly undershot preferable. Muzzle of medium length; a square muzzle is objectionable.

HEAD: Heavy head furnishings with good fall over ears, good whiskers and beard; skull narrow, falling away behind the eyes in a marked degree; not quite flat, but not domed or apple shaped; straight foreface of fair length. Nose black, about one and one-half inches long, or the length from tip of nose to eye to be roughly about one-third of the total length from nose to back of skull.

EYES: Dark brown, neither very large and full, nor very small and sunk.

EARS: Pendant, heavily feathered.

LEGS: Forelegs straight; both fore and hindlegs heavily furnished with hair.

FEET: Well feathered, should be round and catlike, with good pads.

TAIL AND CARRIAGE: Well feathered, should be carried well over back in a screw, there may be a kink at the end. A low carriage of stern is a serious fault.

Approved April 9, 1935

THE UNITED KINGDOM'S DESCRIPTION AND STANDARD OF POINTS

CHARACTERISTICS: The Apso should give the appearance of a well-balanced, solid dog. Gay and assertive, but chary of strangers. Free and jaunty in movement.

HEAD AND SKULL: Heavy head furnishing with good fall over the eyes, good whiskers and beard. Skull moderately narrow, falling away behind the eyes in a marked degree; not quite flat, but not domed or apple shaped. Straight foreface, with medium stop. Nose black. Muzzle about one and one-half inches long, but not square; the length from tip of nose to be roughly one-third the total length from nose to back of skull.

EYES: Dark, medium sized eyes to be frontally placed, not large or full, or small and sunk. No white showing at base or top of eye.

EARS: Pendant, heavily feathered. Dark tips an asset.

MOUTH: Upper incisors should close just inside the lower, i.e., a reverse scissor bite. Incisors should be 'nearly' in a straight line. Full dentition is desirable.

NECK: Strong, well covered with a dense mane which is more pronounced in dogs than in bitches.

FOREQUARTERS: Shoulders should be well laid back. Forelegs straight, heavily furnished with hair.

BODY: The length from point of shoulders to point of buttocks greater than height at withers. Well ribbed up. Level top-line. Strong loin. Well balanced and compact.

HINDQUARTERS: Well developed with good muscle. Good angulation. Heavily furnished. The hocks when viewed from behind should be parallel and not too close together.

FEET: Round and cat-like, with good pads. Well feathered.

TAIL: High set, carried well over back and not like a pot-hook. There is often a kink at the end. Well feathered.

COAT: Top coat heavy, straight and hard, not woolly or silky, of good length. Dense under-coat.

COLOURS: Golden, sandy, honey, dark grizzle, slate, smoke, parti-colour, black, white or brown.

SIZE: Ideal height—10 inches at shoulder for dogs; bitches slightly smaller.

NOTE: Male animals should have two apparently normal testicles fully descended into the scrotum.

THE FIRST STANDARD FOR THE BREED

In 1901, while in the service of the British Government in India, Mr. Lionel Jacob, Sire Lionel after his Knighthood, compiled a description and standard of points for the breed which was published in

KENTUCKY
NNEL CLUB
PTEMBER 1, 1968
BEST IN
SHOW

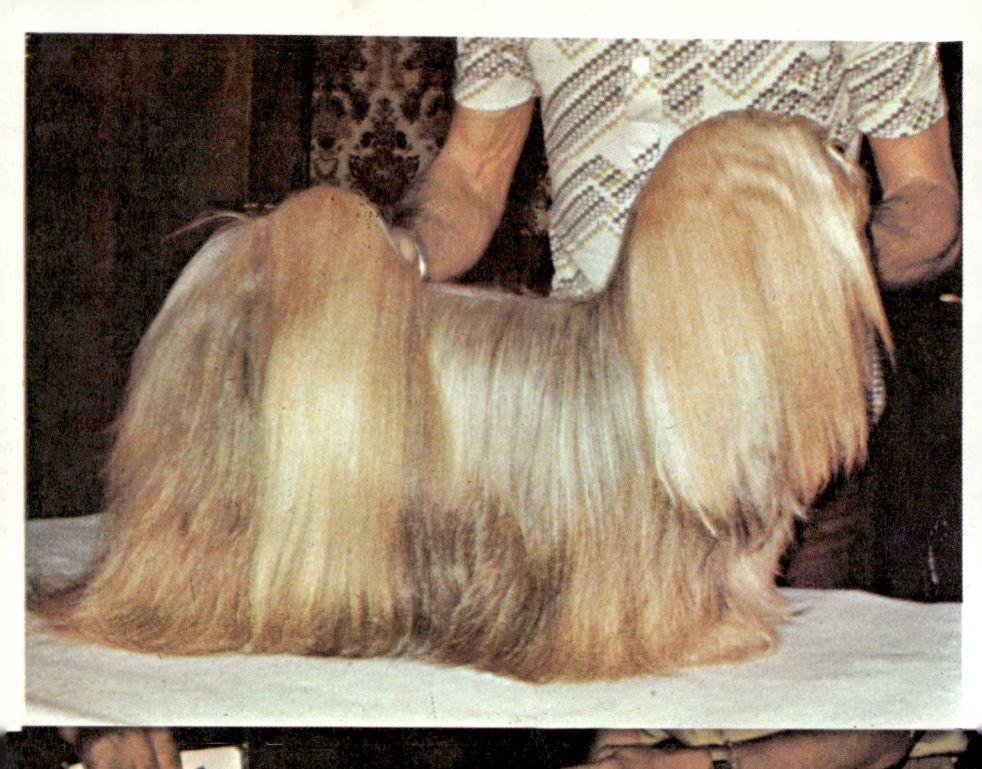

LOUISVILLE, KY.
LHASA APSO
FEB. 23, 1974

the *Kennel Gazette* that same year. He put the height at the shoulder at 11 inches and the weight at 20 pounds.

The following year the Reverend H.W. Bush, recognized as an authority on the various Asiatic breeds, was behind a successful attempt to attain separate classification for the Lhasa Terrier with the Kennel Club in England.

A CHANGE IN NAME

In 1958 the Kennel Club allowed the name to be changed to Tibetan Apso to identify the dog more closely with its country of origin. But in 1968 the Apso Club applied to the Kennel Club for permission to re-

Lovely stamps issued by Bhutan to commemorate the Lhasa Apso as a breed.

Captions for pages 104 and 105
Page 104, top: American Champion Dolsa Tamike, pictured in full show coat, bred by Jean Kausch in the U.S.A. and imported to France by Dr. F.P. Clement of Loire, France. Dr. Clement's Lhasas are in the care of Andre Cuny.
Page 104, bottom: Ch. Karma Frosty Knight O'Everglo is pictured winning his ninth Best In Show at the 1968 Mid-Kentucky Kennel Club Show. Owned by Maria Aspuru and Angela Rossie, Frosty's sire was Ch. Karma Kushag, the sire of 9 champions, and his dam was Ch. Hamilton Sha-Tru. Bred by Dorothy Cohen.
Page 105, top: On-Ba Lho-Bho O'Joymarc is pictured winning at one year of age at the 1974 Kentucky Lhasa Apso Club Show under judge Carolyn Herbel. Owned by Winifred Graye, Joymarc Kennels, Highland, Michigan.
Page 105, bottom: Ch. Ruffway Kara Shing, owned and handled by Georgia Palmer of Addison, Illinois, is pictured winning under the late judge Clara Alford at the 1970 Wheaton Kennel Club Show. This lovely Lhasa is the dam of the Best In Show winner Ch. Ruffway Mashaka, Group winner Ch. Ruffway Marpa and Ch. Ruffway Norru.

turn the name to Lhasa Apso once again. Permission was granted and effective January 1, 1970, Lhasa Apso once again became the official name for the breed. In Europe, of course, the dog is officially named Terrier de Lhassa.

EUROPEAN STANDARD

The Lhasa Apso has now become quite firmly established in all the countries of Europe and the breed is judged according to the rules of the Federation Cynologique International Standard. It is the same as the British Standard. As the breed gains in prestige in Europe, more and more International Championship titles are being attained. Thanks to the advances in modern transportation, exhibitors get to travel with ease from country to country to achieve these titles. Hopefully, the easy exchange of bloodlines through stud service will also allow for the very best breeding in the future.

International Champion Mani de Gandamak and American, French and International Champion SharBo Tsan Chu; owned by Dr. F.P. Clement, Loire, France. Photographed on an oriental antique from their native land.

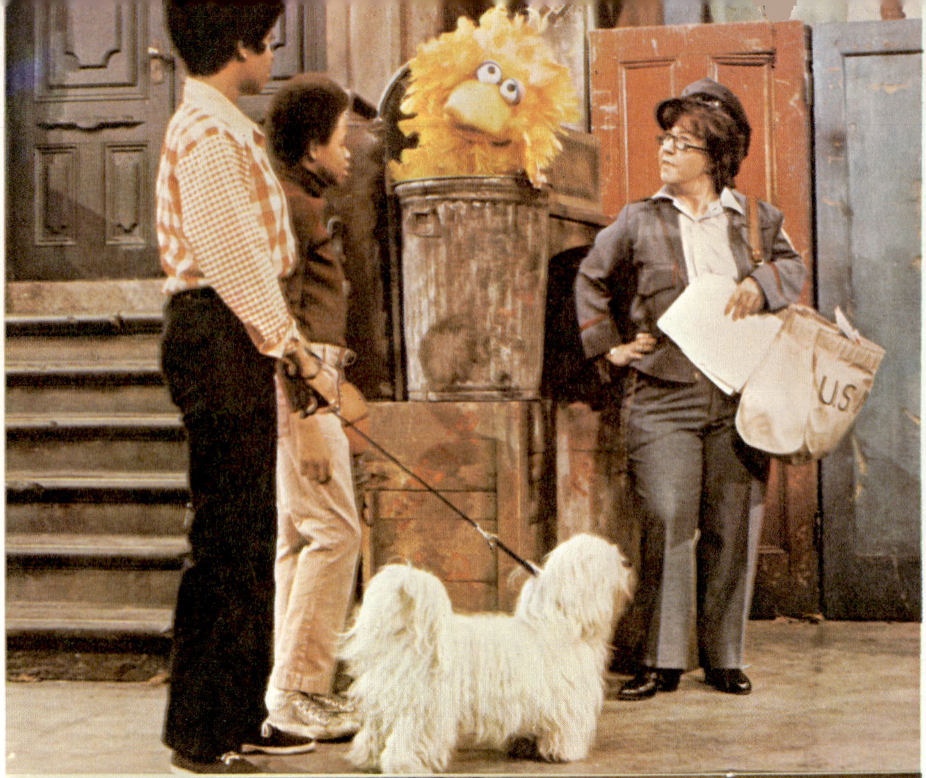
U.S.

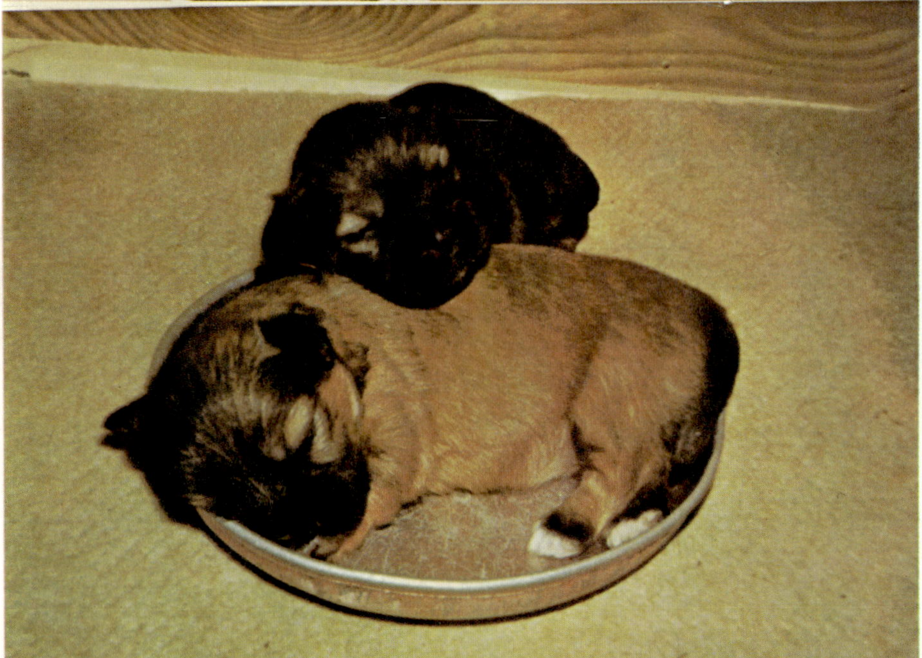

B.O.W.
photo by Gilbert

VARIETY GROUP

NON-SPORTING GROUP 1ST.

THE STANDARD FOR INDIA

While the Lhasa Apso is growing in number in many countries and especially in the United States, Great Britain and Australia, the ones that are seen and shown in India are bred close to the Standard set up for them by the Indian Kennel Club. Their Standard reads as follows:

APPEARANCE: A small, short-legged, shaggy dog with pendent ears and curled tail. Height for dogs 10 to 11 inches; bitches being smaller.

HEAD: Narrow, the skull being neither flat nor domed or apple-headed, but conical. Stop well defined. Muzzle of medium length of skull as 1:3. Mouth with scissor bite, but an undershot jaw is permissible. Eyes dark brown, of medium size and not sunken. Nose black. Ears pendent and well feathered. The head fringe falling over the eyes, and the moustache and beard making the muzzle appear longer than it actually is. Neck of medium length.

BODY: Longer than high, well ribbed up and with straight back. Loins strong and straight, croup not falling away. For and hindlimbs short and straight; well covered with hair and feathered.

TAIL: Carried over the back—never down—and covered with long hair.

FEET: Round, with strong pads and plenty of feather.

COAT: Hard and straight, neither woolly nor silky; of good length and very thick.

COLOUR: Golden, sandy or honey, with dark points to the hairs on the muzzle and ears preferred. May also be dark grey, slate-grey, smoke-grey, or white pied with black and brown.

Captions for pages 108 and 109:

Page 108, top: Rygal Bo-Jangles, C.D., is pictured during his appearance on a Sesame Street television show. Famous character actress Charlotte Rae plays the mail lady, Big Bird is emerging from the trash can and Susan, played by Loretta Long, holds Bo-Jangles on the leash. He is owned by Barbara Wood, Anbara Lhasa Apsos, New York City.

Page 108, bottom: Two-week-old puppies sleeping in their mother's food dish at the Karma Kennels in Las Vegas, Nevada.

Page 109, top: Canadian and American Champion Nonsuch Anme Machin is pictured going Best of Winners at the 1973 Woodstock Kennel Club Show under judge Joseph Faigel. She is breeder-owner-handled by Ann-Marie Adderley of Montreal West, P.Q., Canada.

Page 109, bottom: Multiple Group winner Ch. Tabu's Chubby Checkers is pictured with handler Richard Vaughan after winning the Group at the Brevard Kennel Club Show. Owned by Maria B. Aspura, bred at the Tabu Lhasa Apso Kennels, Lucas, Kansas.

6: BREED TEMPERAMENT AND CHARACTERISTICS

First and foremost the Lhasa Apso is a housedog and anyone considering the breed as a pet or show dog should bear this in mind. The Lhasa is not happy when tied outside or when expected to live out its days between dog shows as just another kennel dog confined to a compartment along with a lot of other dogs.

For all the centuries of its existence the Lhasa has been a member of the household, and is at its best when in a congenial, family atmosphere. Socializing the Lhasa Apso from the time it is a very young puppy enhances this friendly trait which is highly desired in the breed.

The Lhasa has an even temperament and is hardy enough to share the lives of young children. While no dog selected as a companion for children should be abused, you will find that the Lhasa is active and sturdy enough—and smart enough—to pretty much take care of itself when involved in the antics of normal, healthy youngsters. Therefore, when purchasing a Lhasa Apso, temperament should be of utmost concern. An even-tempered Lhasa is typical of the breed; a cranky, snappy, or disinterested Lhasa is to be avoided. As breeds gain in popularity, as the Lhasa Apso has, indiscriminate breeding can produce such faults as bad temperament. Therefore, it is of utmost importance that you buy from a reputable breeder known for not only good bloodlines, but for the proper temperament to insure the desirable disposition called for in a companion dog.

This is not to say that the Lhasa is not selective in his choice of friends. A dog has every right not to have to love everyone. The Standard for the breed specifically states under the heading of temperament that the breed is "gay and assertive, but chary of strangers." But this caution should in no way be confused with hostility or aggression. With proper socialization and a happy family life you will find your Lhasa Apso is perfectly capable of differentiating between the two. You will find they enjoy family life and yet will be alert little "watch dogs" as well if the occasion demands.

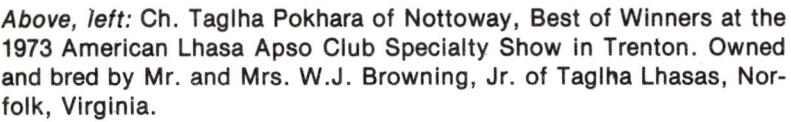

Above, left: Ch. Taglha Pokhara of Nottoway, Best of Winners at the 1973 American Lhasa Apso Club Specialty Show in Trenton. Owned and bred by Mr. and Mrs. W.J. Browning, Jr. of Taglha Lhasas, Norfolk, Virginia.

Above, right: Beautiful headstudy of a Canadian Lhasa provided by Ann-Marie Adderly, Nonsuch Kennels, Montreal West, P.Q., Canada.

Opposite, upper photo: Champion Bella-Mu Go Get 'Em Tiger, winning Best of Breed at the 1975 North Country Kennel Club Show under judge Dr. Samuel Draper. Owned and handled by Ann Sergio of Bella-Mu Kennels, Woodbury, New York.

Opposite, lower photo: Ch. Rgyal-Bu Tompar is shown capturing the Best of Winners title enroute to the championship. Tompar is breeder-owner-handled by Barbara Wood, Anbara Lhasa Apsos, New York.

BEST OF BREED OR VARIETY
NORTH COUNTRY KENNEL CLUB, INC.
AUG. 16, 1975 KLEIN

BEST OF WINNERS
ASHBEY PHOTO

LHASA COATS

One of the most striking features about the Lhasa Apso is the beautiful profusion of coat. A well-groomed Lhasa in full bloom is a joy to behold. It represents a healthy, well-cared-for animal that is seen in the peak of condition.

However, this long full coat is not just to please the eye, or to impress the judge in the show ring. The Lhasa coat is to protect the dog from the elements. And it is this profuse coat that keeps out the heat in summer and the cold in winter that makes this breed an ideal dog for any climate. They survive in the tropics or the mountains with equal comfort. The hair over the eyes protects them from the sun or the glare from the snow. The thickness of the coat over the entire body also protects the body from dampness and insects such as flies, etc., and the hair between the toes protects their feet from ground heat or rocky terrain.

LHASA COLORS

While many different colors and shadings are seen today in the show ring, the gold colored dog is most highly desired by most people who admire the little oriental dogs. The Tibetans, of course, prefer the gold colors since they are, after all, considered to be "little lion dogs" and the gold color rings true with that comparison. In India whites are preferred. However, the blending of the various shades with the tipping found in so many of today's specimens does provide a variety of colors and the matter of color has become strictly a matter of personal preference. Even the solid blacks are beginning to win in the rings today.

Pigmentation must not be sacrificed in any way, however. The good dark brown eye and nose leather called for in the Standard should be preserved.

LHASA MOVEMENT

While there is no mention of the way a Lhasa Apso should move in the official Standard for the breed, needless to say, it is very important that the dog gait correctly. Bad fronts and rears, cow hocks, paddling in front, bowed legs are all objectionable and will spoil the image of the dog. Legs that are out at the shoulders, or hindquarters that are weak, are undesirable and not typical of the breed. When the dog is in motion the gait should be smooth and even and the pads of the hind feet may be visible beneath the coat as the dog reaches its legs directly behind it.

Also, when the dog is gaiting the head should be held up high in the gay manner called for in the Standard, and not sniffing the ground or reached out straight ahead. The tail should be carried up over the back to complete the pretty picture of the Lhasa in motion.

Rgyal Bo-Jangles, C.D., owned and bred by Barbara Wood, Anbara Lhasas, New York City. He finished for his title in three consecutive shows and was trained by his owner.

LHASA SIZE

While Lhasa Apsos in the United States are of a good size and carefully stated in the Standard, the Lhasas in other countries may vary. They tend to be more partial to the smaller size abroad, although they agree that symmetry and type are more important factors. As breeding practices become more and more strict along with the breed's increase in popularity, we are seeing more and more uniformity in litters.

FIRST

ASHBEY PHOTO

BROOKHAVEN K.C.
OCTOBER 14, 1973
BEST PUPPY
NON SPORTING
GROUP

A BUSHMAN PHOTO

Above: Ch. Rygal Khetsa-Po is shown finishing her championship under judge Dr. Samuel Draper at the Newton Kennel Club show of August 3, 1973. Khetsa-Po is owner-handled by Barbara Wood, Anbara Lhasa Apsos, New York City.

Opposite, upper photo: Tabu's Fame and Fortune, bred by Norman and Carolyn Herbel, is owned and shown by Gerrilynn Goldberg to a First Prize in Novice Junior Handling at the Rockland County Kennel Club Show in 1974. Fame was sired by Ch. Tibet of Cornwallis ex Ch. Bindy of Norbulingka. Photo by Ashbey.
Opposite, lower photo: Tyba Ron-nie wins the Non-Sporting Group at the 1973 Brookhaven Kennel Club Match Show. Bred by Mrs. Paula Lieberman and handled by Allan Lieberman, Ron-nie is co-owned by Mrs. Lieberman and Mrs. Dorothy Cohen.

LHASA LONGEVITY

The Lhasa Apso, being a hardy little dog, has proven time and again that it is a long-lived breed. Like many of the ancient sages that reigned in the temples and monasteries of the orient, this dog seemed destined to live for a long time right along with their masters.

While the breed has only been in this country for less than half a century, there has hardly been time to set up any table as to the average life span of the Lhasa Apso that would represent any true picture of what to expect. However, we do know that Ch. Hamilton La Pung lived to be 29 years old. When he died on July 4, 1964, he was just a little more than four-and-a-half months away from his 30th birthday. His owner, Mrs. Elizabeth Finn of Cedar Grove, New Jersey, can attest to the long life of this little white Lhasa.

However, this must be regarded as the exception. While they do live a good long time with the proper loving care, La Pung can in no way be considered as either normal or even occasional: La Pung was surely an exception!

MUGGS: THE CINDERELLA DOG

This is a true story of a rags to riches Lhasa Apso, that with the help of a little girl, chose his own home and a new life for himself.

Late in June of 1971, Mrs. Beverly Stanyon of Auburn, New York, was interrupted during her housework by her daughter Erin, who came running home from school and called to her mother to come see what had followed her home from school. In Beverley Stanyon's own words she said,

"I dropped what I was doing and went to the front door. Out on the lawn stood Erin and next to her was, well, I wasn't sure. It was some kind of little dog but nothing like I had ever seen before. It was a dirty beige-blond color with hair that looked like cotton candy. The first words I said to my daughter were, 'No, we can't keep him!'"

Using the standard speech employed by all mothers whose children bring home strays, Mrs. Stanyon reminded Erin how she would feel if their dog had been lost, and they would have to try very hard to locate the owner. They took the dog around to stores and shopping areas and asked if the dog looked familiar to them, put ads in the newspapers, etc. Mrs. Stanyon located an ad in the paper describing the dog—but advertized as 'found' rather than lost. She called the woman, who explained that she had originally found the dog and advertised for the real owners, but the dog had run away again. The woman also added that she didn't really want the dog anymore and Mrs. Stanyon found herself telling the woman that they would keep him!

The first thought that crossed her mind when she hung up the phone was to give the dog a bath! He appeared to have every disease and parasite in the books, and to protect their Afghan hound, Julius, Mrs. Stanyon made both dog and daughter remain outside. Now the

Winning the Group and then on to Best in Show, the "Cinderella Dog," American and Canadian Champion Gaymans Muggs McGinnis. This rags to riches stray dog followed a little girl home from school one day and eventually became a top show dog! Owned by Beverly Stanyon of Auburn, New York.

bathtub was filled and the shampoo and flea spray was placed alongside and Erin and Mrs. Stanyon put the shaggy dog in the tub.

The dog's coat was like a sponge. The entire body was one solid mat. No matter how much they rinsed, soap kept bubbling out of the mats. However, he survived the bath and the next stop was the veterinarian's office. The veterinarian suggested they get rid of the dog because of its skin condition and Erin's eyes filled with tears. By this time they were really determined to keep the dog no matter what, so the next visit was to Carol Atkins' house. She is a professional groomer who shaved the dog down to the skin except for a little fur on his head and tail. At this stage Carol identified the dog as a Lhasa Apso and determined that the skin problem was flea bites! The mats she shaved off were filled with dead fleas from his earlier shampoo! The pile of mats weighed eight pounds!

Once again the dog went home with the Stanyons. Mrs. Stanyon does not believe in naming animals too quickly, but rather likes to wait until they seem to almost name themselves. Their little tough

BEST OF BREED
OR VARIETY
TRENTON
KENNEL CLUB, INC.
MAY 5,1974

BEST IN SHOW
CLUB CANIN
DE
MONTRÉAL

PACKERLAND
KENNEL CLUB SHOW
APRIL 25, 1970
GREEN BAY, WIS.
BEST NON SPORTING

Captions for pages 120 and 121

Page 120, top: Best in Show winner Ch. BarCon's the Avenger, pictured here winning his second consecutive American Lhasa Apso Club National Specialty show in May 1974 under judge Al Likewise. Bred by the Barry Tompkins, the Avenger is co-owned by Barry Tompkins and Dorothy J. Kendall, his handler. The Avenger went on to Group Second at this same show under judge Peter Knoop. He was the #1 Lhasa Apso and #4 Non-Sporting Dog all-breeds in 1973.

Page 120, bottom: Group 1 and Best In Show from the classes was American and Canadian Champion Gaymans Muggs McGinnis, owned by Mrs. Beverly Stanyon, Crowhaven, Auburn, New York. This win was under breeder-judge John Devlin at the 1975 Club Canin de Montreal, Canada. Parker Harris handled for the owner. Muggs was the top winning Lhasa in Canada for 1975 and has 2 Canadian Bests in Show, 5 Group Firsts and 2 other Group placements, as well as 9 Bests of Breed.

Page 121, top: A photograph of an oil painting by Gourlay Steell, Royal Scottish Academy, born in Edinburgh in 1819. He was called the "Scottish Landseer" and exhibited in the Royal Academy in London. Upon the death of Landseer, Steell was appointed animal painter to the Queen of Scotland and much of his work remains in royal collections abroad. The above painting is thought to have been painted in 1873, the year of his appointment to the Queen, but there is no record of the name of the dog or who owned it at the time of the sitting.

This original painting was discovered by a young couple in a California antique shop. Many Lhasa fanciers offered them considerable money for it, but it was not for sale. Information was taken off the back of the painting and its history traced by dog-man Gerald Massey. The photograph of the painting was done by Dan Adams of Glendale, California.

Page 121, bottom: Ch. Ruffway Mashaka is pictured winning the Non-Sporting Group at the 1970 Packerland Kennel Club Show under judge Joseph Faigel. Mashaka is the winner of six Groups and a Best in Show. This son of Ch. Everglo's Spark of Gold was owner-handled to these impressive wins by Georgia Palmer of Addison, Illinois.

guy eventually became Muggs and he hit it off with Julius, the Afghan, right from the start. From his early appearance Mrs. Stanyon believed Muggs to be an old dog.

"He had eyes that had the look of a dog that had seen a century go by. Happiness for him now was sleeping under the kitchen table with a big bowl of food."

Muggs was learning to be walked on a leash along with Julius and soon learned what the jangle of a chain collar meant. He was as happy as a clam with his new family. But it was inevitable that the real owners would eventually call to claim their dog. Mrs. Stanyon had been warning Erin to be ready for it. Two weeks later the phone did ring and it was Muggs' real owners. All Mrs. Stanyon could manage to say was that this was going to break her daughter's heart. Raggs—his real name she learned from the owner—had run away from them but that they had been considering selling the dog before he took off. The owner told her that they had paid $375 for the dog when he was a puppy and he was now about a year old. Mrs. Stanyon explained that she could not afford that much after all the medical and grooming bills and offered her fifty dollars. The woman had considered offering a twenty-five dollar reward for the dog and so she sold him to her for that!

Later the woman arrived with the papers for Muggs. She was carrying a baby and explained that her husband wasn't too fond of the dog so he was tied out by the barn and had chewed his way through the rope.

After the papers had been signed the lady patted the dog on the head and walked away. Muggs never moved. He obviously was not sorry to see her go. Once the door was closed she called, "Raggs!" but the dog did not respond. She tried "Muggs!" and the little dog came bounding down the hall to her. He knew his new name, and with the papers now in her possession Raggs officially became Gayman's Muggs McGinnis. But the story does not end there with Muggs and the Stanyons just living together happily ever after.

Three years later Julius became very ill. He was operated on for a tumor that turned out to be a massive cancer and there was no hope for a recovery. Young Bill Stanyon and Muggs mourned the hardest and the longest. Muggs stopped eating when Billy turned away from him in his grief. After eight days of starvation they had to force-feed Muggs. He picked up a little but he still mourned the loss of his friend Julius.

Beverly Stanyon realized she had to buy another friend for Muggs. She went to see Carol Atkins who instead recommended showing Muggs after seeing him again. They sent for a five generation pedigree and were amazed to find his background filled with champions from Hamilton and Norbulinka lines. Muggs was taken to Parker Harris, a professional handler, for another opinion on his

WINNERS
ELMIRA
KENNEL CLUB, INC.
JUNE 30, 1975   KLEIN

BEST OF WINNERS
PHOTO BY Graham

BEST OF WINNERS
HATBORO DOG CLUB, INC.
OCT. 4, 1974
KLEIN

quality. While Parker Harris admitted he was lacking in coat he accepted him and a fairytale show career was launched!

Show after show Muggs did well, and was soon a Canadian Champion. But even before earning his championship status he won his first Best in Show from the classes in Canada. Next came his American championship before returning to Canada for another Best in Show! He was top Lhasa Apso in Canada in 1975. His record in eight times shown was two Bests in Show, five Group Firsts, one Group Second, one Group Third and eight Bests of Breed.

The Stanyons have been offered thousands of dollars for Muggs, but the answer, of course, is always a firm "No!" Mrs. Stanyon says, "After all, he picked us and how do you put a price on a fairytale?" In the meantime Muggs has been producing some excellent litters of puppies and the Stanyons have purchased Sharpette's Bo Peep as a mate for him. Their first litter was whelped in January, 1976. The Stanyons say they intend to see to it that Muggs and Bo Peep live happily ever after and that some day one of their offspring will be another kind of fairytale dog.

Captions for pages 124 and 125:

Page 124, top: Tib's Tribulation of Milarepa, whelped in 1974, is pictured winning a 4-point major as Best of Winners under judge Dudley McMillin at the 1975 Denton Kennel Club Show with her handler Beverly Henry. Tribulation is owned by Mary S. Carter of Flower Mound, New Town, Texas.

Page 124, bottom: Dolsa Solo pictured winning Winners Bitch under judge Mrs. Ann Wanner at the 1975 Elmira Kennel Club Show. Solo has 12 points toward championship to date. Bred by Jean Kausch, co-owner with Connie Tompkins, BarCon Kennels, Fulton, New York.

Page 125, top: Ch. Chin-Ti's Ti Ko La is shown finishing his championship with a 4-point Winners Dog and Best of Winners decision by judge C.L. Savage at the Furniture City Kennel Club Show. Handled by Toddie Clark for owners Mr. and Mrs. Scott Hall.

Page 125, bottom: Ch. Karma Lo Lo Ko, bred by Dorothy Cohen and owned by Mrs. Arlene Bloch, pictured winning at the 1974 Hatboro Kennel Club Show under judge Robert Braithwaite. Handled by Joan Pettit for the owner. Klein photograph.

7: THE AMERICAN LHASA APSO CLUB

The American Lhasa Apso Club was organized on February 9, 1959. As with all breed clubs, the intent and purpose of this parent club was to serve as a guide to newcomers to the breed and for the purpose of promoting and encouraging high ethical standards for breeding and showing the Lhasa Apso.

As a method of better serving interested parties, the club publishes a pamphlet entitled *The Lhasa Apso* which may be obtained free of charge by writing to the club secretary. Name and address of the club secretary can be obtained by writing or telephoning the American Kennel Club, 51 Madison Avenue, New York City, New York, 10010.

The pamphlet contains a brief description of the history of the Lhasa Apso, a word about the club, the American Kennel Club approved Standard for the breed, and an application blank for membership in the club. The membership fee is ten dollars per year per person, and fifteen dollars for couples. Membership runs from June first of each year to May 31st of the following year. All prospective members must be recommended by two American Lhasa Apso Club members, must be 18 years of age or over, and in good standing with the American Kennel Club.

Membership is open to all those who express a sincere interest in the Lhasa Apso.

LHASA APSO SPECIALTY CLUBS

As the breed began to flourish in the United States it became more and more obvious that one parent club could no longer handle all the activities that were going on in the breed, and regional clubs, or chapters of the American Lhasa Apso Club, began to mushroom.

As of the mid-seventies there were several clubs which functioned actively on behalf of the breed. A list of them follows which will help you get in touch with the group closest to your locality.

CASCADE LHASA APSO FANCIERS
 Secretary, Margaret Starling
 6722-200th S.W.
 Lynnwood, Washington 98036

GULF COAST LHASA APSO CLUB
 Secretary, Shirley Michalinos
 11110 Sagedown Lane
 Houston, Texas 77034

BEST OF
WINNERS

Americal's Sandur, U.D., owned by Mr. and Mrs. James Wood of Venice, California. Sandur is pictured here at seven years of age still clearing the bar with the greatest of ease.

Opposite, upper photo: Ch. Karma Ka-Sha, bred by Dorothy Cohen and owned by Joan Pettit, Mio Lhasa Apso, New York. Ka-Sha was three years old when this photograph was taken in October, 1973.

Opposite, lower photo: Ch. Sharpette's Galahad pictured taking a Best of Winners decision at the 1971 Southern Adirondack Kennel Club Show under judge Anna Cowie. Handling for owners David and Elizabeth Goldfarb, Xanadu Lhasa Apso, is Robert Sharp. Galahad is the foundation dog at the Goldfarb's kennel.

French and International Ch. Fo de l'Annapurna, who is, without a doubt, the most influential stud in France. Bred and owned by Miss V. Dupont of the Annapurna Kennels, he was sired by Daphnis de l'Annapurna *ex* Int. Ch. Hamilton Kangmar.

KENTUCKIANA LHASA APSO CLUB
   Secretary, Al Vogt
   2611 Pope Lick Road
   Louisville, Kentucky 40299

LHASA APSO CLUB OF HAWAII

LHASA APSO CLUB OF NORTHERN CALIFORNIA
   Secretary, Mrs. Alice Banoff
   P.O. Box 95
   Los Gatos, California 95030

LHASA APSO CLUB OF SOUTHERN CALIFORNIA
   Secretary, Lynn Chertkow
   471 Beverwil Drive
   Beverly Hills, California

LHASA APSO CLUB OF WESTCHESTER, INC.
   Secretary, Barbara Wood
   15 West 84th Street
   New York, New York 10024

NATIONAL CAPITAL AREA LHASA APSO CLUB
   Secretary, Doris Curtis
   2605 Faber Court
   Falls Church, Virginia

NEW ENGLAND LHASA APSO CLUB
   Secretary, Joanne Egan
   169 Linden Drive
   Cohasset, Mass. 02025

Ch. Belazieth's Malcolm, a Best in Show winner, bred and owned by Rob and Doreen Richardson of Essex, England. A Diane Pearce photograph. Malcolm has eight C.C.'s and two all-breed Bests in Show. He was Best Puppy in Show at the 1974 Lhasa Championship show and Best in Show in 1975. He was also Best of Breed at Crufts in 1975.

Chiz Ari Khelev, C.D., with a few of his obedience trophies. He scored in the 190's for his title and was working on his C.D.X. when he died tragically from kidney disease. Owned by Madeline P. Chizever and Joanne P. Baker, Chiz Lhasa Apso, Columbia, Maryland.

These clubs hold Match Shows and issue bulletins or club publications which are informative and helpful to all. There are others as this book goes to press, but full information was not received in time for publication.

THE AWARDS DINNERS

1973 was the year the American Lhasa Apso Club staged its first Annual Awards Dinner. It was held on February 11 at the famous Luchow's Restaurant on 14th Street in New York City along with the annual Club meeting. Chairlady for the event was Raena Wilks, who was complimented on her efforts by the club president, Robert Sharp.

CLUB BULLETIN

The Lhasa Bulletin, created in 1972, is the official voice of the American Lhasa Apso Club. Norman L. Herbel is the editor, and sees to it that members receive show results, articles of interest to members and beautifully presented advertisements from members wishing to promote their dogs and their kennels.

LHASA APSO PUBLICATIONS

In addition to the parent club pamphlet, the American Lhasa Apso Club supplies members with a copy of the Constitution and the Standard. However, there are several publications which provide information regarding the breed.

The Lhasa Apso Reporter, Jean Kausch, editor; P.O. Box 827, Culver City, California 90230. This is a bi-monthly publication and costs ten dollars a year for a subscription.

Lhasa Tales, is another excellent publication edited by Dick Brown and Darrel Smith, at 541 5th Street, West Des Moines, Iowa 50265. *Lhasa Tales* is published each month.

A booklet entitled *The Lhasa Apso* by Frances Sefton of Australia is available at most pet shops for around two dollars and is the true definitive book on the breed, containing excellent photographs of the early greats first imported to England plus current winners from the 1970's.

T.F.H. Publications, Inc., publishers of this book, also publish a small paperback book written by Patricia Chenoweth; and Dr. Robert Berndt has written a book entitled *Your Lhasa Apso* that is available through the club.

Additional information and kennel advertising may be seen through the pages of the various dog magazines which also publish breed columns each month, and the *American Kennel Club Complete Dog Book* also provides information on our breed.

American and Canadian Ch. Reiniets St. Nicholas finished his Canadian championship at four shows in 1972 with four Bests of Breed, and a Group One, a Group Two and a Group Four. You will note from the photograph that in Canada the Lhasa Apso is exhibited in the Terrier Group as compared to the Non-Sporting Group in the U.S.A. Sired by Ch. Americal's Sing Song, C.D., he is owned by Harriet C. Cohrs, Reinet Lhasas, Clinton, Arkansas.

THE UNITED KINGDOM LHASA APSO CLUB

This Lhasa Apso Club exists for the encouragement of the breeding and owning of Lhasas and lists among its members many people of dedication and prominence. The Club's patron is Her Highness The Drenjong Gyalmo, Queen of Sikkim, and the President is Princess Pema Tsedeum Yapshi Pheunkhang Lhacham. Among the Vice-Presidents we find the names of The Hon. Mrs. I. Bailey, Miss B. Harding, Major R. Mayer, The Lady Doreen Prior-Palmer and The Lady Freda Valentine.

A newsletter is sent to all members at intervals during the year, and the club's Chairman, W.M. Brownlie, Esquire, is actively promoting the distribution of the club's handbook, first published in 1975. There is also a club badge, which is available to club members, with a design based on the Tibetan flag.

The club stages two dog shows each year. The Open Show is held in conjunction with the annual meeting in March, and the club's Championship Show, held in September, features the annual Parade of Champions. The club possesses many impressive perpetual trophies, among them the Tibetan Butter Lamp presented by their patron, the Queen of Sikkim, for the Best in Show winner at the Championship Show. Two Tibetan "Chang" Bowls for Best Dog and Best Bitch at this same show have been donated by the Hon. Mrs. Bailey, and the Brackenbury Lhotse Memorial Points Cup is awarded annually to the Lhasa winning the most points in breed and variety classes each year. The club also offers the Mayer Stud Dog Trophy and there is the Verles Cup for the winning Brood Bitch awarded on a point basis for their progeny which win Challenge Certificates and Reserve C.C.'s.

There are also several club trophies available at the general all-breed Championship Shows. The Marjorie Wild Memorial Trophy, presented to the Kennel Club by the late Miss Wild, is awarded each year at Crufts to the Best of Breed Lhasa. This trophy, formerly the Waterloo Cup for Greyhound coursing, was won by a member of Miss Wild's family.

The yearbook and the newsletter both publish the names of the winners of these cups and trophies as well as a list of the judges, list of shows holding classes for the breed, a list of members' names and addresses, and the names of their dogs standing at stud. Also, a four-page booklet telling significant facts about the breed can be obtained by writing the club's Secretary (since 1960), Mrs. D.M. Hesketh-Williams, a most prompt and prolific correspondent for the club.

Interest in the breed in the United Kingdom can be clearly evidenced by the amount of advertising by reputable kennels in the club's yearbook and by the entries now appearing at their shows. At the 1975 Championship Show there was an entry of 108 Lhasas in 20 classes.

8: SOME OF THE TOP KENNELS TODAY

Even though the oriental breeds have always been popular among dog fanciers all over the world, there is no denying the amazing rise in popularity found in the Lhasa Apso breed. In 1974 a record total of 1,103,249 dogs were registered with the American Kennel Club. While registrations were down 7.9% in 1975, only seven breeds continued to show an increase in individual registrations out of the top thirty. One of the seven was the Lhasa Apso. It was #5 as far as a gain in position on the charts; this was published in an article in the March, 1976 issue of the American Kennel Club magazine, *Pure-Bred Dogs*.

While it can be dangerous for any breed to gain too quickly in popularity so that it suffers "growing pains" and risks indiscriminate breeding for commercial gain, it is to the credit of reputable breeders, who by producing fine quality stock have enhanced the breed with the dog-loving public. These dedicated breeder-exhibitors are responsible for presenting their dogs at their best and are responsible for the impressive show records which make history for the breed. The dogs also provide a lot of love and affection for those who take them into their hearts and homes.

The future of the breed lies in the hands of the kennels and breeders of today. We present in this chapter, in alphabetical order, brief resumes of some of today's leading and most active kennels. The success of the breed today and in the decades to come remains with these noted American kennels.

ANBARA

In 1969 Barbara Wood fell in love with the beauty and personality of the Lhasa Apso and established her Anbara line of Lhasas.

Because she lives in a New York City apartment, her breeding is on a very limited scale, and Barbara considers herself strictly a hobby breeder...but a breeder, nonetheless.

Barbara Wood enjoys both the show and obedience ring competition and does her own training and showing. Such was the case in completing the championships on her Ch. Rgyal Khetsa-Po, Ch. Rgyal Zig of Lejo, Ch. Rgyal-Bu Tompar, and Ch. Neika Hi Lah Lieh.

A 5½-week-old litter of Lhasas bred and owned by Barbara Wood, Anbara Kennels, New York City. The sire was Ch. Potala Keke's Tomba Tu *ex* Ch. Tgyal Khetsa-Po. The fourth puppy from left grew up to be Ch. Tgyal Zig of Lejo, now owned by Lee Bankuckas and Barbara Wood, and the fifth puppy is Ch. Tgyal-Bu Tompar owned by Barbara Wood.

Her top obedience dog, Rgyal Bo-Jangles, C.D., finished for his title in three consecutive shows.

In the breeding end of the Anbara operation, Barbara's Khetsa is the dam of two champions and Yeti Rimar's Ginger Snaps has 10 points toward championship.

Through some business connections, Barbara has had her␃hasas used in theatrical appearances and as models on television and in magazines. Bo-Jangles has also appeared on the famous children's show *Sesame Street*, where he made a big hit with everyone. Barbara Wood's hobby is photography and she is responsible for taking many very beautiful photographs of her dogs at all stages of their development.

BARCON

Barry and Connie Tompkins started their BarCon Kennels in 1968 in Fulton, New York. In a vary short span of years they achieved remarkable success with their BarCon's the Avenger. In July, 1974 he was awarded his 14th Best in Show award, making him the top-winning Lhasa Apso of all time to that date. Avenger also won the

Multiple Best in Show winner Ch. Bar Con's the Avenger, the top-winning Lhasa of all time, shown here winning Best in Show at the 1974 Faith City Kennel Club show. Dorothy J. Kendall is handling; she co-owns Avenger with breeders Barry and Connie Tompkins, BarCon Kennels, Fulton, New York.

American Lhasa Apso Club National Specialty in 1973 and 1974 and was awarded the 1973 and 1974 Best in Show and Group Trophies by the Club. By 1975 he had sired four champions as well.

Other Lhasas at the BarCon kennels include American and Canadian Ch. BarCon's Arvergus, Double Trouble, Stage Door Jonny and Ch. Tabu's Double or Nuthin'. There are others, of course, as well as those seen in the show ring.

CHEN

The Chen kennels in California are owned by Patricia and Tom Chenoweth, both ardent enthusiasts in the breed. Pat Chenoweth is a prolific writer and was columnist for *Popular Dogs* magazine for many years. With her husband she also authored the paperback book on the breed entitled *How to Raise and Train a Lhasa Apso* (published by T.F.H. Publications, Inc.).

Pat also has the distinction of being co-breeder, along with Frances Harwell, of Ch. Chen Korum-Ti, one of the really big winners in the breed in the early 1970's. Sired by Ch. Chen Nyun-Ti out of Ch. Chen Karakorum, "Kori" won the breed at Westminster in 1971 under judge Mrs. Augustus Riggs IV and went on to win second in the Non-Sporting Group. This placement is the highest ever achieved by a Lhasa at this show to date.

In the over twenty years that the Chenoweths have been in the dog fancy, they have gathered a wealth of information on the breed and have produced a line of quality dogs that they can really be proud of, in and out of the show ring!

Another of the Lhasas the Chenoweths can surely boast about is Ch. Chen Tukki Dar, handled during his show ring career by Robert Sharp for owners Jean and Don La Fontaine.

CROWHAVEN

Mrs. William (Beverly) Stanyon of Auburn, New York, has Arabian horses and a few Lhasas. The story of her getting into the breed with her first Lhasa is one of the most remarkable tales ever told about the breed. Her Best in Show-winning American and Canadian Ch. Gayman's Muggs McGinnis came to her as a stray dog which she tried to return to its owner and then purchased for $25.00!

Opposite:
Chen Ti-Kara of Karo La, pictured winning Best of Winners at the 1971 Golden Gate Kennel Club show. Tiki made ten points, both majors, on the way toward championship. Tiki is alternately handled by Carol and Bill Stretch of Los Gatos, California, and is co-owned by Mrs. Stretch and Patricia Chenoweth.

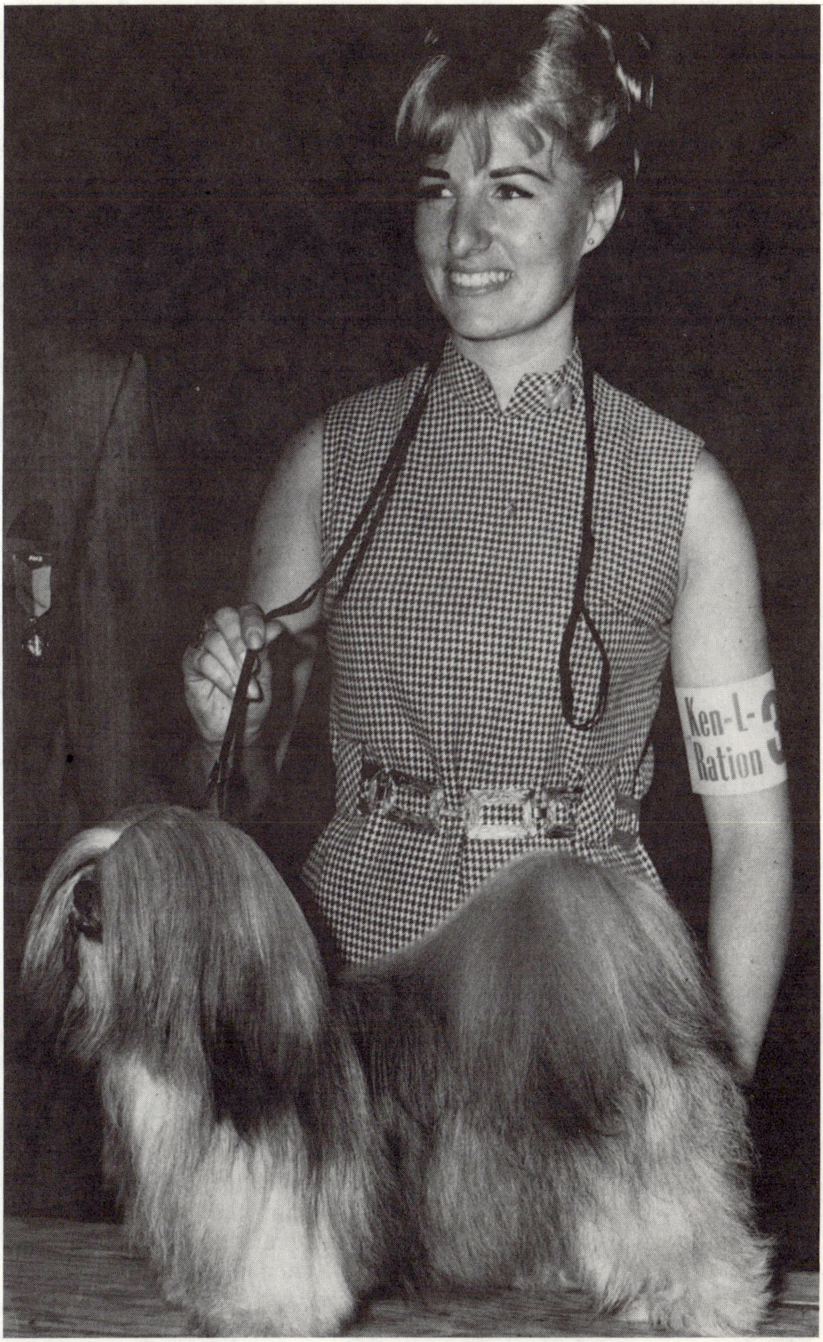
Ken-L-
Ration

Anbara's Popcorn and Anbara's Snowflake, pictured at five weeks of age. Bred and owned by Barbara Wood, New York City.

Opposite:
Ch. BarCon's Double Trouble, pictured taking the Best of Winners ribbon at the 1971 Old Dominion Kennel Club Show with handler Parker Harris. This 5-point win at the age of 13 months finished the championship requirements. Bred by Bar-Con Kennels and owned by Connie and Karey Tompkins, Fulton, New York.

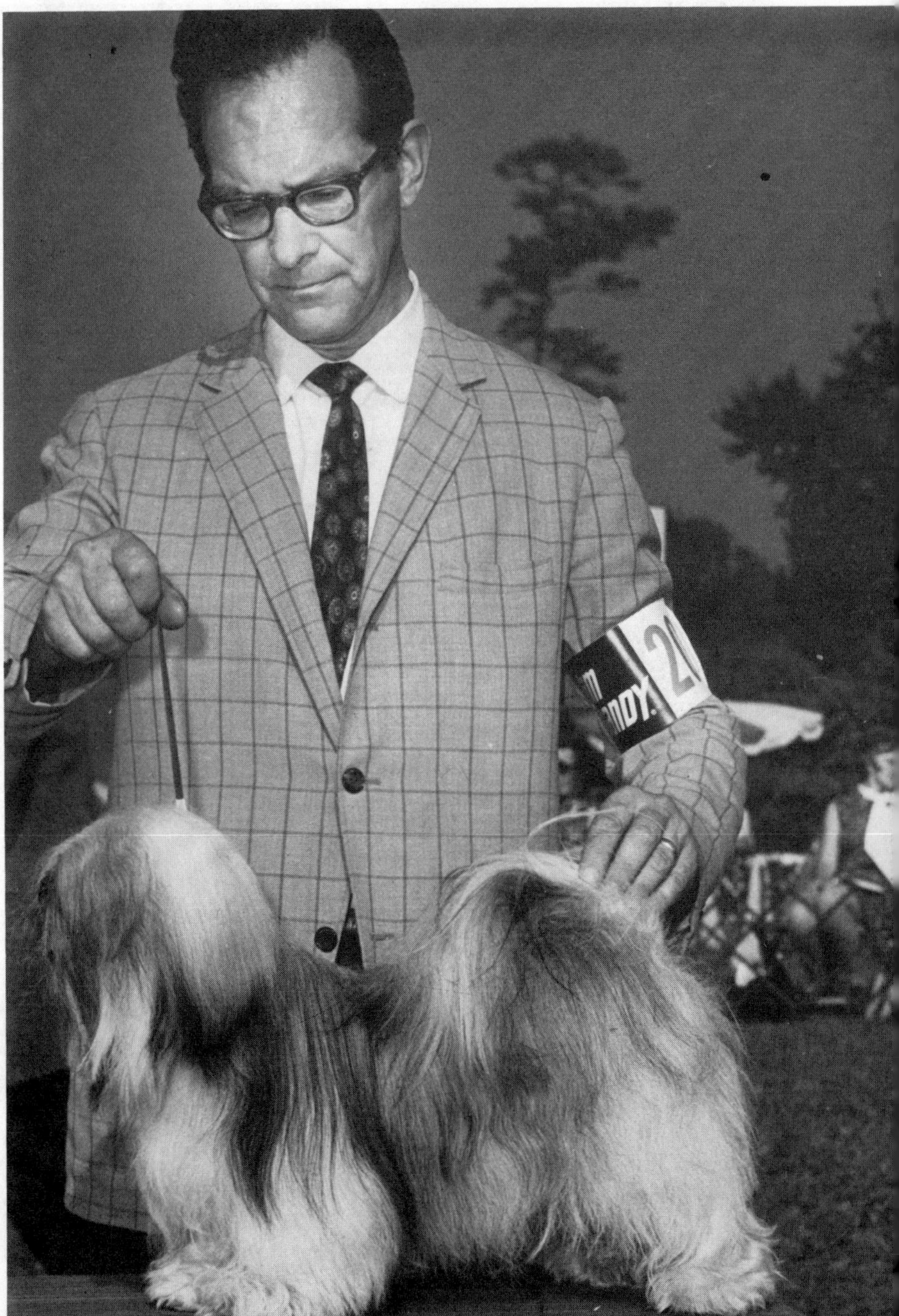

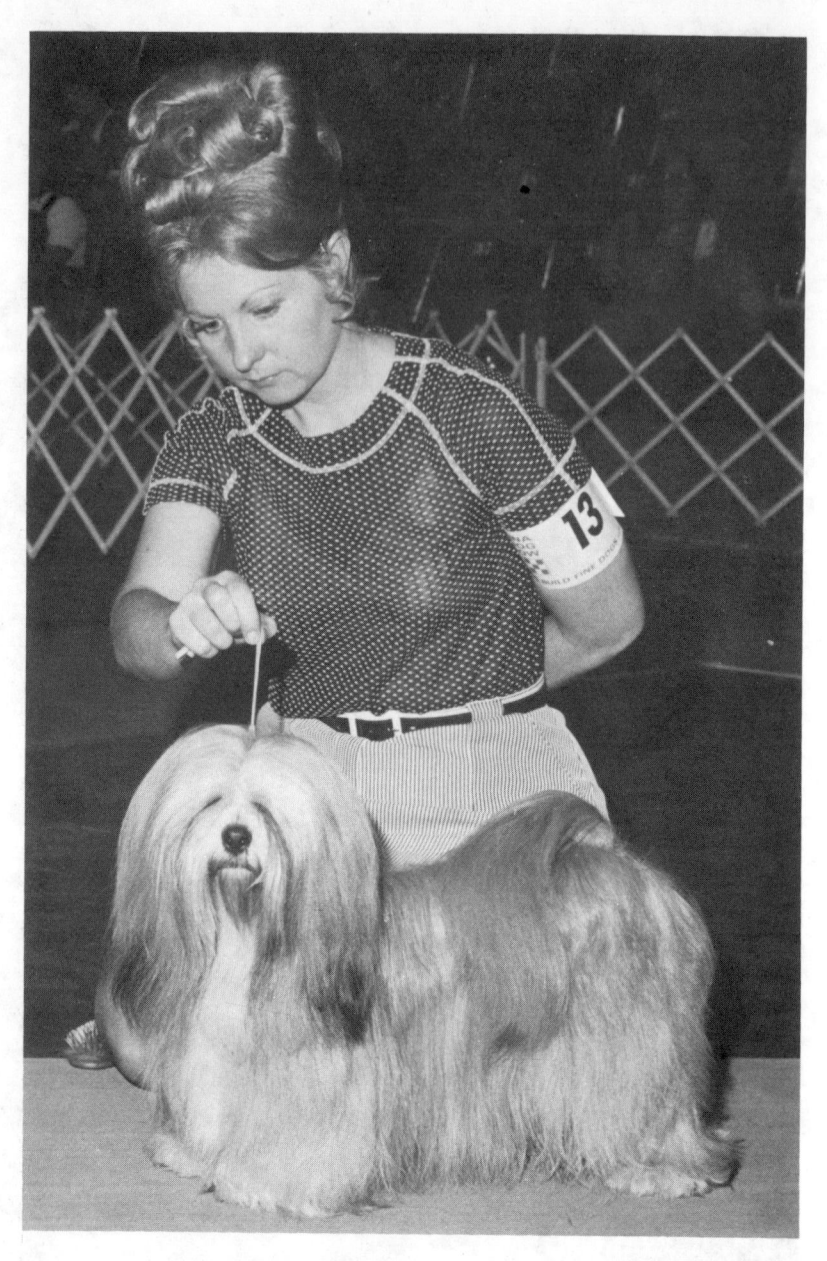

Ch. Joi-San's Khan-Dieh, bred and owned by Joyce Stambaugh, Joi-San Kennels, New Providence, New Jersey. Khan-Dieh is handled here by Annette Lurton and finished with four majors. The sire was Ch. Arborhill's Bhran-Dieh *ex* Chu Shu's Kiri.

Muggs' record includes two Bests in Show, five Group Firsts and a Group Second and Third, with nine Bests of Breed in limited showing in Canada. He was the top-winning Lhasa in Canada for 1975 in spite of his strange introduction into the Stanyon family.

The Stanyons and their two children also own a Lhasa bitch, Sharpettes Bo Peep, a Chen Korum Ti daughter that whelped her first litter in January, 1976. While it took Beverly Stanyon three and a half years after acquiring Muggs to enter him into the show ring, the entire family is proud of his record, and the Stanyons have given him the title of The Cinderella Dog. He has made the entire family become as devoted to Lhasa Apsos as they have always been to the Arabian horse.

JOI-SAN

Mrs. James (Joyce) Stambaugh started her Joi-San kennels in New Providence, New Jersey, in the late 1960's and has produced many champions considering the fact that she breeds very few litters.

Her line was based on her brood bitch, Chu Shu's Kiri, who is the dam of four champions; her top dogs are American and Canadian Ch. Joi-San's King Tu, Ch. Joi-San's Khan-Dieh, Ch. Joi-San's Grundoon and Ch. Joi-San's Ribar's Joker. Gol-Den Mocca of Ky is a multiple all-breed Best in Show winner, and Happieh is a multiple Group winner and has won a Specialty Show.

Joyce's friend Annette Lurton, owner of the Darby Ram Kennels in Lexington, Kentucky, where she breeds and shows both Lhasas and Standard Poodles, claims that Joyce Stambaugh has another claim...that is, she is prone to sell only older puppies, making sure that when she represents her stock as show winners, they really are!

MAGESTIC

The foundation dogs for the Magestic Kennels were purchased by Lois Magette of Long Beach, California, from Mrs. Dorothy Cohen in 1968. She selected Karma Magestic Mah Jong and Ch. Karma Skar-Cen, two beautiful bitches. Mah Jong became her foundation bitch and Skar-Cen became the first bitch ever to win a Non-Sporting Group in California, owner-handled over an entry of 298.

Mah Jong had picked up points toward championship before being bred, first to Ch. Karma Dmar Po, then to Ch. Everglo Zijuh Tomba. Both litters produced champions.

Lois then acquired Karma Rus Timala, a top-producer with six champions from a litter of nine puppies. Two of these placed in the Group from the classes.

Lois Magette is particularly proud of her American, Mexican, and Canadian Ch. Magestic Gyad Po from her first home-bred litter; the evidences of quality have been passed to her succeeding generations in breeding. Lois breeds only for pleasure and showing, not as a commercial venture, and follows up on the well-being of the puppies long after they are sold. The Magestic Kennels are truly dedicated to the breed.

NHAMRHET

The Nhamrhet Lhasa Apso Kennels, established in 1970, are owned by Fred Terman of Englewood Cliffs, New Jersey. Fred Terman had two things foremost in his mind in creating Nhamrhet: the breeding of quality dogs with soundness of body and mind and the betterment of the breed. He produced Lhasas that were house pets first and show dogs second.

Champion Magestic Gro-Mo, owner-bred and handled by Miss Pamela L. Magette of Long Beach, California. The sire was Ch. Everglo Zijuh Tomba *ex* Karma Magestic Mah-Jong.

Ch. Licos Cheti La, whelped in June, 1962 and pictured winning under the late Robert Griffing, Lhasa Apso breed pioneer. Cheti was the dam of Best in Show winner Ch. Tibet of Cornwallis, ROM, and Ch. Willy of Cornwallis. Owned and shown by Carolyn Herbel, Tabu Kennels, Lucas, Kansas.

Fred Terman is active in the showring, however, with Rimar's Alikat and Nhamrhet Chu-Sin Dhree. Nhamrhet is also the home of Sheezmi Dhum Dhum. Mr. Terman's degree in animal science (with a minor in genetics) is a great help to him in his breeding program, and he further extends himself on behalf of better dogs by serving on the board of directors of the Lhasa Apso Club of Greater New York.

Fred Terman does not breed Lhasas often, but when he does it's with an eye toward breeding for soundness and type and certainly good temperament. Fred Terman expects to be in Lhasas for many years and has high hopes for Nhamrhet based on both his knowledge and his great devotion to the breed.

NORBULINGKA

Phyllis Marcy's Norbulingka Kennels are located in Franklin, New Hampshire, but actually began in Anchorage, Alaska. This was back in 1960 when she acquired three Hamilton-line Lhasas. They were Lou-Lan of Garten, Karma Kosala, and Licos Khung-La. It was from a breeding of Kosala and Khung-La that she bred the famous Ch. Kham of Norbulingka. Her dedicated breeding program during the next years produced many champions. In this group were Mighty of Norbulingka, the third top-producing sire in the breed for 1971, Lama, Lady Bug, Korkee, Do-Ani Gindy and Norbu—all with the "of Norbulingka" suffix.

ORLANE

The Orlane Kennels of Mrs. Dorothy Kendall Lohmann of Burlington, Iowa, were established in 1956 with Miniature Schnauzers. The Lhasas arrived in 1962 and were purchased from the Everglow Kennels in California. The two champions were Sparky and Flame, and they produced 49 champions between them! Their sire, Ch. Kai Sangs Clown of Everglow, established a new line of Lhasas which can be found behind many of the top-winning Lhasas in the U.S. today.

Orlane Kennels then based their line-breeding program on the Clown offspring and have themselves produced over 20 champions in less than ten years. There were 14 other champions from breedings to Orlane bitches by outside studs.

Orlane won the American Lhasa Apso Club Award of Top Breeder for 1974, and Sparky was Top ROM (Register of Merit) Sire for 1974. The Clown line has produced three Best in Show dogs, including the 1973 and 1974 National Specialty Show winner, making it the Top Lhasa Apso for those years. Some of the outstanding Orlane show dogs are American and Canadian Ch. Orlane's Good As Gold, a Best in Show winner, Int. Ch. Orlane's Golden Puppet, and Best in Show

Opposite:
Ch. Gindy of Norbulingka, ROM, pictured winning Best of Opposite Sex at the 1970 Kanadasage Kennel Club Show. She is the dam of multiple Group winners: Ch. Tabu's Chubby Checkers, Ch. Tabu's Rhapsody in Red, Ch. Tabu's Raquel, and Ch. Tabu's Double or Nuthin. Owner-handled by Carolyn Herbel, Tabu Kennels, Lucas, Kansas.

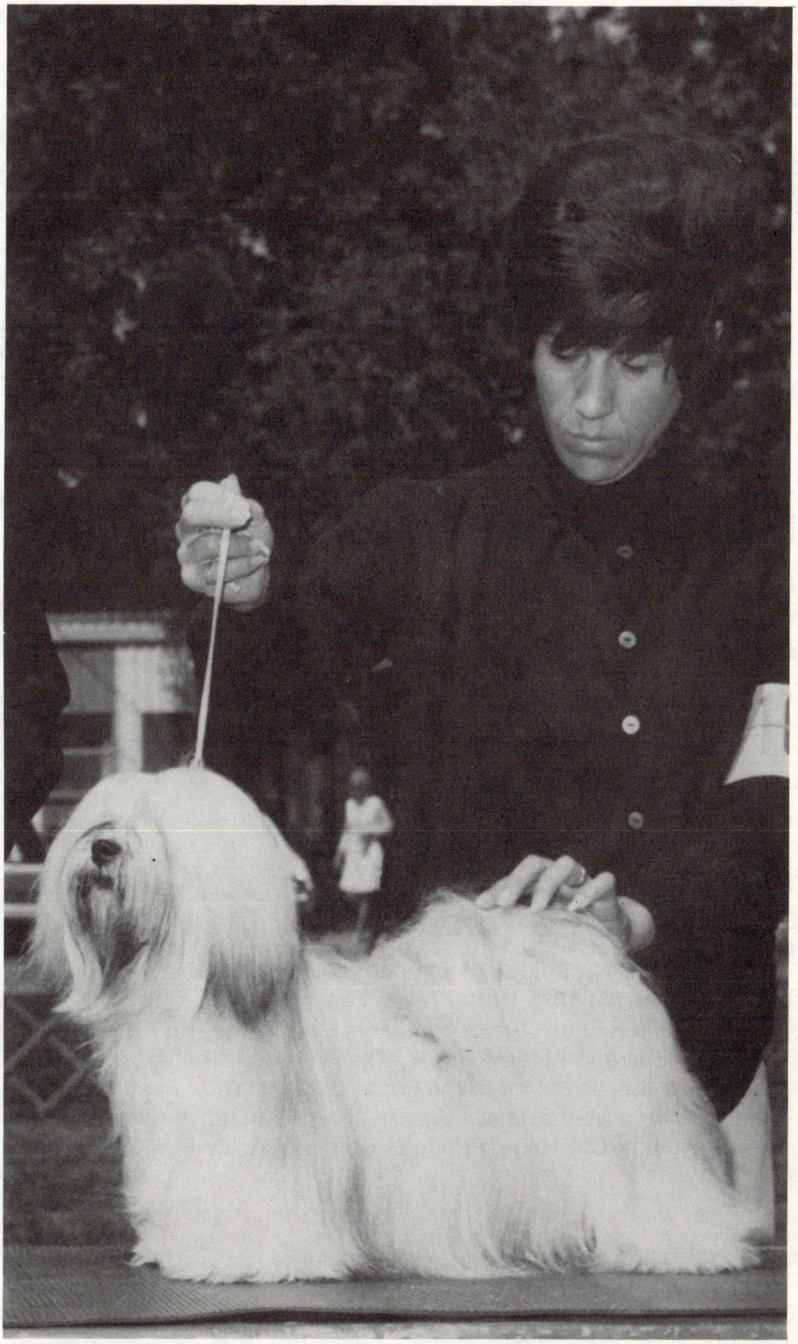

Khasa's Ko Ko Nor, pictured winning Best in Match early in his show ring career at the 1975 North Texas Lhasa Apso Club in Dallas. The judge is Celia Hall, the junior handler is Mark Smith. Ko Ko is breeder-owned by Ben and Barbara Brook, Khasa Lhasas, Richardson, Texas. Ko Ko also has been first in the Puppy Sweepstakes, Best Puppy and Best in Match at the Lhasa Apso Club of Austin; he was sired by Group winning Ch. Hall's Prince Li Chin *ex* Chok's Pin-Ka.

Lingkhor Bhu of Norbulingka, bred by Beverly Deynzer; owned and handled by Phyllis Marcy.

winner Ch. Everglow Spark of Gold. Good as Gold has six Best in Show wins to her credit and was Top Terrier in Canada in 1966 and 1967. She was also a Best of Breed at Westminster.

Mrs. Lohmann's International Champion Orlane's Golden Puppet was exported to Belgium after making his American championship and then earned championship titles in Germany, Austria, Holland and France, as well as in his new homeland, Belgium. Ch. Ever-

The full-coated Lhasa Apso in repose! The beautiful Rimar's Alikat, owned by Fred Terman of Englewood Cliffs, New Jersey, and Stephen G.C. Campbell. The sire was Best in Show winning Ch. Tibet of Cornwallis, ROM, *ex* Ch. Arborhill's Lho-Lha of Rimar. Alikat was bred by Stephen Campbell and Sharon Binkowski.

gow's Spark of Gold was piloted to his Best in Show win by Joe Bousek and was the first Best in Show Lhasa in the Midwestern area. He is the sire of 43 champions (making him the #1 producer in the history of the breed to date) and the sire of three Best in Show champions.

Ch. Orlane's Dulmo, owned by Al and Irene Smith, is the sire of 23 champions. Ch. Kai Sang Flame of Everglow is the dam of six champions, Ch. Ruffway Khambu is the dam of six champions and Ch. Orlane's Chitra of Ruffway is the dam of seven champions. The list of successful Lhasas from the Orlane Kennels goes on and on.

Am. and Can. Ch. Reiniet's St. Nicholas is pictured with handler Mike Shea after going First in the Group at a 1971 show under judge Frank Hayes Burch. He was bred by Harriet C. Cohrs with Ch. Americal's Sing Song as sire, and is owned by Reiniet Lhasas, Clinton, Arkansas.

Tyba Ron-nie, a reddish gold Lhasa male, handled to First in the Sweepstakes at a recent show by 11-year-old Ira Lieberman. Bred by Mrs. Paula Lieberman, Tyba Kennels, Baldwin Harbor, Long Island, New York, Ron-nie is co-owned by Mrs. Lieberman and Dorothy Cohen.

POTALA

Potala and Keke Blumberg, the owner, are very well known in the breed. Since Potala was founded in 1963 there has been a steady stream of top-winning quality dogs that bear the name.

After travelling across America and Europe to visit kennels and look at breeding stock as a foundation for her kennel, Keke Blumberg purchased Ch. Keke's T'Chin T'Chin. Chin quickly finished her championship by the time she was nine months of age.

Chin's success was quickly followed by Ch. Ky-Chu Shara; this bitch's show ring career culminated with the distinct honor of being the second Lhasa Apso bitch to go all the way to Best in Show in the United States. Shara also produced six champions. Shara won the Second Lhasa Apso National Specialty Show under judge Keith Browne on the day she retired from the American showring. However, she did make a few additional appearances in the Canadian showring to earn her Canadian championship!

Best in Show for American and Canadian Champion Potala Keke's Zintora, bred by Keke Blumberg and owned by Dorothy Schottgen. This win was at the 1975 Wilmington Kennel Club show. Handled by Robert Sharp for owner Keke Blumberg, pictured on the right.

Ch. Potala Keke's Golden Gatsby, pictured at his very first dog show. Entered in the American-bred Class, he went on to Best of Breed under judge Robert Braithwaite. Gatsby is handled by Carolyn Herbel. He was 10 months old at this show and went on to finish for his championship in seven shows. A Specials career is planned when he reaches full maturity.

Keke Blumberg imported Ch. Rhamblersholt Verles Rham-Tru from England and finished him in this country. She also purchased Best in Show winner Ch. Tibet of Cornwallis. Tibet not only has had a sparkling showring career but also is one of the breed's top producers to date.

Keke Blumberg has bred or owned four Best in Show winners and many Group winners as well. Her Canadian and American Ch. Potala Keke's Yum Yum was Best in Show in October, 1975, one week before her seventh birthday, and was the 1974 Best of Breed winner at Westminster. She has whelped six champions to date, including Ch. Potala Keke's Tomba Tu. Tomba Tu has won over one hundred Bests of Breed and was a Group winner as well. Yum Yum was the fifth Lhasa bitch to win a Best in Show.

To date Keke Blumberg has bred forty Lhasa champions, and there are many more pointed. Her Potala Kennel is not a kennel, *per se*, because in actuality all the dogs are brought up and live in the house as members of the family. Keke is an American Kennel Club judge as well.

Ch. Daktazl Tsung, pictured winning at a recent show. Handled by Ted Young, Jr., for owners M. Aspuru and Leonard Ripley of Stamford, Connecticut, Tsung was a 1975 Specialty show winner. He is a son of the great Best in Show winner, Ch. Karma Frosty Knight O'Everglo.

Head study of Rimar's Alikat depicting the true Lhasa Apso expression. Owned by Fred Terman (Nhamrhet Lhasa Apso) and Stephen G.C. Campbell (Rimar Lhasa Apso).

RIMAR

Remarkable success has been achieved by Stephen G.C. Campbell since he started his Rimar Kennels in West Trenton, New Jersey, in 1968. Within a very few years his outstanding show dog, Ch. Tabu's King of Hearts, ROM, has become a multiple Group winner in widespread competition at the top shows. Stephen Campbell is also the owner of another multiple Group winner, Ch. Rimar's J.G. King Richard, home-bred that he is most proud of.

While breeding and showing is just a hobby, he is proud of his fourth generation of Lhasa breeding. Stephen is also a member of the Board of Directors, the Awards Chairman, and Delegates to the American Kennel Club for the American Lhasa Apso Club.

He is particularly proud of the fact that his brood bitch, Ch. Rimar's Tipit, was listed by *Lhasa Reporter* magazine as Top Producer in 1975, while King of Hearts was named Top Producer in the male category by both *Lhasa Reporter* and *Kennel Review* magazines. Stephen Campbell is a well-known figure in the breed both in the ring with his lovely dogs and outside the ring in an administrative capacity.

RIMMON

Leonard and Adrienne Ripley of the Rimmon Kennels in Stamford Connecticut, are relatively new to the breed. They got their first Lhasa in 1971 and have done some fine winning since they first ventured into the show ring. Their Ch. Daktazl Tsung was a winner at the 1975 Specialty held in conjunction with the Trenton Kennel Club show, and their homebred Ch. Rimmon Ripsnorter won a Specialty Show in 1974. Tsung has produced two Specialty winners in two litters.

The Ripleys are particularly proud of the Daktari, a Group winner that has 75 Bests of Breed to his credit. They also own Ch. Potala Keke's Andromeda, a lovely bitch of perfect balance and luxurious coat. For having just begun in the early 1970's they are off to a good start and expect to be active in the breed and in the showring in the future.

SHENG-LA

The Dickersons formed their Sheng-La Kennel in Marion, Ohio, in 1965. Admittedly, they consider themselves a small kennel, maintaining that their Lhasas are first and foremost members of their household and *then* show dogs.

The Dickersons breed very few litters, but they have excellent show-quality stock to breed from when they do. Their accent is on producing dogs of quality and good temperament, and placing them in the best possible homes.

The Dickersons enjoy the shows and finishing their own champions, training and competing for obedience degrees and bringing up the young puppies. By the mid-1970's, after a decade in the breed, the Dickersons have four adult Lhasas in Sheng-La. Their Ch. Sheng-La's Chun King is their stud dog and a homebred they are proud of. Ch. Tashi Norbu Tizi of Sheng-La and Dunklehaven Shawnee of Sheng-La are their two little bitches, and a third bitch, the homebred Sheng-La's Tashi Tamima, has a C.D.X. title.

TABU

The famous name of Tabu in the Lhasa Apso world belongs to Norman and Carolyn Herbel; it has been synonymous with quality dogs since 1967. Situated now in Lucas, Kansas, Carolyn is a past secretary of the American Lhasa Apso Club, and Norman is editor of the *Lhasa Bulletin*, the official club magazine. He was also President of the club in the 1970's.

The Herbels have been represented in the obedience rings with their American and Canadian C.D. dog, Tabu's Digger O'Dell, which they bred. But it is in the show ring where they excel, and they have had many Best in Show winners. These include American, Bermudian and Canadian Champion Ku Ka Boh of Pickwick, Ch. Tibet of Cornwallis, ROM, and American and Bermudian Ch. Kinderland's Tonka. Tonka became one of the top-winning Lhasa bitches in the history of the breed.

Their stud force was equally impressive. Karma Tharpa was sister of both Tibet and Ku Ka Boh; she sired 28 champions, including two Best in Show winners and four Group Winners.

Tabu has bred many champions, including the multiple Group-winning Ch. Tabu's King of Hearts, ROM, the multiple Group-winning Ch. Tabu's Chubby Checkers, and the Group-winning Ch. Tabu's Gold Galaxy.

The Herbel's purchased their first Lhasa from Paul Williams. It was the now-famous dog Ch. Tibet of Cornwallis, ROM. They were so pleased with this remarkable 13-month-old dog that a short time later they purchased another male, KuKa Boh of Pickwick. Then the search for a bitch began. The fantastic Tonka was their choice, and she made history in the breed. The Herbels were off to a marvelous start and on a winning streak that has continued ever since.

TAGLHA

Mr. and Mrs. Wilson Browning, Jr. of Norfolk, Virginia, first got interested in Lhasas in 1967. In the years that followed they showed Ch. Kimricks Jeh Sah Cah to a championship and put championship titles on three homebreds, Ch. Taglha Pokhara of Nottoway, Ch. Taglha Sinsa of Kinderland and Ch. Taglha Dum Cho, Ch. Kinderland Tonka Tu is another champion at their kennel.

In 1969 they won Best of Winners at the Westminster Kennel Club show with Ch. Kimricks Jeh Sah Cah, and her granddaughter, Ch.

Ch. Rimmon Ripsnorter, a winner at the First Independent National Specialty show in November, 1974. Rip is a home bred and is always owner-handled by Leonard Ripley, Rimmon Kennels, Stamford, Connecticut. He is pictured here being exhibited at a mock dog show at the Manhattan Savings Bank in New York City in May, 1975.

Taglha Pokhara, had a big win at the Eastern Specialty Show held in conjunction with the Trenton Kennel Club show in 1973. Pokhara had several Bests of Breed and Group placements to her credit as well before her retirement from the showring in 1974.

The three bitches at Taglha are the basis of their breeding program, with Sinsa their only male and stud. Sinsa won the Midwestern Futurity from the Puppy Class in 1974 and has Group placements as well.

Champion Sheng-La's Chun King finished for his championship under judge Edd Biven at the 1973 Indianapolis Kennel Club show with a 4-point major; handler, Peggy Hogg. King is owned by the Dickersons, Sheng-La Apsos, Marion, Ohio.

Ch. Taglha Pokhara of Nottoway, pictured winning Best of Breed at the 1974 Durham, North Carolina Kennel Club show. Pokhara is owned by Mr. and Mrs. Wilson J. Browning, Jr., Taglha Lhasas, Norfolk, Virginia, and handled by Mrs. Browning.

TAL-HI

In 1960 A. Ann Hoffman began breeding the Tal-Hi Lhasas at her Talmadge Hill Kennels in Waverly, New York.

While her original breed was smooth standard Dachshunds, when she decided to switch to "longhairs" she purchased two from Keke

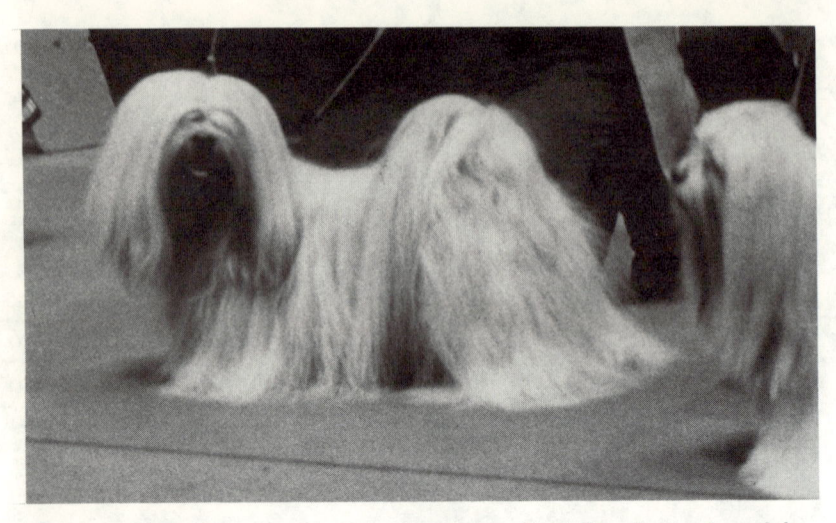

Ch. Tabu's King of Hearts, Top Producing Stud Dog in the breed for 1975 according to the *Kennel Review* magazine and *Lhasa Reporter* systems. King of Hearts is pictured here in the ring at the 1973 Westminster Kennel Club show. Owner-handled by Stephen G.C. Campbell, Rimar Lhasa Apso, West Trenton, New Jersey.

Blumberg. These were Chia, or Ch. Keke's T'ChinChia, and Ch. Keke's Ha-Le.

Ha-Le passed away, but Chia is still going strong and a few other Lhasas have joined the ranks. Ch. Kasha's Tsony of Tal-Hi came along and two of her offspring, Ch. Tal-Hi Kori Ti Ko and Ch. Tal-Hi Presto Celeste, are very much in evidence at this busy kennel. In 1970 a Skye Terrier joined the kennel, but there is no denying that the Lhasas reign supreme!

TSAN

LaVerne Payton of Cloverdale, California, is no longer an active breeder, but her interest in the Lhasa is as strong as it was in the early days when she established her Tsan Kennels (1955). And there is no denying that two of her dogs, Ch. Hamilton Jimpa and Ch. Tsan's Drima, played a major role in the history of the Lhasa Apso in this country.

Drima was a champion in both this country and Mexico and was the winner of seven Groups. Drima was born in 1964 and was a grandson of the famous Ch. Hamilton Jimpa. In 1965, he won his championship and his first group at just 14 months of age. In 1966 he won the Mexican championship also with a Group First. In 1967 he won 15

Ch. Tsan's Drima, pictured winning the Non-Sporting Group at the 1967 Beverly Hills Kennel Club Show in California. Handled by his owner, La Verne Payton of Cloverday, California. Drima, a champagne gold, won his championship and his first Group at 14 months of age in 1965. A grandson of the famous Ch. Hamilton Jimpa, he finished his Mexican title in 1966 by winning the Group in that country. He was also Top-winning Lhasa Apso in the West for three consecutive years, and he was honored with the nomination for top Non-Sporting Dog by *Kennel Review* Magazine. He had seven Groups and many Group placements to his credit during his show ring career during 1966 and 1967.

Ch. Windsong Madoros Mai Li Chin, owned by Shirley Ruth and Don Ross of Houston, Texas. Buttons is pictured here winning at the 1975 ALAC Midwest Futurity show under judge Stephen G.C. Campbell; also shown are, extreme left, Shirley Ruth Ross, the judge, and Marie Ross; extreme right is Elisabeth Moseley, the co-breeder. This little bitch was Best Puppy at three Lhasa Apso Club Match shows and won her first major at seven months at her first show, winning over Specials as Best of Opposite Sex. Her second major, a 5-pointer, was at 12 months of age.

Ch. Tashi Norbu Tizi of Sheng-La, pictured finishing for her championship at the 1973 Palouse Empire Show in Colfax, Washington. Tizi was Best of Winners and Best Opposite Sex for a 4-point major win.

Madoros Chien Foo Te Ko Tu, owned by Mrs. Marie J. Ross, Houston, Texas. Ko Tu will soon be campaigned for his championship.

Ch. Shangrelu Sneak Preview, pictured winning at the 1975 Eastern Futurity show under judge Georgia Palmer. Sneak Preview's owner is Wendy Fotheringham Penn of Shangrelu Kennels, Columbus, Ohio.

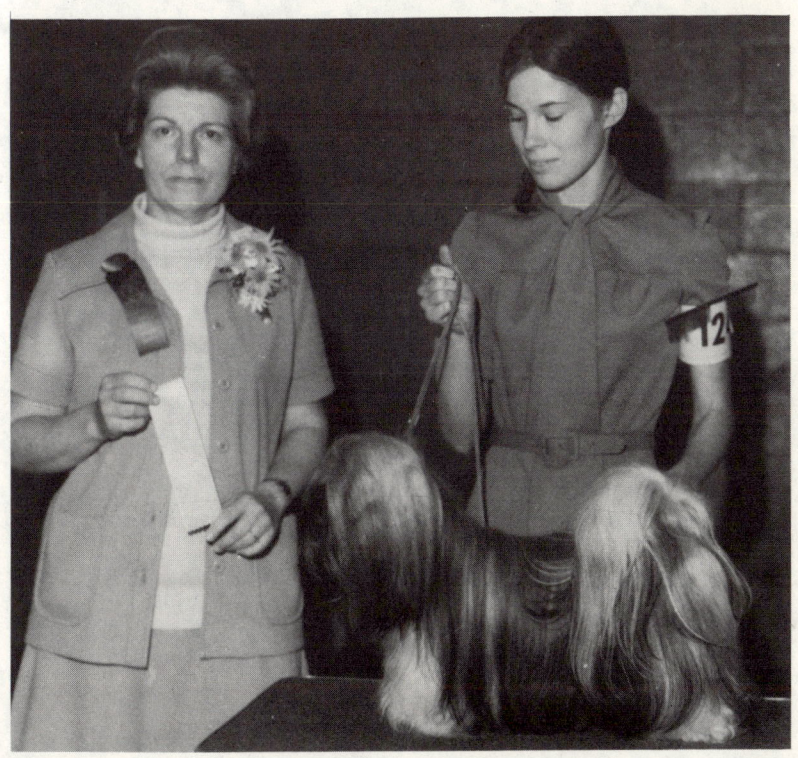

Group placements, including three firsts out of 18 appearances in the showring, one of which was at the Beverly Hills Kennel Club, one of the largest dog shows in the United States.

Drima was top-winning Lhasa Apso in the western states for three consecutive years, according to Kennel Review Magazine Awards, and was nominated for Top Non-Sporting Dog. He was always breeder-owner handled by LaVerne Payton.

Ch. Hamilton Jimpa was a busy stud dog at the Tsan Kennels. He was a favorite of Mrs. Sydham Cutting and was sold to LaVerne Payton with the understanding that he be used extensively at stud on the West Coast to spread his great quality. Over his ten years at stud he did just that, proving his prepotency time and time again. He produced 12 champion sons and daughters and 43 champion descendants, including five Group winners and three Best in Show winners, among them the well-known Ch. Kyi Chu Friar Tuck.

The Peytons feel that Jimpa was handicapped in his show career by the fact that they were professional handlers, and their clients' dogs always had to come first. That meant that Jimpa could not go to too many shows, though when he did go he certainly did his share of winning!

XANADU

Xanadu Lhasa Apso was started by David and Elizabeth Goldfarb in 1969. David Goldfarb worked closely with Robert Sharp, President of the American Lhasa Apso Club, to have the club recognized and made a member of the American Kennel Club. He also served on the board of directors of the American Lhasa Apso Club and as a Chairman of their Forum Committee. Both David and Elizabeth are charter members of the Lhasa Apso Club of Greater New York and David was elected its first President.

Xanadu's foundation stock includes Ch. Sharpette's Galahad, Ch. Sharpette's Bobette, and American and Canadian Ch. Taou Chin of Al-Mar.

In the mid-1970's they introduced two young show stars to the fancy, Xanadu's Antares and Xanadu's Raphael. Antares' sire was Ch. Tabu's King of Hearts and the dam was Xanadu's Snapdragon. Raphael was sired by Ch. Joi-San's Happieh-Go-Luckieh out of their Ch. Sharpette's Bobette.

The Goldfarbs enjoy the show aspect of the fancy as well as breeding and showing their dogs all along the eastern seaboard from New York to Florida and as far west as Kansas.

Champion Xanadu's Antares finished for his championship with three 4-point majors by 17 months of age: The sire was Ch. Tabu's King of Hearts, ROM, *ex* Xanadu's Snapdragon. Bred by David and Liz Goldfarb, who co-own him with Fred Terman, his handler of Englewood Cliffs, New Jersey.

9. GROOMING AND BATHING THE LHASA APSO

Since the luxurious coat of the Lhasa Apso is perhaps its most outstanding attribute, it is essential that it be preserved. Grooming the coat in the proper manner is the most obvious way to keep the dog looking its best and, if a schedule is observed, the actual care of the coat need not be a full-time job.

Grooming or brushing on a regular basis will keep the coat clean and relatively tangle-free. Every few days, better still, every other day, will maintain a good coat and this regimen should begin early. Hopefully the breeder will start the grooming process, beginning with a tooth brush when the puppy in only weeks old. If started at this early age, and done in the proper manner with the proper affection, the dog will grow up to consider the grooming routine as a very special time of devotion between the two of you, rather than a necessary evil inflicted upon them.

The key word is gentle, and if the dog is restless or wiggles constantly it probably is because YOU are doing something wrong. Either you're using the brush or comb too heavily, or you are holding him to tightly! When the puppy is very young start getting him acquainted with a grooming table. Make sure he has solid footing, a rubber mat is best, and then spray the coat lightly with warm water or a coat dressing which can be obtained (usually in a spray bottle) at any pet store. Then gently brush dry with a bristle brush.

For the legs and underside of the body you can place the puppy upside down in your lap, but make sure the head isn't hanging or dangling off the end of your knees. This is the proper way to cut their nails at this age as well. Be sure you get them used to having their nails cut early, also. This can best be done by holding the hair back off the nails with the thumb and using the regular nail clippers with the other hand.

As the dog grows older the grooming can be done entirely on the grooming table. The light spraying for general coat care and the bristle brush still should be used. Start by lying the dog first on one side and then the other, brushing in layers from the skin outward to the ends of the hair. When all the coat has been brushed, stand the dog up and make the part.

Using the comb, start the part at the nose and make the part from there back to the base of the tail. If, when brushing the hair down on the side, you find there is too much electricity in the coat and the hair "flies," a light spraying of water and smoothing it down with your hands will take care of it. After smoothing down the outer coat and tail, use the fine-tooth comb on the beard, tail and whiskers. Above all, use both brush and comb most carefully around the dog's eyes! This flying steel can not only injure, but can make the dog hand-shy.

SHEDDING

All dogs shed, but they shed only the barest minimum of hair. This factor combined with weekly brushing will prevent the heavy shedding you hear about with other long haired breeds. Once they shed their puppy coats, which can be anywhere between six months to a year and a half, you will find your house and clothes are seldom covered with dog hairs.

Licos Omorfo La, photographed here at 10 months of age, was considered to be one of the best ever bred by breeder-owner Grace Licos of Beverly Hills, California. The sire was Ch. Licos Kulu La *ex* Ch. Hamilton Pluti.

The typical Lhasa Apso hair style for the breed. Shown is the beautifully coated Ch. Hamilton Torma ready for the show ring.

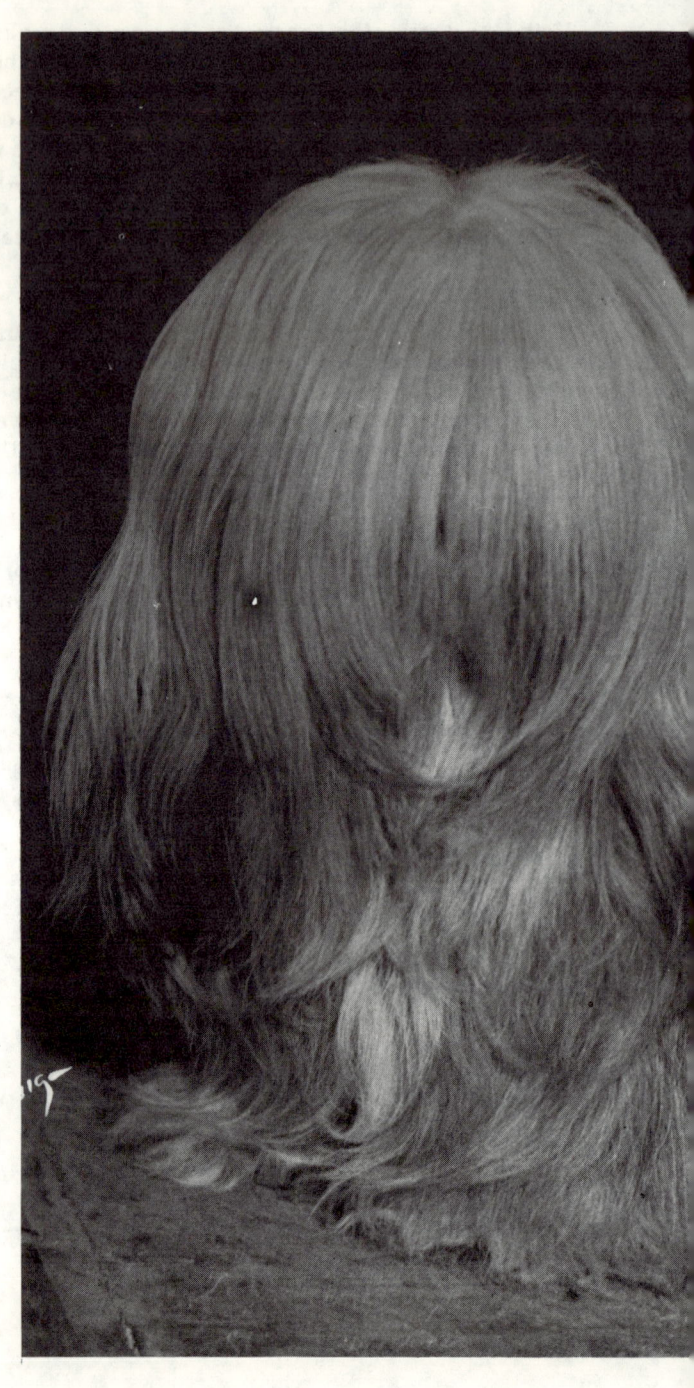

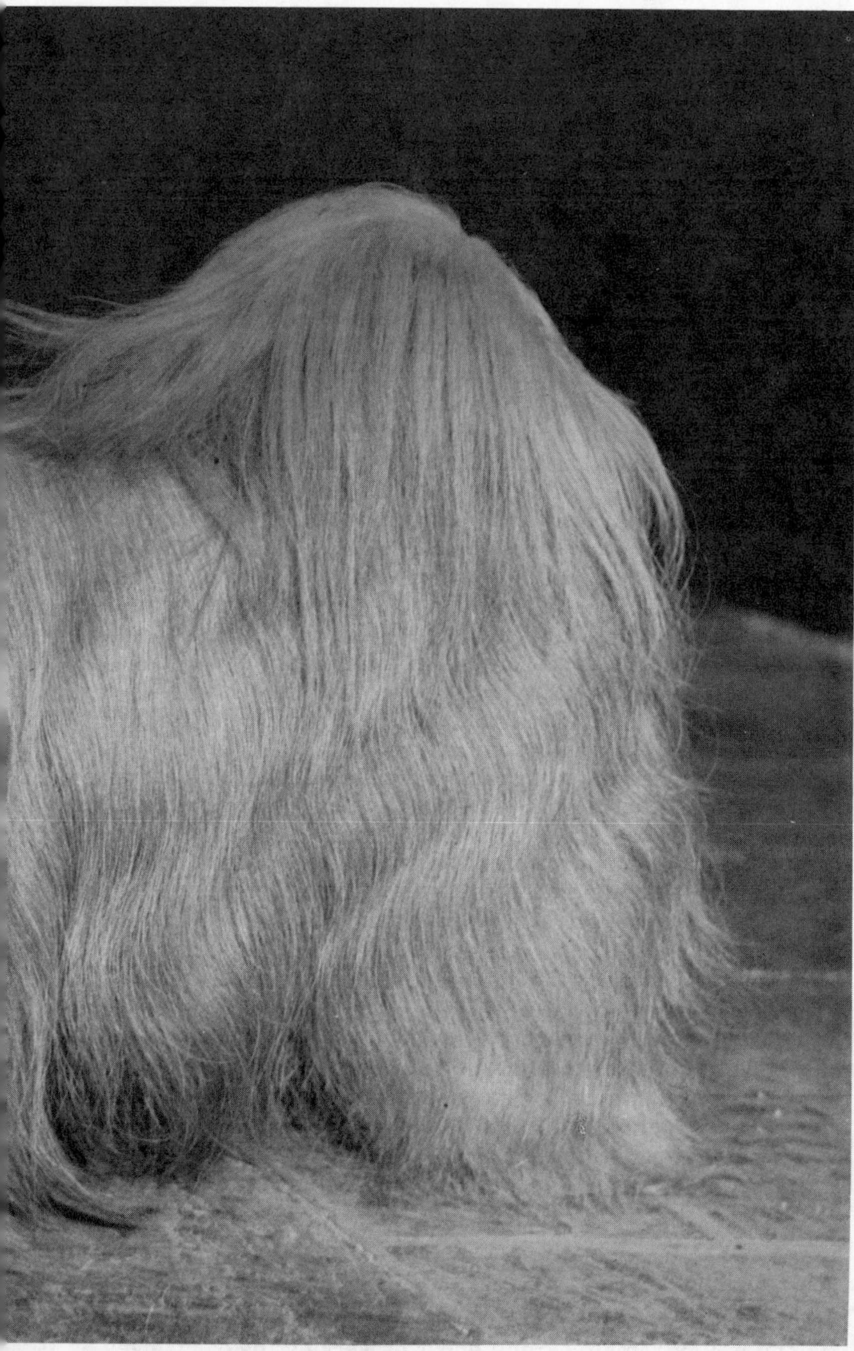

BATHING

Note that the grooming out of dead hair and mats BEFORE the bath is essential, and while Lhasas seldom require a full bath, show dogs can be bathed weekly without any danger to their coats, if done properly. You will find that the part will stay better if put in while the dog is still wet from the bath.

DIRTY ENDS

With Lhasas, as with all long haired breeds, the hair soils at both ends because of its length. Whiskers or beards are frequently stained as food and water are consumed and unless they are cleaned up after each feeding, dust and dirt are bound to gather on them giving both an unsightly appearance and an unpleasant odor.

The beards and whiskers can be kept clean after drinking by merely squeezing them dry with a paper towel and/or running a fine tooth comb through them. Where solid foods are concerned it is necessary to wash them off with a wet towel, or perhaps sprinkle corn starch through the hair and brush dry. It all depends on how "neat" an eater your dog is. There is also the alternative of putting the hair up in papers or pulling it back with rubber bands until after the meal.

Where show dogs are concerned and every hair must be preserved, individual care should be given at meal times to see that every last bit of food is out of the coat and the face and ear fringes are 100% clean, otherwise, you risk staining.

As for the rear end, here again, special attention must be given to see that no excrement sticks to the coat. Staining and odor and great discomfort to the dog can result. Should this happen, place the dog in the bathtub under running water (warm water, of course) and use a wide-toothed comb to part the hair until it is completely rinsed out. Then squeeze dry with paper towels, spray with a coat conditioner, and brush dry.

If your dog is inclined to have a soft stool (and this is always a probable occurence) you can save yourself a lot of work by brushing the hair under the tail toward the outside of the body and holding it to the side with rubber bands. Do this before eating and leave it on until the dog has been walked or has eliminated after eating. Since the Lhasa Apso is by nature a clean dog, it will appreciate your help in avoiding this unpleasant occurrence whenever possible.

EAR CARE

We have just mentioned wrapping the beards and the hair of the tail and hindlegs in papers and rubber bands. Many Lhasa owners do this and are extremely careful about preserving the ear fringes by keeping them wrapped in paper almost constantly. Others just wrap the ears while the dogs are eating or at play. The papers prevent the hair from being soiled or caught up with debris which might make the hair ends break off.

While this wrapping process is a matter of individual choice, I must caution here about careful and proper wrapping. If the ears are wrapped you must be certain that none of the ear leather is wrapped in the paper. Should it be, and the rubber band secured over the skin, all circulation in the ear leather will be cut off and infection may result. There have been cases where some of the ear leather had to be removed surgically it was so badly damaged.

The best way to make sure that you have not wrapped any of the leather, and only the hair, is to secure the paper with the rubber band and then be sure you can put the comb entirely through the hair between the paper and the end of the ear leather. If the comb touches the leather, rewrap!

We have discussed wrapping with wax paper, but there are many materials which can be used to wrap hair. Some owners are using tissue paper, others use net material preferring the hair to "breathe" rather than be completely covered, others use saran wrap. Here again, it is a matter of preference with the most important thing being to keep the hair clean.

Wrapping is a fairly simple procedure once you get the hang of it. Depending upon the amount of hair you wish to wrap, cut a piece of paper wide enough to fold over the hair from each side, about six to eight inches long. Place the hair down the center, fold over each side and then fold upwards toward the base of the ear, stopping just below the leather. Tie the wrap with a rubber band much as you would the end of a child's braid. Check with the comb to see that you have not tied any of the ear leather, and make sure that there are no hairs pulling at the dog. The body wraps should not be so tight to the body that the dog cannot lie down comfortably, and the beard or whisker wraps should not be so tight that he cannot use his mouth normally.

THE TOP KNOT

Wrapping of the hair, which normally falls over the eyes, is common practice today, and for many reasons. One is that it prevents the eyes from tearing and staining the hair on the face and also the wrapping protects the hair for the show ring. Perhaps the most important reason of all is that the wraps, or the berets they use to hold it back off the eyes, makes them look so cute!

While the top knot is "Standard" for the Shih Tzu, more and more Lhasa owners are using the top knots at home so they can enjoy their breed both ways! Some use the single top knot; others maintain the required part in the hair from the nose on back and tie up two top knots. Some use the berets, others use little bows or ribbons, but regardless of the method the purpose is still accomplished.

Rimar's U Bet Cha Buttons displays the way the hair on the ears and head can be held back off the face "between shows" and while eating. Soft rubber bands are used and then cut off with scissors so as not to break the hair.

    If you are going to "wrap" your Lhasa it is essential that you get someone familiar with the technique of wrapping properly to show you how to do it the first time. You will see the correct size of paper, benefit from their experience on the best kind of paper, and will get the "feel" of the correct size the wrap should be on each part of the body.

10. BUYING YOUR LHASA APSO PUPPY

There are several paths that will lead you to a litter of puppies where you can find the puppy of your choice. Write to the parent club and ask for the names and addresses of members who have puppies for sale. The addresses of breed clubs can be obtained by writing the American Kennel Club, 51 Madison Avenue, New York, N.Y. 10010. They keep an accurate, up-to-date list of reputable breeders from whom you can seek information on obtaining a good healthy puppy. You might also check listings in the classified ads of major newspapers. The various dog magazines also carry listings and usually a column each month which features information and news on the breed.

It is to your advantage to attend a few dog shows in the area where purebred dogs of just about every breed are being exhibited in the show ring. Even if you do not wish to buy a show dog, you should be familiar with what the better specimens look like so that you may at least get a decent looking representative of the breed for your money. You will learn a lot by observing the dogs in action in the show ring, or in a public place where their personalities come to the fore. The dog show catalog will list the dogs and their owners with local kennel names and breeders whom you can visit to see the types and colors they are breeding and winning with at the shows. Exhibitors at these shows are usually delighted to talk to people about their dogs and the specific characteristics of their particular breed.

Once you have chosen your breed above all others because you admire its exceptional beauty, intelligence and personality, and because you feel the breed will fit in with your family's way of life, it is wise to do a little research on it. The American Kennel Club library, your local library, bookshops and the breed clubs can usually supply you with a list of reading matter or written material on the breed, past and present. Then, once you have drenched yourself in the breed's illustrious history and have definitely decided that this is the breed for you, it is time to start writing letters and making phone calls to set up appointments to see litters of puppies.

A word of caution here: don't let your choice of a kennel be determined by its nearness to your home, and then buy the first cute puppy that races up to you or licks the end of your nose. All puppies are cute, and naturally you will have a preference among those you see. But don't let preferences sway you into buying the wrong puppy.

If you are buying your dog as a family pet, a preference might not be a serious offense. But if you have had, say, an age preference since you first considered this breed, you would be wise to stick to it. If you are buying a show dog, all physical features must meet with the Standard for the breed. In considering your purchase you must think clearly, choose carefully, and make the very best possible choice. You will, of course, learn to love whichever puppy you finally decide upon, but a case of "love at first sight" can be disappointing and expensive later on if a show career was your primary objective.

To get the broadest possible concept of what is for sale and the current market prices, it is recommended that you visit as many kennels and private breeders as you can. With today's reasonably safe, inexpensive and rapid non-stop flights on the major airlines, it is possible to secure dogs from far-off places at nominal additional charges, allowing you to buy the valuable bloodlines of your choice, if you have a thought toward a breeding program in the future.

While it is always safest to actually *see* the dog you are buying, there are enough reputable breeders and kennels to be found for you to buy a dog with a minimum of risk once you have made up your mind what you want, and when you have decided whether you will buy in your own country or import to satisfy your concept of the breed Standard. If you are going to breed dogs, breeding Standard type can be a moral obligation, and your concern should be with buying the best bloodlines and individual animals obtainable, in spite of cost or distance.

It is customary for the purchaser to pay the shipping charges, and the airlines are most willing to supply flight information and prices upon request. Rental of the shipping crate, if the owner does not provide one for the dog, is nominal. While unfortunate incidents have occurred on the airlines in the transporting of animals by air, the major airlines are making improvements in safety measures and have reached the point of reasonable safety and cost. Barring unforeseen circumstances, the safe arrival of a dog you might buy can pretty much be assured if both seller and purchaser adhere to and follow up on even the most minute details from both ends.

Opposite:
The late Sylvia Hee's Bai Jai's Phu Tuu wins Best of Breed at a Lancaster Kennel Club show.

177

THE PUPPY YOU BUY

Let us assume you want to enjoy all the cute antics of a young puppy and decide to buy a six-to-eight-week-old puppy. This is about the age when a puppy is weaned, wormed and ready to go out into the world with a responsible new owner. It is better not to buy a puppy under six weeks of age; it simply is not yet ready to leave the mother or the security of the other puppies. At eight to twelve weeks of age you will be able to notice much about the appearance and the behavior. Puppies, as they are recalled in our fondest childhood memor-

A classic "doggie bag"! This Lhasa Apso puppy peers out from a United Air Lines Pet Liner kennel which is provided free by the airline to passengers for the carrying of puppies and kittens.

An indication of things to come: seven-month-old Bella-Mu Go Get 'Em Tiger wins Best of Breed and First in the Non-Sporting Group at the 1973 Riverhead Kennel Club Match Show under judge Arlene Thompson. Owner-handled by Ann Sergio of Woodbury, Long Island, New York.

ies, are gay and active and bouncy, as well they should be! The normal puppy should be interested, alert and curious, especially about a stranger. If a puppy acts a little reserved or distant, however, such need not be misconstrued as shyness or fear. It merely indicates he hasn't made up his mind whether he likes you as yet! By the same token, he should not be fearful or terrified by a stranger—and especially should not show any fear of his owner!

In direct contrast, the puppy should not be ridiculously overactive either. The puppy that frantically bounds around the room and is never still is not especially desirable. And beware of the "spinners"! Spinners are the puppies or dogs that have become neurotic from being kept in cramped quarters or in crates and behave in an emotionally unstable manner when let loose in adequate space. When let out they run in circles and seemingly "go wild." Puppies with this kind of traumatic background seldom ever regain full composure or adjust to the big outside world. The puppy which has had the proper exercise and appropriate living quarters will have a normal, though spirited, outlook on life and will do his utmost to win you over without having to go into a tailspin.

If the general behavior and appearance of the dog thus far appeal to you, it is time for you to observe him more closely for additional physical requirements. First of all, you cannot expect to find in the puppy all the coat he will bear upon maturity. That will come with time and good food, and will be additionally enhanced by the many wonderful grooming aids which can be found on the market today. Needless to say, the healthy puppy's coat should have a nice shine to it, and the more dense at this age, the better the coat will be when the dog reaches adulthood.

Look for clear, dark, sparkling eyes, free of discharge. Dark eye rims and lids are indications of good pigmentation, which is important in a breeding program and enhances their generally pleasing good looks.

When the time comes to select your puppy, take an experienced breeder along with you if this is possible. If it is not possible, take the Standard for the breed with you. Try to interpret the Standard as best you can by making comparisons between the puppies you see.

Check the bite completely and carefully. While the first set of teeth can be misleading, even the placement of teeth at this young age can be a fairly accurate indication of what the bite will be in the grown dog. The gums should be a good healthy pink in color and the teeth should be clear, clean and white. Any brown cast to them could mean a past case of distemper and would assuredly count against the dog in the show ring and against the dog's general appearance at maturity.

Puppies take anything and everything into their mouths to chew on while they are teething, and a lot of infectious diseases are transmitted this way. The aforementioned distemper is one, and the brown teeth as a result of this disease never clear. The puppy's breath should not be sour or even unpleasant or strong. Any acrid odor could indicate a poor mixture of food, or low quality of meat, especially if it is being fed raw. Many breeders have compared the breath of a healthy puppy to that of frest toast, or as being vaguely like garlic. At any rate, a puppy should never be fed just table scraps, but should have a well-balanced diet containing a good dry puppy chow and a good grade of fresh meat. Poor meat and too much cereal or fillers tend to make the puppy too fat. We like puppies to be in good flesh, but not fat from the wrong kind of food.

It goes without saying that we want to find clean puppies. The breeder or owner who shows you a dirty puppy is one from whom to

Janet and Marvin Whitman's darling little Lhasa puppy, photographed in July, 1974. The sire was Ch. Mor-Knoll's Alex-A-Hente *ex* Ch. Lifelong's Stolen Hours. The Whitmans' Ja-Ma Lhasas are situated in Spring Valley, New York.

steer away! Look closely at the skin. Rub the fur the wrong way or against the grain; make sure it is not spotted with insect bites or red, blotchy sores or dry scales. The vent area around the tail should not show evidences of diarrhea or inflammation. By the same token, the puppy's fur should not be matted with dry excrement or smell of urine.

True enough, you can wipe dirty eyes, clean dirty ears and give the puppy a bath when you get it home, but these things are all indications of how the puppy has been cared for during the important formative first months of its life, and can vitally influence its future health and development. There are many reputable breeders raising healthy puppies that have been reared in proper places and under the proper conditions in clean housing, so why take a chance on a series of veterinary bills and a questionable constitution?

MALE OR FEMALE

The choice of sex in your puppy is also something that must be given serious thought before you buy. For the pet owner, the sex that would best suit the family life you enjoy would be the paramount choice to consider. For the breeder or exhibitor, there are other vital considerations. If you are looking for a stud to establish a kennel, it is essential that you select a dog with both testicles evident, even at a tender age, and verified by a veterinarian before the sale is finalized if there is any doubt.

The visibility of one testicle, known as monorchidism, automatically disqualifies the dog from the show ring or from a breeding program, though monorchids are capable of siring. Additionally, it must be noted that monorchids frequently sire dogs with the same deficiency, and to introduce this into a bloodline knowingly is an unwritten sin in the fancy. Also, a monorchid can sire dogs that are completely sterile. Such dogs are referred to as cryptorchids and have no testicles.

If you want the dog to be a member of the family, the best selection would probably be a female. You can always go out for stud service if you should decide to breed. You can choose the bloodlines doing the most winning because they should be bred true to type, and you will not have to foot the bill for the financing of a show career. You can always keep a male from your first litter that will bear your own "kennel name" if you have decided to proceed in the kennel "business."

An additional consideration in the male versus female decision for the private owners is that with males there might be the problem of leg-lifting and with females there is the inconvenience while they are in season. However, this need not be the problem it used to be—pet shops sell "pants" for both sexes, which help to control the situation.

Lhasa Apso puppies being "socialized" at the Karma Kennels. It is essential that puppies be accustomed to visitors and human companionship if they are to lead normal lives.

THE PLANNED PARENTHOOD BEHIND YOUR PUPPY

Never be afraid to ask pertinent questions about the puppy, as well as questions about the sire and dam. Feel free to ask the breeder if you might see the dam, the purpose of your visit to determine her general health and her appearance as a representative of the breed. Ask also to see the sire if the breeder is the owner. Ask what the puppy has been fed and should be fed after weaning. Ask to see the pedigree, and inquire if the litter or the individual puppies have been registered with the American Kennel Club, how many of the temporary and/or permanent inoculations the puppy has had, when and if the puppy has been wormed and whether it has had any illness, disease or infection.

You need not ask if the puppy is housebroken. . . it won't mean much. He may have gotten the idea as to where "the place" is where he lives now, but he will need new training to learn where "the place" is in his new home! And you can't really expect too much from puppies at this age anyway. Housebreaking is entirely up to the new owner. We know puppies always eliminate when they first awaken and sometimes dribble when they get excited. If friends and relatives are coming over to see the new puppy, make sure he is walked just before he greets them at the front door. This will help.

The normal time period for puppies around three months of age to eliminate is about every two or three hours. As the time draws near, either take the puppy out or indicate the newspapers for the same purpose. Housebreaking is never easy, but anticipation is about 90 per cent of solving the problem. The schools that offer to housebreak your dog are virtually useless. Here again the puppy will learn the "place" at the schoolhouse, but coming home he will need special training for the new location.

A reputable breeder will welcome any and all questions you might ask and will voluntarily offer additional information, if only to brag about the tedious and loving care he has given the litter. He will also sell a puppy on a 24-hour veterinary approval. This means you have a full day to get the puppy to a veterinarian of your choice to get his opinion on the general health of the puppy before you make a final

A typical quality puppy from the Sorcis' Shangri-La Kennels.

A basketful of beauties from the Miradel Lhasa Kennels, pictured in 1957. Miradel is in Los Gatos, California.

Little Lyn Sorci's first Lhasa winning her first Winners Cup...at her first dog show! Judge Beatrice Godsol awarded the prize to Tara Toy of Shangri-La at a 1958 show.

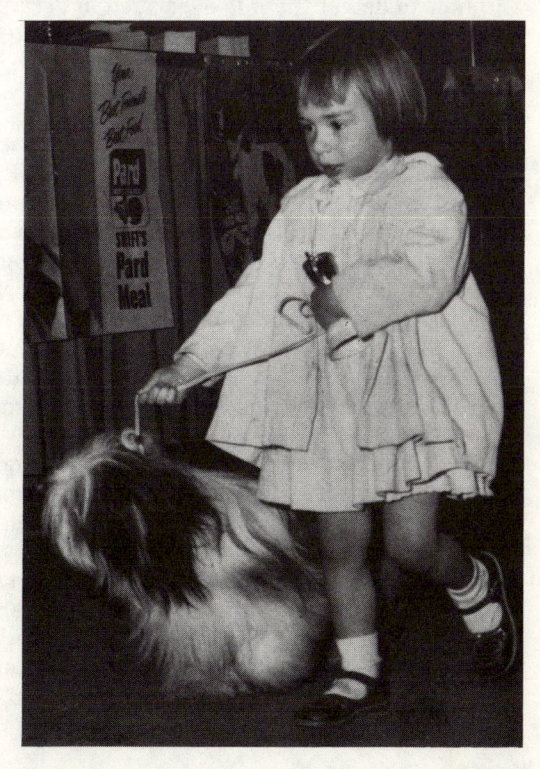

decision. There should also be veterinary certificates and full particulars on the dates and types of inoculations the puppy has been given up to that time.

PUPPIES AND WORMS

Let us give further attention to the unhappy and very unpleasant subject of worms. Generally speaking, almost all puppies—even those raised in clean quarters—come into contact with worms early in life. The worms can be passed down from the mother before birth or picked up during the puppies' first encounters with the earth or their kennel facilities. To say that you must not buy a puppy because of an infestation of worms is nonsensical. You might be passing up a fine animal that can be freed of worms in one short treatment, although a heavy infestation of worms of any kind in a young dog is dangerous and debilitating.

The extent of the infection can be readily determined by a veterinarian, and you might take his word as to whether the future health and conformation of the dog has been damaged. He can prescribe the dosage and supply the medication at the time and you will already have one of your problems solved. The kinds and varieties of worms and how to detect them is described in detail elsewhere in this book and we advise you to check the matter out further if there is any doubt in your mind as to the problems of worms in dogs.

VETERINARY INSPECTION

While your veterinarian is going over the puppy you have selected to purchase, you might just as well ask him for his opinion of it as a specimen of the breed as well as the facts about its general health. While few veterinarians can claim to be breed conformation experts, they usually have a good eye for a worthy specimen and can advise you where to go for further information. Perhaps your veterinarian could also recommend other breeders if you should want another opinion. The veterinarian can point out structural faults or organic problems that affect all breeds and can usually judge whether an animal has been abused or mishandled and whether it is oversized or undersized.

I would like to emphasize here that it is only through this type of close cooperation between owners and veterinarians that we can expect to reap the harvest of modern research in the veterinary field. Most reliable veterinarians are more than eager to learn about various breeds of purebred dogs, and we in turn must acknowledge and apply what they have proved through experience and research in their field. We can buy and breed the best dog in the world, but when disease strikes we are only as safe as our veterinarian is capable—so let's keep them informed breed by breed, and dog by dog. The veterinarian represents the difference between life and death!

THE CONDITIONS OF SALE

While it is customary to pay for the puppy before you take it away with you, you should be able to give the breeder a deposit if there is any doubt about the puppy's health. You might also (depending on local laws) postdate a check to cover the 24-hour veterinary approval. If you decide to take the puppy, the breeder is required to supply you with a pedigree, along with the puppy's registration paper. He is also obliged to supply you with complete information about the inoculations and American Kennel Club instructions on how to transfer ownership of the puppy into your name.

Ch. Rgyal Khetsa-Po, photographed at eight months of age. Owned by Barbara Wood, Anbara Lhasas, New York City.

Ch. Rgyal-Bu Tompar, owned and bred by Barbara Wood, Anbara Lhasas, New York City, is shown here at the age of 4½ weeks.

Some breeders will offer buyers time payment plans for convenience if the price on a show dog is very high or if deferred payments are the only way you can purchase the dog. However, any such terms must be worked out between buyer and breeder and should be put in writing to avoid later complications.

You will find most breeders cooperative if they believe you are sincere in your love for the puppy and that you will give it the proper home and the show ring career it deserves (if it is sold as a show quality specimen of the breed). Remember, when buying a show dog, it is impossible to guarantee nature. A breeder can only tell you what he *believes* will develop into a show dog... so be sure your breeder is an honest one.

Also, if you purchase a show prospect and promise to show the dog, you definitely should show it! It is a waste to have a beautiful dog that deserves recognition in the show ring sitting at home as a family pet, and it is unfair to the breeder. This is especially true if the breeder offered you a reduced price because of the advertising his kennel and bloodlines would receive by your showing the dog in the ring. If you want a pet, buy a pet. Be honest about it, and let the breeder decide on this basis which is the best dog for you. Your conscience will be clear and you'll both be doing a real service to the breed.

BUYING A SHOW PUPPY

If you are positive about breeding and showing your dog, make it clear that you intend to do so so that the breeder will sell you the best possible puppy. If you are dealing with an established kennel, you will have to rely partially, if not entirely, on their choice, since they know their bloodlines and what they can expect from the breeding. They know how their stock develops, and it would be foolish of them to sell you a puppy that could not stand up as a show specimen representing their stock in the ring.

However, you must also realize that the breeder may be keeping the best puppy in the litter to show and breed himself. If this is the case, you might be wise to select the best puppy of the opposite sex so that the dogs will not be competing against one another in the show ring for their championship title.

THE PURCHASE PRICE

Prices vary on all puppies, of course, but a good show prospect at six weeks to six months of age will sell for several hundred dollars. If the puppy is really outstanding, and the pedigree and parentage is also outstanding, the price will be even higher. Honest breeders, however, will be around the same figure, so price should not be a deciding factor in your choice. If there is any question as to the current price range, a few telephone calls to different kennels will give you a good

A litter bred by Barbara Wood of New York City. This basketful of charm was sired by Ch. Potala Keke's Tomba Tu *ex* Ch. Rgyal Khetsa-Po.

average. Breeders will usually stand behind their puppies; should something drastically wrong develop, such as hip dysplasia, etc., their obligation to make an adjustment is usually honored. Therefore, your cost is covered.

THE COST OF BUYING ADULT STOCK

Prices for adult dogs fluctuate greatly. Some grown dogs are offered free of charge to good homes; others are put out with owners on breeder's terms. But don't count on getting a "bargain" if it doesn't cost you anything! Good dogs are always in demand, and worthy studs or brood bitches are expensive. Prices for them can easily go up into the four-figure range. Take an expert with you if you intend to make this sort of investment. Just make sure the "expert" is free of professional jealousy and will offer an unprejudiced opinion. If you are reasonably familiar with the Standard, and get the expert's opinion, between the two you can usually come up with a proper decision.

Buying grown stock does remove some of the risk if you are planning a kennel. You will know exactly what you are getting for your foundation stock and will also save time on getting your kennel started.

11. BREEDING YOUR LHASA APSO

Let us assume the time has come for your dog to be bred, and you have decided you are in a position to enjoy producing a litter of puppies that you hope will make a contribution to the breed. The bitch you purchased is sound, her temperament is excellent and she is a most worthy representative of the breed.

You have taken a calendar and counted off the ten days since the first day of red staining and have determined the tenth to fourteenth day, which will more than likely be the best days for the actual mating. You have additionally counted off 63 to 65 days before the puppies are likely to be born to make sure everything necessary for their arrival will be in good order by that time.

From the moment the idea of having a litter occurred to you, your thoughts should have been given to the correct selection of a proper stud. Here again the novice would do well to seek advice on analyzing pedigrees and tracing bloodlines for your best breedings. As soon as the bitch is in season and you see color (or staining) and a swelling of the vulva, it is time to notify the owner of the stud you selected and make appointments for the breedings. There are several pertinent questions you will want to ask the stud owners after having decided upon the pedigree. The owners, naturally, will also have a few questions they wish to ask you. These questions will concern your bitch's bloodlines, health, age, how many previous litters if any, etc.

THE HEALTH OF THE BREEDING STOCK

Some of your first questions should concern whether or not the stud has already proved himself by siring a normal healthy litter. Also inquire as to whether or not the owners have had a sperm count made to determine just exactly how fertile or potent the stud is. Also ask whether he has been X-rayed for hip dysplasia and found to be clear. Determine for yourself whether the dog has two normal testicles.

When considering your bitch for this mating, you must take into consideration a few important points that lead to a successful breeding. You and the owner of the stud will want to recall whether she has had normal heat cycles, whether there were too many runts in the litter and whether Caesarean section was ever necessary. Has she ever had a vaginal infection? Could she take care of her puppies by herself, or was there a milk shortage? How many surviving puppies were there from the litter, and what did they grow up to be in comparison to the requirements of the breed Standard?

Don't buy a bitch that has problem heats and has never had a litter. But don't be afraid to buy a healthy maiden bitch, since chances are, if she is healthy and from good stock, she will be a healthy producer. Don't buy a monorchid male, and certainly not a cryptorchid. If there is any doubt in your mind about his potency, get a sperm count from the veterinarian. Older dogs that have been good producers and are for sale are usually not too hard to find at good established kennels. If they are not too old and have sired quality puppies, they can give you some excellent show stock from which to establish your own breeding lines.

THE DAY OF THE MATING

Now that you have decided upon the proper male and female combination to produce what you hope will be—according to the pedigrees—a fine litter of puppies, it is time to set the date. You have selected the two days (with a one day lapse in between) that you feel are best for the breeding, and you call the owner of the stud. The bitch always goes to the stud, unless, of course, there are extenuating circumstances. You set the date and the time and arrive with the bitch *and* the money.

Standard procedure is payment of a stud fee at the time of the first breeding, if there is a tie. For the stud fee, you are entitled to two breedings with ties. Contracts may be written up with specific conditions on breeding terms, of course, but this is general procedure. Often a breeder will take the pick of a litter to protect and maintain his bloodlines. This can be especially desirable if he needs an outcross for his breeding program or if he wishes to continue his own bloodlines if he sold you the bitch to start with, and this mating will continue his line-breeding program. This should all be worked out ahead of time and written and signed before the two dogs are bred. Remember that the payment of the stud fee is for the services of the stud—not for a guarantee of a litter of puppies. This is why it is so important to make sure you are using a proven stud. Bear in mind

Opposite, upper photo: Mi-Luv and Mi-Lo, photograhed at their first dog show after reaching six months of age! Owned by Mrs. C.H. Wearmouth, Near Chepstow, Gwent., England.

Opposite, lower photo: BarCon's Double Up, pictured winning Winners Bitch honors at the 1974 Kanadasaga Kennel Club Show under judge Ed Bracy. 8-year-old Karey Tompkins is the handler for the win. She is the daughter of Barry and Connie Tompkins, BarCon Kennels, Fulton, New York.

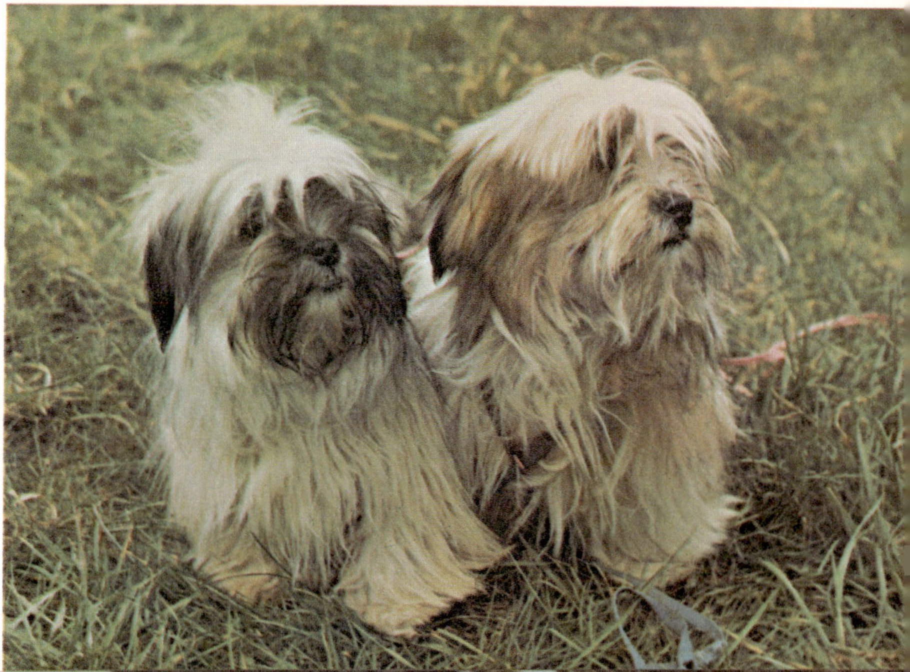

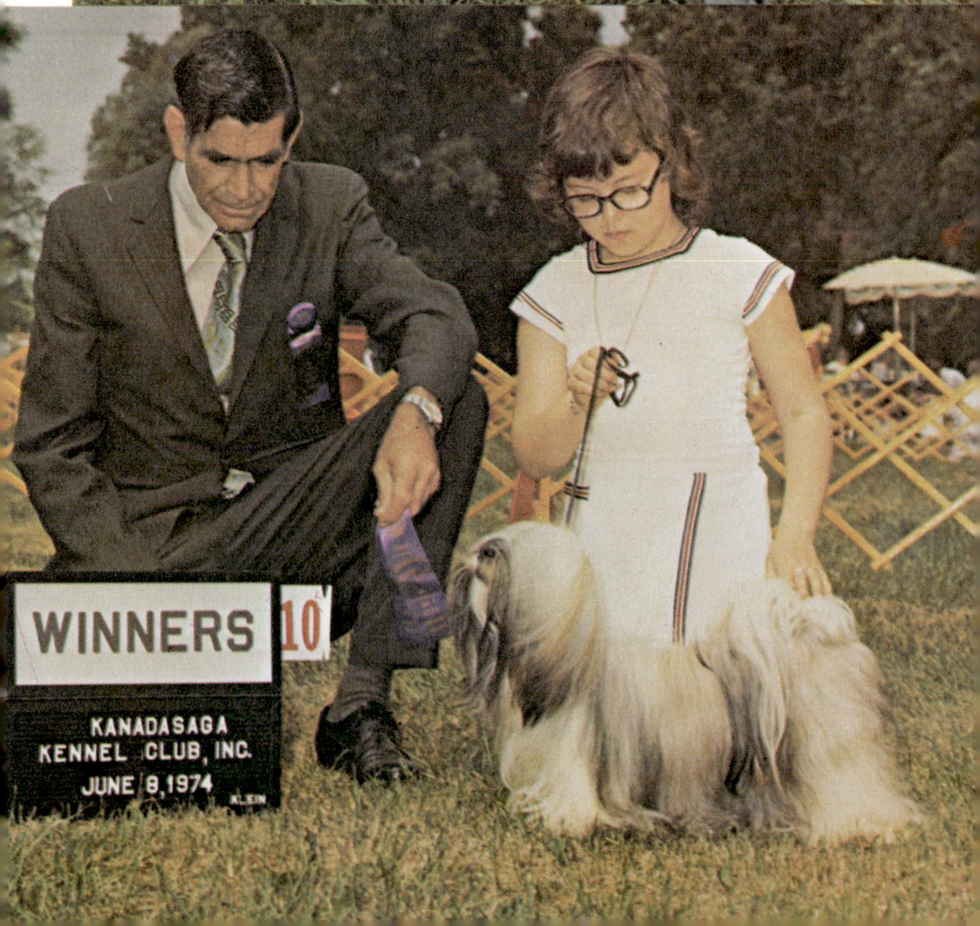
WINNERS
10
KANADASAGA
KENNEL CLUB, INC.
JUNE 8, 1974

also that the American Kennel Club will not register a litter of puppies sired by a male that is under eight months of age. In the case of an older dog, they will not register a litter sired by a dog over 12 years of age, unless there is a witness to the breeding in the form of a veterinarian or other responsible person.

Many studs over 12 years of age are still fertile and capable of producing puppies, but if you do not witness the breeding there is always the danger of a "substitute" stud being used to produce a litter. This brings up the subject of sending your bitch away to be bred if you cannot accompany her.

The disadvantages of sending a bitch away to be bred are numerous. First of all, she will not be herself in a strange place, so she'll be difficult to handle. Transportation if she goes by air, while reasonably safe, is still a traumatic experience, and there is the danger of her being put off at the wrong airport, not being fed or watered properly, etc. Some bitches get so upset that they go out of season and the trip, which may prove expensive, especially on top of a substantial stud fee, will have been for nothing.

If at all possible, accompany your bitch so that the experience is as comfortable for her as it can be. In other words, make sure before setting this kind of schedule for a breeding that there is no stud in the area that might be as good for her as the one that is far away. Don't sacrifice the proper breeding for convenience, since bloodlines are so important, but put the safety of the bitch above all else. There is always a risk in traveling, since dogs are considered cargo on a plane.

HOW MUCH DOES THE STUD FEE COST?

The stud fee will vary considerably—the better the bloodlines, the more winning the dog does at shows, the higher the fee. Stud service from a top winning dog could run up to $500.00. Here again, there may be exceptions. Some breeders will take part cash and then, say, third pick of the litter. The fee can be arranged by a private contract rather than the traditional procedure we have described.

Here again, it is wise to get the details of the payment of the stud fee in writing to avoid trouble.

THE ACTUAL MATING

It is always advisable to muzzle the bitch. A terrified bitch may fear-bite the stud, or even one of the people involved, and the wild bitch may snap or attack the stud, to the point where he may become discouraged or lose interest in the breeding. Muzzling can be done with a lady's stocking tied around the muzzle with a half knot, crossed under the chin and knotted at the back of the neck. There is enough "give" in the stocking for her to breathe or salivate freely and yet not open her jaws enough to bite. Place her in front of her own-

Ch. Arborhill's Rapsodieh, owned by Robert and Sharon Binkowski. Pictured winning the Supreme award...Best in Show at the 1971 Ravenna Kennel Club Show under Australian judge G. Head. Handled for owners by Jerry B. Edwards.

er, who holds onto her collar and talks to her and calms her as much as possible.

If the male will not mount on his own initiative, it may be necessary for the owner to assist in lifting him onto the bitch, perhaps even in guiding him to the proper place. But usually, the tie is accomplished once the male gets the idea. The owner should remain close at hand, however, to make sure the tie is not broken before an adequate

Above: Ch. Majoma's Sum Sundae, pictured winning a 3-point major under judge Vincent Perry at the 1972 Wachusett Kennel Club Show. Owned by John and Mary Mahan, Majoma's Lhasas, Westwood, Massachusetts.

Opposite, upper photo: Ch. Tabu's Miss Chimney Sweep is pictured going Winners Bitch at the 1975 Green Mountain Kennel Club Show under judge Peter Knoop on the way to her championship. She was Best of Winners at the 1975 Westminster Kennel Club Show, handled by Carolyn Herbel, who co-owns her with Nancy Clarke of Lucas, Kansas.
Opposite, lower photo: Best of Winners and Best of Opposite Sex over Specials is Rimar's Alikat, being shown at the June, 1975 Queensboro Kennel Club Show under judge James Reynolds. Co-owned by breeder Stephen G.C. Campbell and Fred Terman, Nhamrhet Lhasas, Englewood Cliffs, New Jersey.

WINNERS BITCH

BEST OF WINNERS

breeding has been completed. After a while the stud may get bored and try to break away. This could prove injurious. It may be necessary to hold him in place until the tie is broken.

We must stress at this point that while some bitches carry on physically, and vocally, during the tie, there is no way the bitch can be hurt. However, a stud can be seriously or even permanently damaged by a bad breeding. Therefore the owner of the bitch must be reminded that she must not be alarmed by any commotion. All concentration should be devoted to the stud and a successful and properly executed service.

Many people believe that breeding dogs is simply a matter of placing two dogs, a male and a female, in close proximity, and letting nature take its course. While often this is true, you cannot count on it. Sometimes it is hard work, and in the case of valuable stock it is essential to supervise to be sure of the safety factor, especially if one or both of the dogs are inexperienced. If the owners are also inexperienced it may not take place at all!

ARTIFICIAL INSEMINATION

Breeding by means of artificial insemination is usually unsuccessful, unless under a veterinarian's supervision, and can lead to an infection for the bitch and discomfort for the dog. The American Kennel Club requires a veterinarian's certificate to register puppies from such a breeding. Although the practice has been used for over two decades, it now offers new promise, since research has been conducted to make it a more feasible procedure for the future.

Great dogs may eventually look forward to reproducing themselves years after they have left this earth. There now exists a frozen semen concept that has been tested and found successful. The study, headed by Dr. Stephen W.J. Seager, M.V.B., an instructor at the University of Oregon Medical School, has the financial support of the American Kennel Club, indicating that organization's interest in the work. The study is being monitored by the Morris Animal Foundation of Denver, Colorado.

Dr. Seager announced in 1970 that he had been able to preserve dog semen and to produce litters with the stored semen. The possibilities of selective world-wide breedings by this method are exciting. Imagine simply mailing a vial of semen to the bitch! The perfection of line-breeding by storing semen without the threat of death interrupting the breeding program is exciting, also.

As it stands today, the technique for artificial insemination requires the depositing of semen (taken directly from the dog) into the bitch's vagina, past the cervix and into the uterus by syringe. The correct temperature of the semen is vital, and there is no guarantee of success. The storage method, if successfully adopted, will present a new era in the field of purebred dogs.

Judge Maxwell Riddle declares it a family affair! Pandan Hy-Lan Korba of Karo-La, on the left, and Ch. Likalas Kar-Ba of Pandan take Best of Winners and Best of Breed, respectively, at a Richmond Kennel Club Show. Kari's Best of Breed win was over Specials, and she went on to Group Fourth. Both were sired by Ch. Potala Pandan's Apollo. Korbi is handled by Carol Stretch and is co-owned by her and Wendy Harper. Kari is owned and handled by Mrs. James Kaiser of Stockton, California.

THE GESTATION PERIOD

Once the breeding has taken place successfully, the seemingly endless waiting period of about 63 days begins. For the first ten days after the breeding, you do absolutely nothing for the bitch—just spin dreams about the delights you will share with the family when the puppies arrive.

BEST OF OPP. SEX
WINNEGAMIE D.C.
MAY 18, 1975
OLSON PHOTO
BEST OF WINNERS

GROUP
SECOND

ANDERSON PHOTO

FIRST IN GROUP
COUNCIL BLUFFS K.C.
MAY 4, 1975
OLSON PHOTO

NON-SPORTING

Around the tenth day it is time to begin supplementing the diet of the bitch with vitamins and calcium. We strongly recommend that you take her to your veterinarian for a list of the proper or perhaps necessary supplements and the correct amounts of each for your partticular bitch. Guesses, which may lead to excesses or insufficiencies, can ruin a litter. For the price of a visit to your veterinarian, you will be confident that you are feeding properly.

The bitch should be free of worms, of course, and if there is any doubt in your mind, she should be wormed now, before the third week of pregnancy. Your veterinarian will advise you on the necessity of this and proper dosage as well.

PROBING FOR PUPPIES

Far too many breeders are overanxious about whether the breeding "took" and are inclined to feel for puppies or persuade a veterinarian to radiograph or X-ray their bitches to confirm it. Unless there is reason to doubt the normalcy of a pregnancy, this is risky. Certainly 63 days are not too long to wait, and why risk endangering the litter by probing with your inexperienced hands? Few bitches give no evidence of being in whelp, and there is no need to prove it for yourself by trying to count puppies.

Captions for pages 200 and 201:

Page 200, top: Ch. Karma Skar-Cen, pictured winning the Veteran Bitch class at the age of 11 years at the American Lhasa Apso Club Specialty Show under judge Keke Blumberg. Owned and handled by Lois M. Magette of Long Beach, California.

Page 200, bottom: Ch. Tibaron's Dahlia of Reiniet, pictured finishing for championship with another 3-point major at the 1975 Winnegamie Dog Club Show as Best of Winners. Bred by J.R. Ballestrin and Harriet C. Cohrs, Fred Pederson handled Dahlia to this win for owner Harriet Cohrs, Reiniet Lhasas, Clinton, Arkansas.

Page 201, top: Mohican's Liberty Belle of Bellu-Mu, 4-months-old, pictured winning Best of Breed and Group Second over adult competition under English judge Mrs. Adam Block. Belle is shown by Mary Sergio, age 13, daughter of Robert and Ann Sergio of Woodbury, Long Island, New York.

Page 201, bottom: Ch. Windsong's Gusto of Innsbrook, pictured winning the Non-Sporting Group under judge Joseph Gregory at the 1975 Council Bluffs Kennel Club Show. "Buzz" is handled exclusively by Dorothy Kendall Lohmann for owner John W. Lang of Somerset, New Jersey.

ALERTING YOUR VETERINARIAN

At least a week before the puppies are due, you should telephone your veterinarian and notify him that you expect the litter and give him the date. This way he can make sure that there will be someone available to help, should there be any problems during the whelping. Most veterinarians today have answering services and alternate vets on call when they are not available themselves. Some veterinarians suggest that you call them when the bitch starts labor so that they may further plan their time, should they be needed. Discuss this matter with your veterinarian when you first take the bitch to him for her diet instructions, etc., and establish the method which will best fit in with his schedule.

The Bryants' Ch. Licos Shor-Shan La, handled by Maxine Beam to this Non-Sporting Group win under judge Maxwell Riddle in October, 1962. The Bryants were owners of the Milbryan Kennels in Bridgeport, Texas.

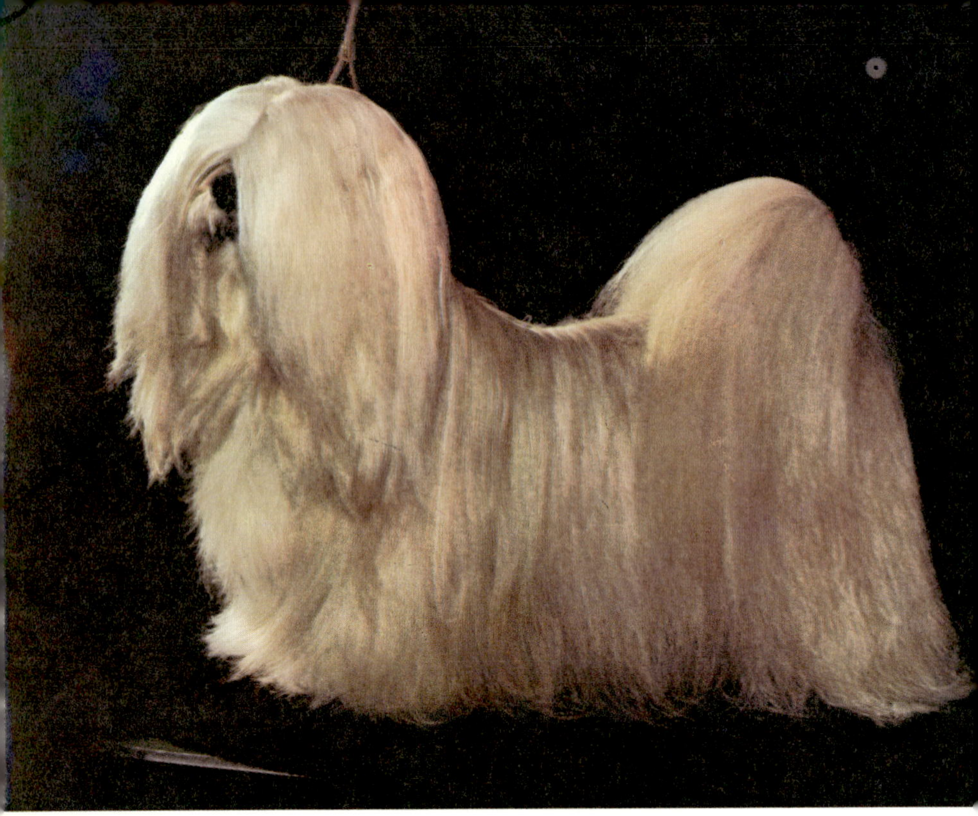

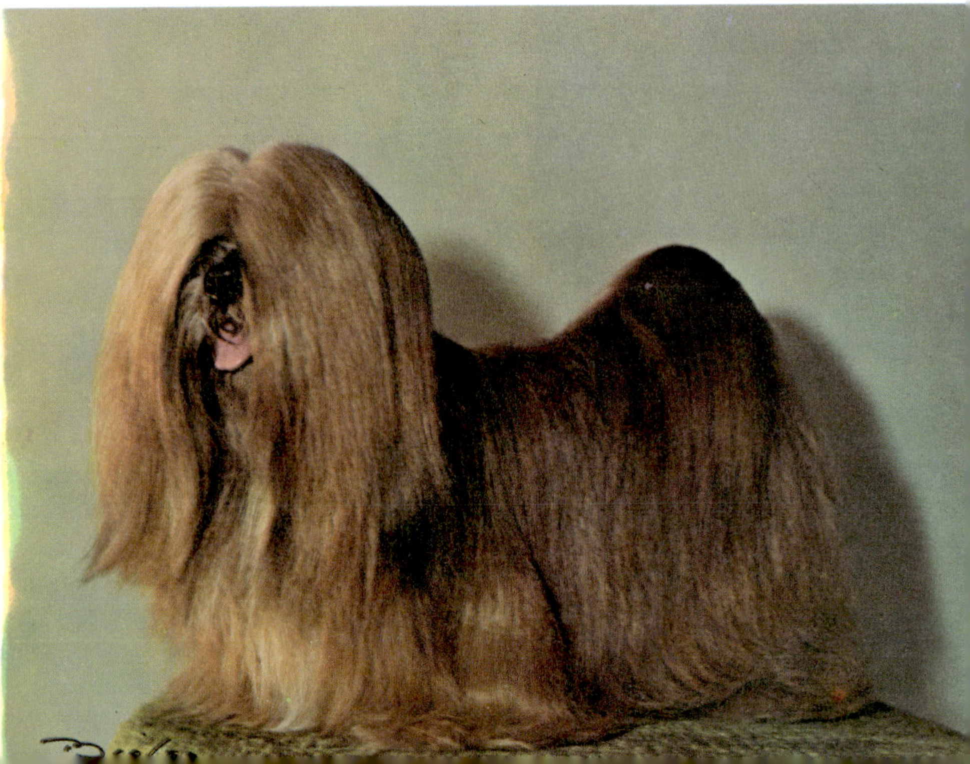

Above: Magestic Yon-Ten Again, pictured winning Best of Winners at the 1975 Superstition Kennel Club Show, is shown with his handler, Marvin Cates. Yon-Ten Again was sired by Karma Yon-Ten ex Ch. Karma Rus-Timala, ROM. Bred and owned by Lois M. Magette, Long Beach, California.

Opposite, upper photo: A lovely portrait of multiple Best In Show winner Am. & Can. Ch. Arborhills' Rapso-Dieh. "Soda" is owned by Janet and Marvin Whitman, Ja-Ma Lhasas, Spring Valley, N.J. and was bred by Sharon and Robert Binkowski.
Opposite, lower photo: Ch. Karma Rus-Tilopa, the multiple Group-winning Lhasa of Maria Aspuru and Angela Rossie. Tilopa is one of Ch. Karma Rus-Ti's nine champion offspring. Bred by Dorothy Cohen, Karma Kennels, Las Vegas, Nevada.

DO YOU NEED A VETERINARIAN IN ATTENDANCE?

Even if this is your first litter, I would advise that you go through the experience of whelping without panicking and calling desperately for the veterinarian. Most animal births are accomplished without complications, and you should call for assistance only if you run into trouble.

When having her puppies, your bitch will appreciate as little interference and as few strangers around as possible. A quiet place, with her nest, a single familiar face and her own instincts are all that is necessary for nature to take its course. An audience of curious children squealing and questioning, other family pets nosing around or strange adults should be avoided. Many a bitch which has been distracted in this way has been known to devour her young. This can be the horrible result of intrusion into the bitch's privacy. There are other ways of teaching children the miracle of birth, and there will be plenty of time later for the whole family to enjoy the puppies. Let them be born under proper and considerate circumstances.

LABOR

Some litters—many first litters—do not run the full term of 63 days. So, at least a week before the puppies are actually due, and at the time you alert your veterinarian as to their arrival, start observing the bitch for signs of the commencement of labor. This will manifest itself in the form of ripples running down the sides of her body, which will come as a revelation to her as well. It is most noticeable when she is lying on her side—and she will be sleeping a great deal as the arrival date comes closer. If she is sitting or walking about, she will perhaps sit down quickly or squat peculiarly. As the ripples become more frequent, birth time is drawing near; you will be wise not to leave her. Usually within 24 hours before whelping, she will stop eating, and as much as a week before she will begin digging a nest. The bitch should be given something resembling a whelping box with layers of newspaper (black and white only) to make her nest. She will dig more and more as birth approaches, and this is the time to begin making your promise to stop interfering unless your help is specifically required. Some bitches whimper and others are silent, but whimpering does not necessarily indicate trouble.

THE ARRIVAL OF THE PUPPIES

The sudden gush of green fluid from the bitch indicates that the water or fluid surrounding the puppies has "broken" and they are about to start down the canal and come into the world. When the water breaks, birth of the first puppy is imminent. The first puppies are usually born within minutes to a half hour of each other, but a couple of hours between the later ones is not uncommon. If you notice the bitch straining constantly without producing a puppy, or if a puppy remains partially in and partially out for too long, it is cause for concern. Breech births (puppies born feet first instead of head first) can often cause delay or hold things up, and this is often a problem which requires veterinarian assistance.

FEEDING THE BITCH BETWEEN BIRTHS

Usually the bitch will not be interested in food for about 24 hours before the arrival of the puppies, and perhaps as long as two or three days after their arrival. The placenta which she cleans up after each puppy is high in food value and will be more than ample to sustain her. This is nature's way of allowing the mother to feed herself and her babies without having to leave the nest and hunt for food during the first crucial days. The mother always cleans up all traces of birth in the wild so as not to attract other animals to her newborn babies.

However, there are those of us who believe in making food available should the mother feel the need to restore her strength during or after delivery—especially if she whelps a large litter. Raw chopmeat, beef boullion, and milk are all acceptable and may be placed near the whelping box during the first two or three days. After that, the mother will begin to put the babies on a sort of schedule. She will leave the whelping box at frequent intervals, take longer exercise periods, and begin to take interest in other things. This is where the fun begins for you. Now the babies are no longer soggy little pinkish blobs. They begin to crawl around and squeal and hum and grow before your very eyes!

It is at this time, if all has gone normally, that the family can be introduced gradually and great praise and affection given to the mother.

BREECH BIRTHS

Puppies normally are delivered head first. However, some are presented feet first or in other abnormal positions, and this is referred to as a "breech birth." Assistance is often necessary to get the puppy out of the canal, and great care must be taken not to injure the puppy or the dam.

Aid can be given by grasping the puppy with a piece of turkish toweling and pulling gently during the dam's contractions. Be careful not to squeeze the puppy too hard; merely try to ease it out by moving it gently back and forth. Because even this much delay in delivery may mean the puppy is drowning, do not wait for the bitch to remove the sac. Do it yourself by tearing the sac open to expose the face and head. Next, cut the chord anywhere from one-half to three-quarters of an inch away from the navel. If the chord bleeds excessively, pinch the end of it with your fingers and count five. Repeat if necessary.

Ch. Karma Ka-Sha is pictured winning at the 1973 Queensboro Kennel Club Show. Bred by Dorothy Cohen, Ka-Sha is owned by Joan Pettit, Mio Lhasas, Woodmere, New York.

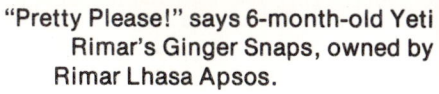

"Pretty Please!" says 6-month-old Yeti Rimar's Ginger Snaps, owned by Rimar Lhasa Apsos.

Right, upper photo:
Mrs. Dwain K. Rowan of Centereach, New York, is pictured with her treasured "Tasha." Photo by Miceli Studios, Ltd.

Right, lower photo:
Ch. Yeti's Paper Tiger, owned by Stephen Campbell; Rimar Lhasa Apsos.

Pry open the mouth with your finger and hold the puppy upside-down for a moment to drain any fluids from the lungs. Next, rub the puppy briskly with turkish or paper toweling. You should get it wriggling and whimpering by this time.

If the litter is large, this assistance will help conserve the strength of the bitch and will probably be welcomed by her. However, it is best to allow her to take care of at least the first few herself to preserve the natural instinct and to provide the nutritive values obtained by her consumption of the afterbirths.

DRY BIRTHS

Occasionally the sac will break before the delivery of a puppy and will be expelled while the puppy remains inside, thereby depriving the dam of the necessary lubrication to expel the puppy normally. Inserting vaseline or mineral oil via your finger will help the puppy pass down the birth canal. This is why it is essential that you be present during the whelping so that you can count puppies and afterbirths and determine when and if assistance is needed.

THE TWENTY-FOUR-HOUR CHECKUP

It is smart to have a veterinarian check the mother and her puppies within 24 hours after the last puppy is born. The vet can check the puppies for cleft palates or umbilical hernia and may wish to give the dam—particularly if she is a show dog—an injection of Pituitin to make sure of the expulsion of all afterbirths and to tighten up the uterus. This can prevent a sagging belly after the puppies are weaned and the bitch is being readied for the show ring.

FALSE PREGNANCY

The disappointment of a false pregnancy is almost as bad for the owner as it is for the bitch. She goes through the gestation period with all the symptoms—swollen stomach, increased appetite, swollen nipples—even makes a nest when the time comes. You may even take an oath that you noticed the ripples on her body from the labor pains. Then, just as suddenly as you made up your mind that she was definitely going to have puppies, you will know that she definitely is not! She may walk around carrying a toy as if it were a puppy for a few days, but she will soon be back to normal and acting just as if nothing happened—and nothing did!

CAESAREAN SECTION

Should the whelping reach the point where there is complication, such as the bitch's not being capable of whelping the puppies herself, the "moment of truth" is upon you and a Caesarean section may be necessary. The bitch may be too small or too immature to expel the

Ch. Mil Bryan Kim Ly Shim (born in 1969), pictured winning at a 1970 show in Oklahoma as Best of Breed. Shim finished with two 5-point and one 3-point majors and was handled here by Maxine Beam for owner Mary S. Carter of Flower Mound New Town, Texas.

Head study of American Champion Dolsa Tamika, bred by Mrs. Jean Kausch and owned by Dr. F.P. Clement, Loire, France.

Opposite, upper photo:
Ch. Karma Rgyal-Po-Chan photographed at one year of age. Bred by Dorothy Cohen and owned by Joan Pettit, Mio Lhasa Apso, Woodmere, Long Island, New York.

Opposite, lower photo:
16-year-old Debbie Hartmann holds a 7-week-old Lhasa Apso puppy for its first photograph on April 6, 1975. The puppy was bred and is owned by Ann Sergio, Bella-Mu Kennels, Woodbury, Long Island, New York.

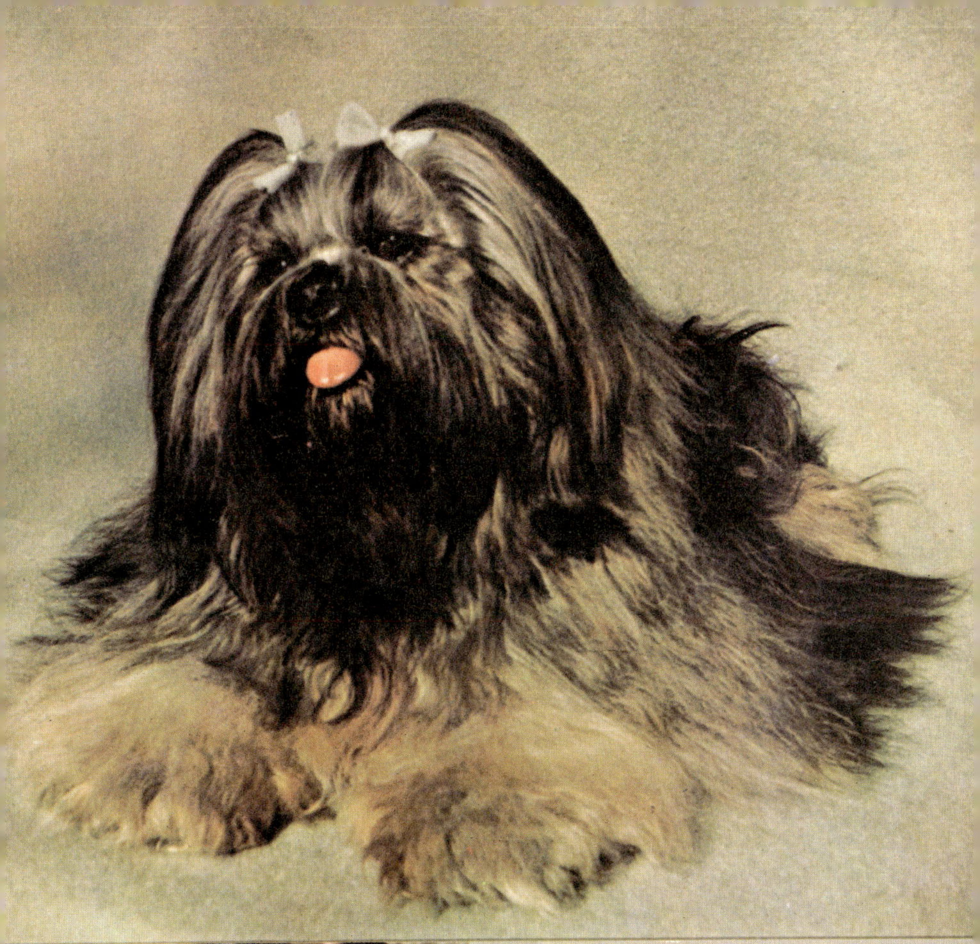

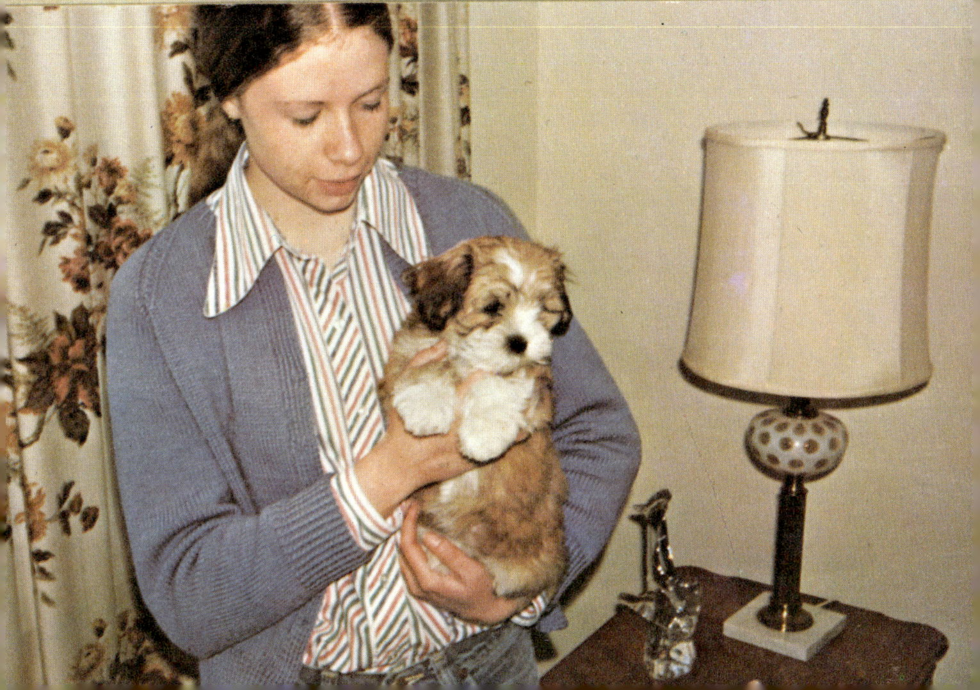

puppies herself; or her cervix may fail to dilate enough to allow the young to come down the birth canal; or there may be torsion of the uterus, a dead or monster puppy, a sideways puppy blocking the canal or perhaps toxemia. A Caesarean section will be the only solution. No matter what the cause, get the bitch to the veterinarian immediately to insure your chances of saving the mother and/or puppies.

The Caesarean section operation (the name derived from the idea that Julius Caesar was delivered by this method) involves the removal of the unborn young from the uterus of the dam by surgical incision into the walls through the abdomen. The operation is performed when it has been determined that for some reason the puppies cannot be delivered normally. While modern surgical methods have made the operation itself reasonably safe, with the dam being perfectly capable of nursing the puppies shortly after the completion of the surgery, the chief danger lies in the ability to spark life into the puppies immediately upon their removal from the womb. If the mother dies, the time element is even more important in saving the young, since the oxygen supply ceases upon the death of the dam, and the difference between life and death is measured in seconds.

After surgery, when the bitch is home in her whelping box with the babies, she will probably nurse the young without distress. You must be sure that the sutures are kept clean and that no redness or swelling or ooze appears in the wound. Healing will take place naturally, and no salves or ointments should be applied unless prescribed by the veterinarian, for fear the puppies will get it into their systems. If there is any doubt, check the bitch for fever, restlessness (other than the natural concern for her young), or a lack of appetite, but do not anticipate trouble.

EPISIOTOMY

Even though large dogs are generally easy whelpers, any number of reasons might occur to cause the bitch to have a difficult birth. Before automatically resorting to Caesarean section, many veterinarians are now trying the technique known as episiotomy.

Used rather frequently in human deliveries, episiotomy (pronounced A-PEASE-E-*OTT*-O-ME) is the cutting of the membrane between the rear opening of the vagina back almost to the opening of the anus. After delivery it is stitched together, and barring complications, heals easily, presenting no problem in future births.

SOCIALIZING YOUR PUPPY

The need for puppies to get out among other animals and people cannot be stressed enough. Kennel-reared dogs are subject to all sorts of idiosyncrasies and seldom make good house dogs or normal members of the world around them when they grow up.

A darling eight-week-old puppy, photographed by Joan Ludwig in the 1960's for owner Grace Licos of Beverly Hills, California.

The crucial age, which determines the personality and general behavior patterns which will predominate during the rest of the dog's life, are formed between the ages of three and ten weeks. This is particularly true during the 21st to 28th day. It is essential that the puppy be socialized during this time by bringing him into family life as much as possible. Floor surfaces, indoor and outdoor, should be experienced; handling by all members of the family and visitors is important; preliminary grooming gets him used to a lifelong necessity; light training, such as setting him up on tables and cleaning teeth and ears and cutting nails, etc., has to be started early if he is to become a show dog. The puppy should be exposed to car riding, shopping tours, a leash around its neck, children—your own and others—and in all possible ways develop relationships with humans.

It is up to the breeder, of course, to protect the puppy from harm or injury during this initiation into the outside world. The benefits

Mrs. Claire Wearmouth's grandchildren Miranda and Jennifer-Jane are shown at home in New Zealand with Ch. Havvi, Ch. Wampum, Ch. Min, the puppy Delphinkum and Ch. Rah.

Ch. Kinderlands Tonka Tu winning Best of Winners at the 1972 Reston Show under the handling of Bob Sharp. Tonka is one of the brood bitches of the Taglha Lhasa Kennels of Mr. and Mrs. W.J. Browning, Jr. of Norfolk, Virginia.

Anbara puppies pictured at five weeks of age. Bred and owned by Barbara Wood.

Ch. Little Fir's Shel Ari of Chiz winning Best of Breed on the way to a Group Second under judge Edward Bracy at the 1975 Mispillion Kennel Club Show. "Ari" is co-owned by Madeline P. Chizever of Columbia, Maryland, and handler Joanne P. Baker.

reaped from proper attention will pay off in the long run with a well-behaved, well-adjusted grown dog capable of becoming an integral part of a happy family.

REARING THE FAMILY

Needless to say, even with a small litter there will be certain considerations which must be adhered to in order to insure successful rearing of the puppies. For instance, the diet for the mother should be appropriately increased as the puppies grow and take more and more nourishment from her. During the first few days of rest while the bitch just looks over her puppies and regains her strength, she should be left pretty much alone. It is during these first days that she begins to put the puppies on a feeding schedule and feels safe enough about them to leave the whelping box long enough to take a little extended exercise.

It is cruel, however, to try and keep the mother away from the puppies any longer than she wants to be because you feel she is being too attentive or to give the neighbors a chance to peek in at the puppies. The mother should not have to worry about harm coming to her puppies for the first few weeks. The veterinary checkup will be enough of an experience for her to have to endure until she is more like herself once again.

As the puppies continue to thrive and grow, you will notice that they take on individual characteristics. If you are going to keep and

Two of Marie and Alfred Stillman's Lhasas in the early days of the breed in this country.

show one of the puppies, this is the time to start observing them for various outstanding characteristics.

EVALUATING THE LITTER

A show puppy prospect should be outgoing, (probably the first one to fall out of the whelping box!) and all efforts should be made to socialize the puppy which appears to be the most shy. Once the puppies are about three weeks old, they can and should be handled a great deal by friends and members of the family.

During the third week they begin to try to walk instead of crawl, but they are unsteady on their feet. Tails are used for balancing, and they begin to make sounds.

The crucial period in a puppy's life occurs when the puppy is from 21 to 28 days old, so all the time you can devote to them at this time will reap rewards later on in life. This is the age when several other important steps must be taken in a puppy's life. Weaning should start if it hasn't already, and it is the time to check for worms. Do not worm unnecessarily. A veterinarian should advise on worming and appropriate dosage and can also discuss with you at this time the schedule for serum or vaccination, which will depend on the size of the puppies as well as their age.

Exercise and grooming should be started at this time, with special care and consideration given to the diet. You will find that the dam will help you wean the puppies, leaving them alone more and more as she notices that they are eating well on their own. Begin by leaving them with her during the night for comfort and warmth; eventually, when she shows less interest, keep them separated entirely.

By the time the fifth week of their lives arrives you will already be in love with every one of them and desperately searching for reasons to keep them all. They recognize you—which really gets to you!—and they box and chew on each other and try to eat your finger and a million other captivating antics which are special with puppies. Their stomachs seem to be bottomless pits, and their weight will rise. At eight to ten weeks, the puppies will be weaned and ready to go.

SPAYING AND CASTRATING

A wise old philosopher once said, "Timing in life is everything!" No statement could apply more readily to the age-old question which every dog owner is faced with sooner or later... to spay or not to spay.

For the one-bitch pet owner, spaying is the most logical answer, for it solves many problems. The pet is usually not of top breeding quality, and therefore there is no great loss to the bloodline; it takes the pressure off the family if the dog runs free with children and cer-

Ch. Karma Dmar-Pos and Karma Karha-Ta, photographed as puppies. Owned and bred by Dorothy Cohen of Las Vegas, Nevada.

Ch. Karma Dmar-Po, sire of 14 Karma-bred champions. Owned by Dorothy Cohen, Karma Kennels, Los Vegas, Neveda.

This darling 5-month-old Lhasa was photographed in 1972 and grew up to be Ch. Karma Rgyal-Po Chan, bred by Dorothy Cohen and owned by Joan Pettit.

Viento Chang-Tang, a three-month-old puppy, by Ch. Wyrley Hermes ex Viento Mame. Bred and owned by Mr. and Mrs. F.E. Wallis, Viento Kennels, Southampton, England.

tainly eliminates the problem of repeated litters of unwanted puppies or a backyard full of eager males twice a year.

But for the owner or breeder, the extra time and protection which must be afforded a purebred quality bitch can be most worthwhile—even if it is only until a single litter is produced after the first heat. It is then not too late to spay, the progeny can perpetuate the bloodline, the bitch will have been fulfilled—though it is merely an old wives' tale that bitches should have at least one litter to be "normal"—and she may then be retired to her deserved role as family pet once again.

With spaying the problem of staining and unusual behavior around the house is eliminated without the necessity of having to keep her in "pants" or administering pills, sprays or shots. . . which most veterinarians do not approve of anyway.

In the case of males, castration is seldom contemplated, which to me is highly regrettable. The owner of the male dog merely overlooks the dog's ability to populate an entire neighborhood, since they do not have the responsibility of rearing and disposing of the puppies. But when you take into consideration all the many females the male dog can impregnate it is almost more essential that the males be taken out of circulation than that the females be. The male dog will still be inclined to roam but will be less frantic about leaving the grounds, and you will find that a lot of the wanderlust has left him.

STERILIZING FOR HEALTH

When considering the problem of spaying or castrating, the first consideration after the population explosion should actually be the health of the dog or bitch. Males are frequently subject to urinary diseases, and sometimes castration is a help. Your veterinarian can best advise you on this problem. Another aspect to consider is the kennel dog which is no longer being used at stud. It is unfair to keep him in a kennel with females in heat when there is no chance for him to be used. There are other more personal considerations for both kennel and one-dog owners, but when making the decision remember that it is final. You can always spay or castrate, but once the deed is done there is no return!

12. TRAINING YOUR LHASA APSO

There are few things in the world a dog would rather do than please his master. Therefore, obedience training, or even the initial basic training, will be a pleasure for your dog, if taught correctly, and will make him a much nicer animal to live with for the rest of his life.

WHEN TO START TRAINING

The most frequently asked question by those who consider training their dog is, naturally, "What is the best age to start training?" The answer is "not before six months." A dog simply cannot be sufficiently or permanently trained before this age and be expected to retain all he has been taught. If too much is expected of him, he can become frustrated and it may ruin him completely for any serious training later on, or even jeopardize his disposition. Most things a puppy learns and repeats before he is six months of age should be considered habit rather than training.

THE REWARD METHOD

The only proper and acceptable kind of training is the kindness and reward method which will build a strong bond between dog and owner. A dog must have confidence in and respect for his teacher. The most important thing to remember in training any dog is that the quickest way to teach, especially the young dog, is through repetition. Praise him when he does well, and scold him when he does wrong. This will suffice. There is no need or excuse for swinging at a dog with rolled up newspapers or flailing hands which will only tend to make the dog hand shy the rest of his life. Also, make every word count. Do not give a command unless you intend to see it through. Pronounce distinctly with the fewest possible words, and use the same words for the same command every time.

Include the dog's name every time to make sure you have his undivided attention at the beginning of each command. Do not go on to another command until he has successfully completed the previous one and is praised for it. Of course, you should not mix play with the

American, French and International Champion SharBo Tsan Chu, winner in Europe of 21 Toy Group Firsts. Bred by American Sharon Rouse and owned by Dr. F.P. Clement, Loire, France.

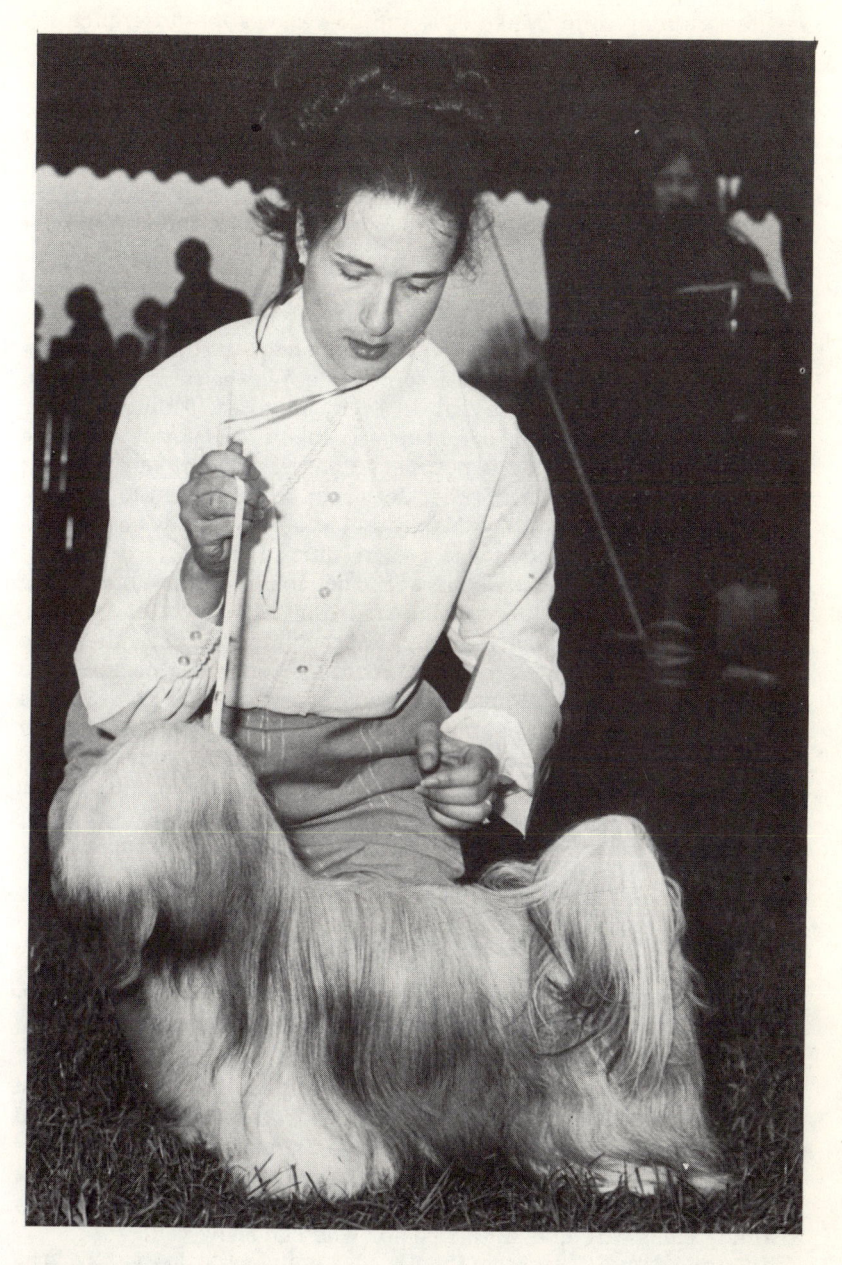

Ch. Milton's Tam-me Ko, owned by Sharon DeCoopman and bred by the Drax Kennels, is pictured going Best of Winners at the 1971 parent club Specialty Show in Trenton, New Jersey.

serious training time. Make sure the dog knows the difference between the two.

In the beginning, it is best to train without any distractions whatsoever. After he has learned to concentrate and is older and more proficient, he should perform the exercises with interference, so that the dog learns absolute obedience in the face of all distractions: Needless to say, whatever the distractions, you never lose control. You must be in command at all times to earn the respect and attention of your dog.

HOW LONG SHOULD THE LESSONS BE?

The lessons should be brief with a young dog, starting at five minutes, and as the dog ages and becomes adept in the first lessons, increase the time all the way up to thirty minutes. Public training classes are usually set for one hour, and this is acceptable since the full hour of concentration is not placed on your dog alone. Working under these conditions with other dogs, you will find that he will not be as intent as he would be with a private lesson where the commands are directed to him alone for the entire thirty minutes.

If you should notice that your dog is not doing well, or not keeping up with the class, consider putting off training for awhile. Animals, like children, are not always ready for schooling at exactly the same age. It would be a shame to ruin a good obedience dog because you insist on starting his training at six months rather than at, say, nine months, when he would be more apt to be receptive both physically and mentally. If he has particular difficulty in learning one exercise, you might do well to skip to a different one and come back to it again at another session. There are no set rules in this basic training, except, "don't push!"

WHAT YOU NEED TO START TRAINING

From three to six months of age, use the soft nylon show leads, which are the best and safest. When you get ready for the basic training at six months of age, you will require one of the special metal-link choke chains sold for exactly this purpose. Do not let the word "choke" scare you. It is a soft, smooth chain and should be held slack whenever you are not actually using it to correct the dog. This chain should be put over the dog's head so that the lead can be attached over the dog's neck rather than underneath against his throat. It is wise when you buy your choke collar to ask the salesperson to show you how it is put on. Those of you who will be taking your dog to a training class will have an instructor who can show you.

To avoid undue stress on the dog, use both hands on the lead. The dog will be taught to obey commands at your left side, and therefore, your left hand will guide the dog close to his collar on a six-foot training lead. The balance of the lead will be held in your right hand.

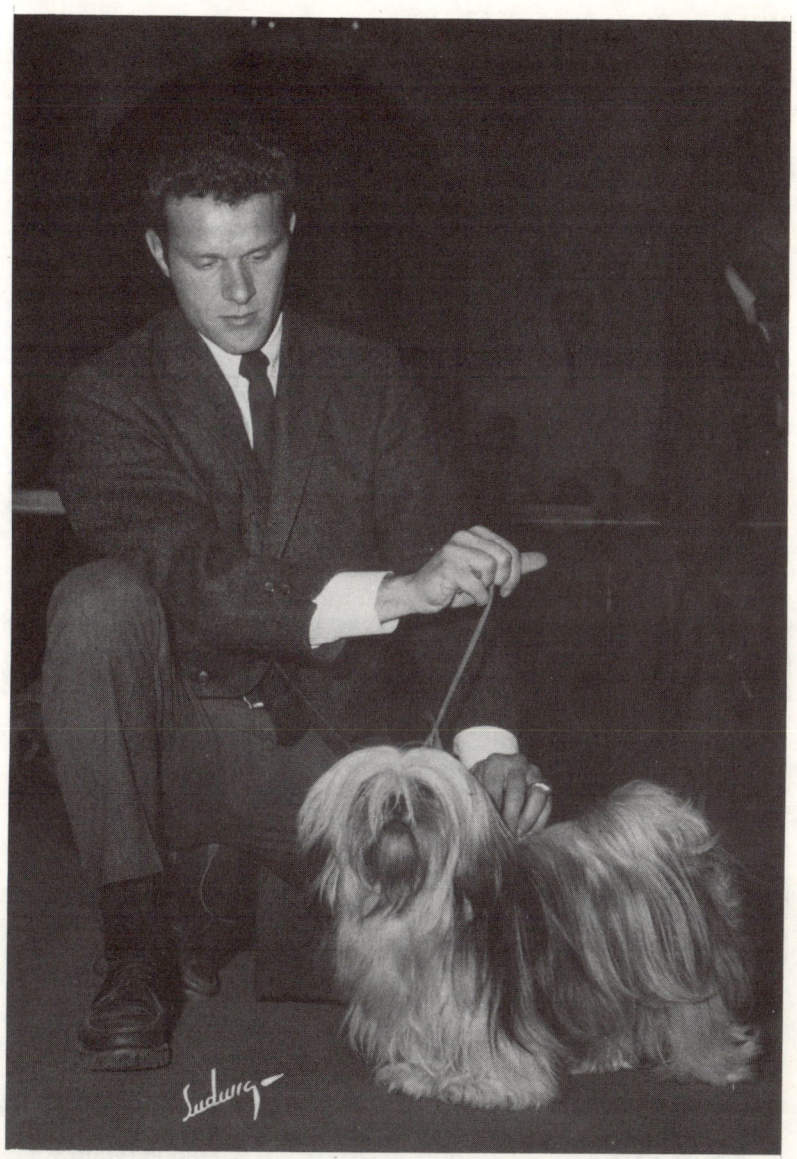

Mexican and American Ch. Karma Sangpo, bred and owned by Dorothy Cohen of Las Vegas, Nevada, is pictured winning with handler Frank Sabella.

Learn at the very beginning to handle your choke collar and lead correctly. It is as important in training a dog as is the proper equipment for riding a horse.

WHAT TO TEACH FIRST

The first training actually should be to teach the dog to know his name. This, of course, he can learn at an earlier age than six months, just as he can learn to walk nicely on a leash or lead. Many puppies will at first probably want to walk around with the leash in their mouths. There is no objection to this if the dog will walk while doing it. Rather than cultivating this as a habit, you will find that if you don't make an issue of it, the dog will soon realize that carrying the lead in his mouth is not rewarding and he'll let it fall to his side where it belongs.

We also let the puppy walk around by himself for a while with the lead around his neck. If he wishes to chew on it a little, that's all right too. In other words, let it be something he recognizes and associates with at first. Do not let the lead start out being a harness.

If the dog is at all bright, chances are he has learned to come on command when you call him by name. This is relatively simple with sweet talk and a reward. On lead, without a reward, and on command without a lead is something else again. If there has been, or is now, a

Sheng-La's Tashi Tamima, C.D.X., caught in full flight over the jump with her dumbbell. This photograph was taken in June, 1974 when Tam was finishing for her titles. Her scores were all over 185 and up into the 190's. Tam was owner-handled and trained by Florence Dickerson, Sheng-La Lhasas, Marion, Ohio.

problem, the best way to correct it is to put on the choke collar and the six-foot lead. Then walk away from the dog, and call him, "Pirate, come!" and gently start reeling him in until the dog is in front of you. Give him a pat on the head and/or reward.

Walking, or heeling, next to you is also one of the first and most important things for him to learn. With the soft lead training starting very early, he should soon take up your pace at your left side. At the command to "heel" he should start off with you and continue alongside until you stop. Give the command, "Pirate, sit!" This is taught by leaning over and pushing down on his hindquarters until he sits next to you, while pulling up gently on his collar. When you have this down pat on the straightaway, then start practicing it in circles, with turns and figure eights. When he is an advanced student, you can look forward to the heels and sits being done neatly, spontaneously, and off lead as well.

THE "DOWN" COMMAND

One of the most valuable lessons or commands you can teach your dog is to lie down on command. Some day it may save his life, and is invaluable when traveling with a dog or visiting, if behavior and manners are required even beyond obedience. While repeating the words, "Pirate, down!" lower the dog from a sitting position in front of you by gently pulling his front legs out in front of him. Place your full hand on him while repeating the command, "Pirate, down!" and hold him down to let him know that you want him to *stay* down. After he gets the general idea, this can be done from a short distance away on a lead along with the command, by pulling the lead down to the floor. Perhaps you can slip the lead under your shoe (between the heel and sole) and pull it directly to the floor. As the dog progresses in training, a hand signal with or without verbal command or with or without lead, can be given from a considerable distance by raising your arm and extending the palm down.

THE "STAY" COMMAND

The stay command eventually can be taught from both a sit and a down position. Start with the sit. With the dog on your left side in the sitting position, give the command, "Pirate, stay!" Reach down with the left hand open and palm side to the dog and sweep it in close to his nose. Next, walk a short distance away and face him. He will at first, having learned to heel immediately as you start off, more than likely start off with you. The trick in teaching this is to make sure he hears "stay" before you start off. It will take practice. If he breaks, sit him down again, stand next to him, and give the command all over again. As he masters the command, let the distance between you and your dog increase while the dog remains seated. Once the command is learned, advance to the stay command from the down position.

THE STAND FOR EXAMINATION

If you have any intention of going on to advanced training in obedience with your dog, or if you have a show dog which you feel you will enjoy showing yourself, a most important command which should be mastered at six months of age is the stand command. This is essential for a show dog since it is the position used when the show judge goes over your dog. This is taught in the same manner as the stay command, but this time with the dog remaining up on all four feet. He should learn to stand still, without moving his feet and without flinching or breaking when approached by either you or strangers. The hand, with palm open wide and facing him, should be firmly placed in front of his nose with the command, "Pirate, stand!" After he learns the basic rules and knows the difference between stand and stay, ask friends, relatives and strangers to assist you with this exercise by walking up to the dog and going over him. He should not react physically to their touch. A dog posing in this stance should show all the beauty and pride of being a sterling example of his breed.

Six-week-old puppies bred by Mrs. John Licos of Beverly Hills, California, and photographed by Joan Ludwig. These two puppies were from a 1959 Christmas litter.

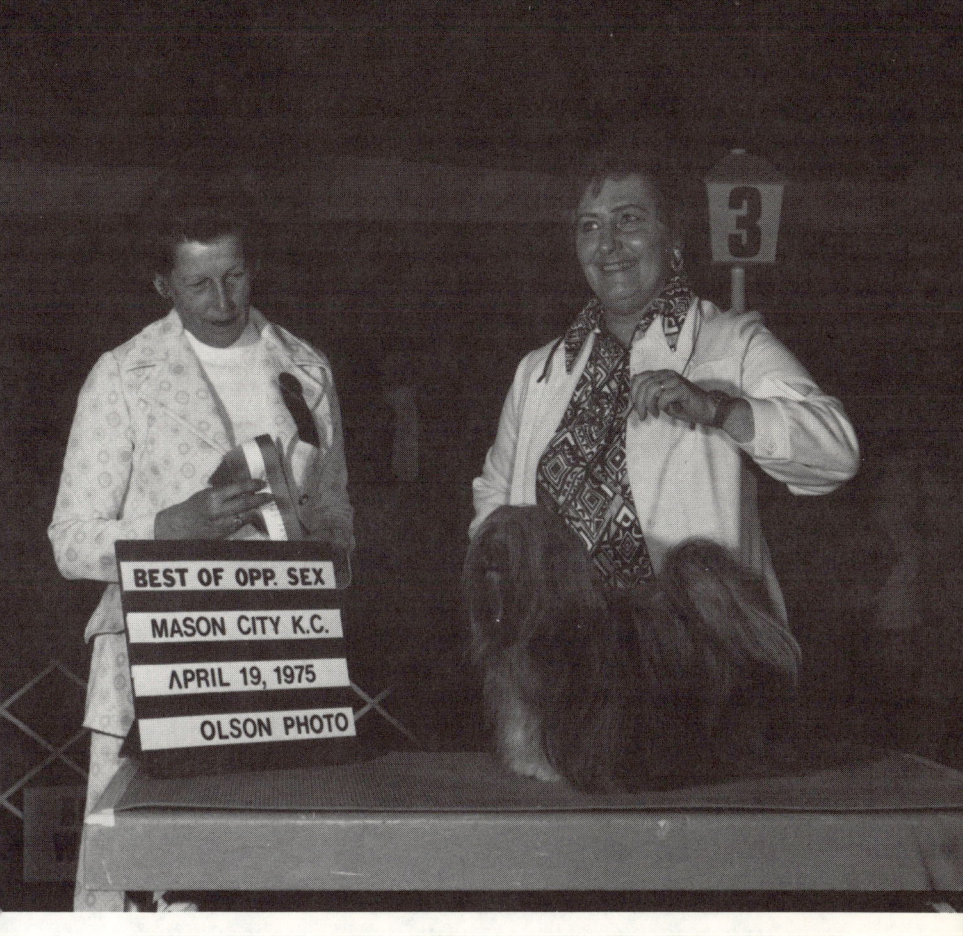

Ch. Joval's Midnight Lace, golden with black overlay, is pictured winning Best Opposite Sex at a 1975 show with handler Rena Martin. The sire was Ch. Potala Chiang *ex* Ch. Tabu's Rhapsody in Red. Co-owned by Janet Whitman and Maxine Felberg, Spring Valley, New York.

FORMAL SCHOOL TRAINING

We mentioned previously about the various training schools and classes given for dogs. Your local kennel club, newspaper or the yellow pages of the telephone book will put you in touch with organizations in your area where this service is performed. You and your dog will learn a great deal from these classes. Not only do they offer formal training, but the experience for you and your dog in public, with other dogs of approximately the same age and with the same purpose in mind, is excellent. If you intend to show your dog, this training is valuable ring experience for later on. If you are having difficulty with the training, remember, it is either too soon to start—or YOU are doing something wrong!

ADVANCED TRAINING AND OBEDIENCE TRIALS

The A.K.C. obedience trials are divided into three classes: Novice, Open and Utility.

In the Novice Class, the dog will be judged on the following basis:

TEST	MAXIMUM SCORE
Heel on lead	35
Stand for examination	30
Heel free—on lead	45
Recall (come on command)	30
One-minute sit (handler in ring)	30
Three-minute down (handler in ring)	30
Maximum total score	*200*

If the dog "qualifies" in three shows by earning at least 50% of the points for each test, with a total of at least 170 for the trial, he has earned the Companion Dog degree and the letters C.D. (Companion Dog) are entered after his name in the A.K.C. records.

After the dog has qualified as a C.D., he is eligible to enter the Open Class competition, where he will be judged on this basis:

TEST	MAXIMUM SCORE
Heel free	40
Drop on Recall	30
Retrieve (wooden dumbbell) on flat	25
Retrieve over obstacle (hurdle)	35
Broad jump	20
Three-minute sit (handler out of ring)	25
Five-minute down (handler out of ring)	25
Maximum total score	*200*

Again he must qualify in three shows for the C.D.X. (Companion Dog Excellent) title and then is eligible for the Utility Class, where he can earn the Utility Dog (U.D.) degree in these rugged tests:

TEST	MAXIMUM SCORE
Scent discrimination (Article #1)	30
Scent discrimination (Article #2)	30
Directed retrieve	30
Signal exercise (heeling, etc., on hand signal)	35
Directed jumping (over hurdle and bar jump)	40
Group examination	35
Maximum total score	*200*

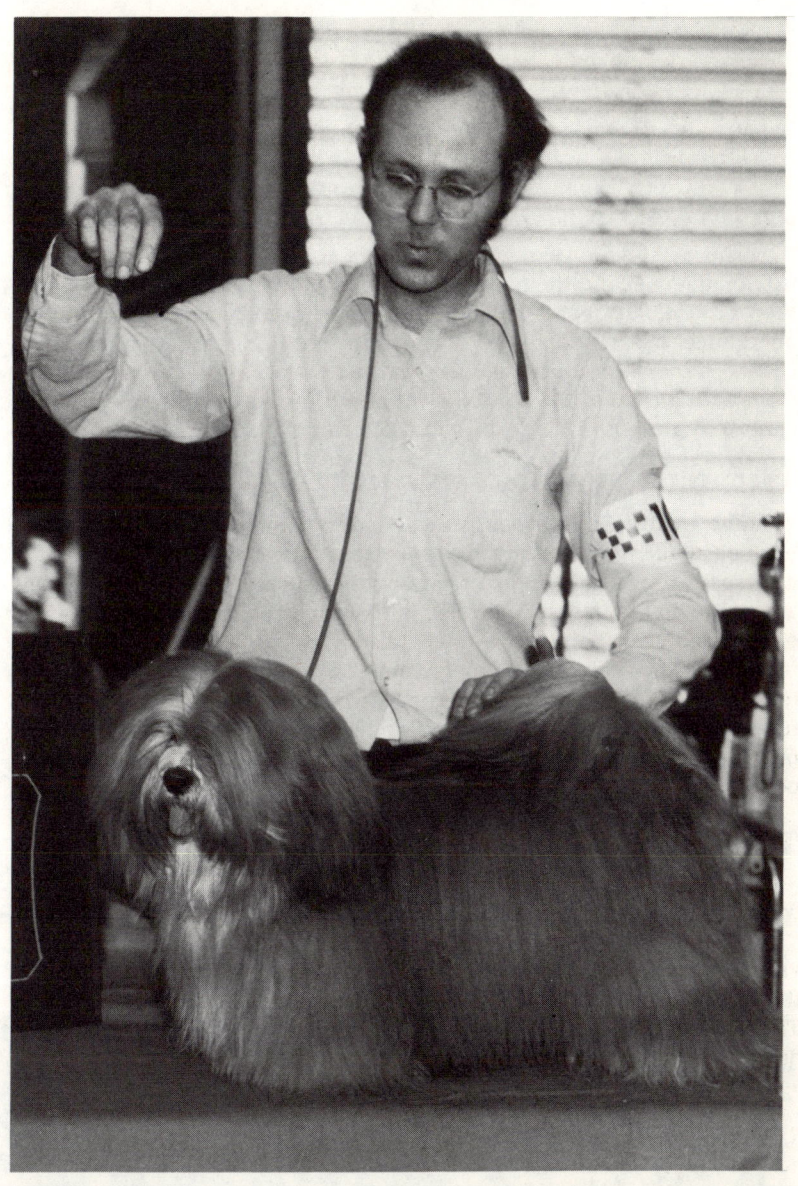

Xanadu's Raphael, pictured winning at a 1976 match. His sire was Best in Show-winning Ch. Joi-Sans Happieh-Go-Luckieh *ex* Ch. Sharpette's Bobette. Bred and owned by David and Liz Goldfarb.

For more complete information about these obedience trials, write for the American Kennel Club's *Regulations and Standards for Obedience Trials*. Dogs that are disqualified from breed shows because of alteration or physical defects are eligible to compete in these trials.

THE COMPANION DOG EXCELLENT DEGREE

There are seven exercises which must be executed to achieve the C.D.X. degree and the percentages for achieving these are the same as for the U.D. degree. Candidates must qualify in three different obedience trials and under three different judges and must have received scores of more than 50% of the available points in each exercise, with a total of 170 points or more out of the possible 200. At that time they may add the letters C.D.X after their name.

THE UTILITY DOG DEGREE

The Utility Dog degree is awarded to dogs which have qualified by successfully completing six exercises under three different judges at three different obedience trials, with a score of more than 50% of available points in each exercise, and with a score of 170 or more out of a possible 200 points.

These six exercises consist of scent discrimination, with two different articles for which they receive thirty points each if successfully completed; direct retrieving, for 30 points; signal exercise for 35 points; directed jumping for 40 points and a group examination for 35 points.

THE TRACKING DOG DEGREE

The Tracking Dog trials are not held as the others are, with the dog shows, and need be passed only once.

The dog must work continuously on a strange track at least 440 yards long and with two right angle turns. There is no time limit, and the dog must retrieve an article laid at the other end of the trail. There is no score given; the dog either earns the degree or fails. The dog is worked by his trainer on a long leash, usually in harness.

13. SHOWING YOUR LHASA APSO

Let us assume that after a few months of tender loving care, you realize your dog is developing beyond your wildest expectations and that the dog you selected is very definitely a show dog! Of course, every owner is prejudiced. But if you are sincerely interested in going to dog shows with your dog and making a champion of him, now is the time to start casting a critical eye on him from a judge's point of view.

There is no such thing as a perfect dog. Every dog has some faults, perhaps even a few serious ones. The best way to appraise your dog's degree of perfection is to compare him with the Standard for the breed, or before a judge in a show ring.

MATCH SHOWS

For the beginner there are "mock" dog shows, called Match Shows, where you and your dog go through many of the procedures of a regular dog show, but do not gain points toward championship. These shows are usually held by kennel clubs, annually or semiannually, and much ring poise and experience can be gained there. The age limit is reduced to two months at match shows to give puppies four months of training before they compete at the regular shows when they reach six months of age. Classes range from two to four months; four to six months; six to nine months; and nine to twelve months. Puppies compete with others of their own age for comparative purposes. Many breeders evaluate their litters in this manner, choosing which is the most outgoing, which is the most poised, the best showman, etc.

For those seriously interested in showing their dogs to full championship, these match shows provide important experience for both the dog and the owner. Class categories may vary slightly, according to number of entries, but basically include all the classes that are included at a regular point show. There is a nominal entry fee and, of course, ribbons and usually trophies are given for your efforts as well. Unlike the point shows, entries can be made on the day of the show right on the show grounds. They are unbenched and provide an

Ch. Hamilton Katha, pictured winning the Non-Sporting Group at the 1960 Sahuaro Kennel Club Show with the late judge R.A. Cross presenting the award. George Payton handled for owner Mrs. John Licos of Beverly Hills, California.

informal, usually congenial atmosphere for the amateur, which helps to make the ordeal of one's first adventures in the show ring a little less nerve-wracking.

THE POINT SHOWS

It is not possible to show a puppy at an American Kennel Club sanctioned point show before the age of six months. When your dog reaches this eligible age, your local kennel club can provide you with the names and addresses of the show-giving superintendents in your area who will be staging the club's dog show for them, and where you must write for an entry form.

The forms are mailed in a pamphlet called a premium list. This also includes the names of the judges for each breed, a list of the prizes and trophies, the name and address of the show-giving club and where the show will be held, as well as rules and regulations set up by the American Kennel Club which must be abided by if you are to enter.

A booklet containing the complete set of show rules and regulations may be obtained by writing to the American Kennel Club, Inc., 51 Madison Avenue, New York, N.Y., 10010.

When you write to the Dog Show Superintendent, request not only your premium list for this particular show, but ask that your name be added to their mailing list so that you will automatically receive all premium lists in the future. List your breed or breeds and they will see to it that you receive premium lists for Specialty shows as well.

American and Bermudian Champion Kinderland's Tonka, dam of multiple group winners Ch. Tabu's King of Hearts, ROM, and Ch. Tabu's Kiss Me Kate (dam of group winner Ch. Tabu's Gold Galaxy). Tonka is a Best in Show winner owned by Norman and Carolyn Herbel, Tabu Kennels, Lucas, Kansas.

Unlike the match shows where your dog will be judged on ring behavior, at the point shows he will be judged on conformation to the breed Standard. In addition to being at least six months of age (on the day of the show) he must be a purebred for a point show. This means both of his parents and he are registered with the American Kennel Club. There must be no alterations or falsifications regarding his appearance. Females cannot have been spayed and males must have both testicles in evidence. No dyes or powders may be used to enhance the appearance, and any lameness or deformity or major deviation from the Standard for the breed constitutes a disqualification.

With all these things in mind, groom your dog to the best of your ability in the specified area for this purpose in the show hall and walk into the show ring with great pride of ownership and ready for an appraisal of your dog by the judge.

The presiding judge on that day will allow each and every dog a certain amount of time and consideration before making his deci-

Hardacre Sinful Skinful, sired by American and Canadian Ch. Hardacre Kinderlands Bhu-Sun *ex* Ch. Tungwei of Coburg. Sinful Skinful is now a champion and was bred by owner Mrs. A. Matthews, Hardacre Kennels, Sussex, England.

Mrs. Anne Griffing of Mountainside, New Jersey, shows her Ch. Ming Toy Nola at the Hunterdon Hills Kennel Club Show in August, 1959. The judge was William E. Henry, who gave Nola the Group First. Nola also won a Non-Sporting Group at the Bryn Mawr Kennel Club Show in 1956 under Judge Hays. Shafer photo.

sions. It is never permissible to consult the judge regarding either your dog or his decision while you are in the ring. An exhibitor never speaks unless spoken to, and then only to answer such questions as the judge may ask—the age of the dog, the dog's bite, or to ask you to move your dog around the ring once again.

However, before you reach the point where you are actually in the ring awaiting the final decisions of the judge, you will have had to decide in which of the five classes in each sex your dog should compete.

POINT SHOW CLASSES

The regular classes of the AKC are: Puppy, Novice, Bred-by-Exhibitor, American-Bred, Open; if your dog is undefeated in any of the regular classes (divided by sex) in which it is entered, he or she is *required* to enter the Winners Class. If your dog is placed second in the class to the dog which won Winners Dog or Winners Bitch, hold the dog or bitch in readiness as the judge must consider it for Reserve Winners.

PUPPY CLASSES shall be for dogs which are six months of age and over but under twelve months, which were whelped in the U.S.A. or Canada, and which are not champions. Classes are often divided six and (under) nine and nine and (under) twelve months. The age of a dog shall be calculated up to and inclusive of the first day of a show. For example, a dog whelped on January 1st is eligible to compete in a puppy class on July 1st and may continue to compete up to and including December 31st of the same year, but is not eligible to compete January 1st of the following year.

THE NOVICE CLASS shall be for dogs six months of age or over, whelped in the U.S.A. or Canada which have not, prior to the closing of entries, won three first prizes in the Novice Class, a first prize in Bred-by-Exhibitor, American-Bred or Open Class, nor one or more points toward a championship title.

THE BRED-BY-EXHIBITOR CLASS shall be for dogs whelped in the U.S.A. which are six months of age and over, which are not champions and which are owned wholly or in part by the person or by the spouse of the person who was the breeder or one of the breeders of record. Dogs entered in the BBE Class must be handled by an owner or by a member of the immediate family of an owner, i.e., the husband, wife, father, mother, son, daughter, brother or sister.

THE AMERICAN-BRED CLASS is for all dogs (except champions) six months of age or over, whelped in the U.S.A. by reason of a mating that took place in the U.S.A.

THE OPEN CLASS is for any dog six months of age or over, except in a member specialty club show held for only American-Bred dogs, in which case the class is for American-Bred dogs only.

WINNERS DOG and WINNERS BITCH: After the above male classes have been judged, the first-place winners are then *required* to compete in the ring. The dog judged "Winners Dog" is awarded the points toward his championship title.

RESERVE WINNERS are selected immediately after the Winners Dog. In case of a disqualification of a win by the AKC, the Reserve Dog moves up to "Winners" and receives the points. After all male classes are judged, the bitch classes are called.

BEST OF BREED OR BEST OF VARIETY COMPETITION is limited to Champions of Record or dogs (with newly acquired points, for a 90-day period prior to AKC confirmation) which have completed championship requirements, and Winners Dog and Winners Bitch (or the dog awarded Winners if only one Winners prize has been awarded), together with any undefeated dogs which have been shown only in non-regular classes; all compete for Best of Breed or Best of Variety (if the breed is divided by size, color, texture or length of coat hair, etc.).

BEST OF WINNERS: If the WD or WB earns BOB or BOV, it automatically becomes BOW; otherwise they will be judged together for BOW (following BOB or BOV judging).

BEST OF OPPOSITE SEX is selected from the remaining dogs of the opposite sex to Best of Breed or Best of Variety.

OTHER CLASSES may be approved by the AKC: STUD DOGS, BROOD BITCHES, BRACE CLASS, TEAM CLASS; classes consisting of local dogs and bitches may also be included in a show if approved by the AKC (special rules are included in the AKC Rule Book).

Ch. Chen Krisna Nor, co-owned and handled by Wendy Harper and Patricia Chenoweth. He was sired by Ch. Chen Nyun-Ti out of Chen Pho Nimo.

Ch. Chig-Chig and daughter Ch. Chig Jo-Mo photographed for distribution on doggie notepaper by photographers Albert and Creszentia Allen. Both Lhasas are owned by Robert and Anne Griffing of Mountainside, New Jersey.

The MISCELLANEOUS CLASS shall be for purebred dogs of such breeds as may be designated by the AKC. No dog shall be eligible for entry in this class unless the owner has been granted an Indefinite Listing Privilege (ILP) and unless the ILP number is given on the entry form. Application for an ILP shall be made on a form provided by the AKC and when submitted must be accompanied by a fee set by the Board of Directors.

All Miscellaneous Breeds shall be shown together in a single class except that the class may be divided by sex if so specified in the premium list. There shall be *no* further competition for dogs entered in this class. Ribbons for 1st, 2nd, 3rd and 4th shall be rose, brown, light green and gray, respectively. This class is open to the following Miscellaneous dog breeds: Australian Cattle Dogs, Australian Kelpies, Border Collies, Cavalier King Charles Spaniels, Ibizan Hounds, Miniature Bull Terriers, and Spinoni Italiani.

A charming headstudy of English and Australian Champion Cheska Jesta, bred and owned by Frances Sefton of New South Wales, Australia.

If Your Dog Wins a Class...

Study the classes to make certain your dog is entered in a proper class for his or her qualifications. If your dog wins his class, the rule states: *You are required* to enter classes for Winners, Best of Breed and Best of Winners (no additional entry fees). The rule states, "No eligible dog may be withheld from competition." It is not mandatory that you stay for group judging. *If your dog wins a group,* however, *you must stay for Best-in-Show competition.*

THE PRIZE RIBBONS AND WHAT THEY STAND FOR

No matter how many entries there are in each class at a dog show, if you place first through fourth position you will receive a ribbon. These ribbons commemorate your win and can be impressive when collected and displayed to prospective buyers when and if you have puppies for sale or if you intend to use your dog at public stud.

All ribbons from the American Kennel Club licensed dog shows will bear the American Kennel Club seal, the name of the show, the date and the placement. In the classes the colors are blue for first, red for second, yellow for third, and white for fourth. Winners Dog or Winners Bitch ribbons are purple, while Reserve Dog and Reserve Bitch ribbons are purple and white. Best of Winners ribbons are blue and white; Best of Breed, purple and gold; and Best of Opposite Sex ribbons are red and white.

In the six groups, first prize is a blue rosette or ribbon, second placement is red, third yellow and fourth white. The Best in Show rosette is either red, white and blue or incorporates the colors used in the show-giving club's emblem.

QUALIFYING FOR CHAMPIONSHIP

Championship points are given for Winners Dog and Winners Bitch in accordance with a scale of points established by the American Kennel Club based on the popularity of the breed in entries and the number of dogs competing in the classes. This scale of points varies in different sections of the country, but the scale is published in the front of each dog show catalog. These points may differ between the dogs and the bitches at the same show. You may, however, win additional points by winning Best of Winners, if there are fewer dogs than bitches entered, or vice versa. Points never exceed five at any one show, and a total of fifteen points must be won to constitute a championship. These fifteen points must be won under at least three different judges, and you must acquire at least two major wins. Anything from a three to five point win is a major, while one and two point wins are minor wins. Two major wins must be won under two different judges to meet championship requirements.

Ch. Hardacre Hitchcock of Belazieth, photographed by Diane Pearce for owners Doreen and Rob Richardson of Essex, England. This fabulous Lhasa really brought attention to the breed in England with his outstanding record of 27 Bests In Show, all-breeds, and a Best In Show win at the Lhasa Apso Club's 1971 championship show. He was top-winning Lhasa four years in a row in the United Kingdom *Dog World* competition. He was also Best of Breed at Crufts in 1971 and is the sire of many champions both in England and abroad.

OBEDIENCE TRIALS

Some shows also offer Obedience Trials, which are considered as separate events. They give the dogs a chance to compete and score on performing a prescribed set of exercises intended to display their training in doing useful work.

There are three obedience titles for which they may compete. First, the Companion Dog or C.D. title; second the Companion Dog Excellent or C.D.X.; and third, the Utility Dog or U.D. Detailed information on these degrees is contained in a booklet entitled Official Obedience Regulations and may be obtained by writing to the American Kennel Club.

JUNIOR SHOWMANSHIP COMPETITION

Junior Showmanship Competition is for boys and girls in different age groups handling their own dogs or one owned by their immediate family. There are four divisions: Novice A, for the ten to twelve year olds; Novice B, for those thirteen to sixteen years of age, with no previous junior showmanship wins; Open C, for ten to twelve year olds; and Open D, for thirteen to sixteen years old who have earned one or more JS awards.

As Junior Showmanship at the dog shows increased in popularity, certain changes and improvements had to be made. As of April 1, 1971, the American Kennel Club issued a new booklet containing the Regulations for Junior Showmanship which may be obtained by writing to the A.K.C. at 51 Madison Avenue, New York, N.Y. 10010.

DOG SHOW PHOTOGRAPHERS

Every show has at least one official photographer who will be more than happy to take a photograph of your dog with the judge, ribbon and trophies, along with you or your handler. These make marvelous remembrances of your top show wins and are frequently framed along with the ribbons for display purposes. Photographers can be paged at the show over the public address system, if you wish to obtain this service. Prices vary, but you will probably find it costs little to capture these happy moments and the photos can always be used in the various dog magazines to advertise your dog's wins.

TWO TYPES OF DOG SHOWS

There are two types of dog shows licensed by the American Kennel Club. One is the all-breed show which includes classes for all the recognized breeds, and groups of breeds; i.e., all terriers, all toys, etc. Then there are the specialty shows for one particular breed which also offer championship points.

BENCHED OR UNBENCHED DOG SHOWS

The show-giving clubs determine, usually on the basis of what facilities are offered by their chosen show site, whether their show will be benched or unbenched. A benched show is one where the dog show superintendent supplies benches (cages for toy dogs). Each bench is numbered and its corresponding number appears on your entry identification slip which is sent to you prior to the show date. The number also appears in the show catalog. Upon entering the show you should take your dog to the bench where he should remain until it is time to groom him before entering the ring to be judged. After judging, he must be returned to the bench until the official time of dismissal from the show. At an unbenched dog show the club makes no provision whatsoever for your dog other than an enormous tent (if an outdoor show) or an area in a show hall where all crates and grooming equipment must be kept.

Benched or unbenched, the moment you enter the show grounds you are expected to look after your dog and have it under complete control at all times. This means short leads in crowded aisles or getting out of cars. In the case of a benched show, a "bench chain" is needed. It should allow the dog to move around, but not get down off the bench. It is also not considered "cute" to have small tots leading enormous dogs around a dog show where the child might be dragged into the middle of a dog fight.

Ch. Ruffway Mashaka (owned and handled by Georgia Palmer), pictured winning Best in Show at the 1971 Wheaton Kennel Club show.

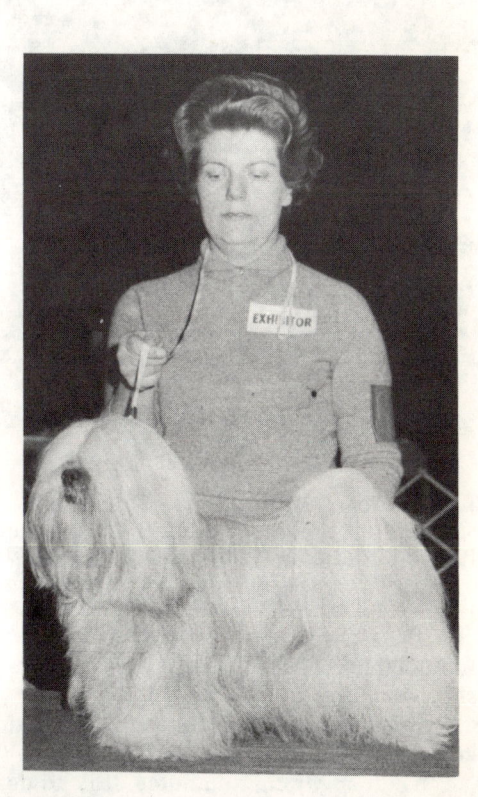

PROFESSIONAL HANDLERS

If you are new in the fancy and do not know how to handle your dog to his best advantage, or if you are too nervous or physically unable to show your dog, you can hire a licensed professional handler who will do it for you for a specified fee. The more successful or well-known handlers charge slightly higher rates, but generally speaking there is a pretty uniform charge for this service. As the dog progresses with his wins in the show ring, the fee increases proportionately.

Judge Robert Griffing, one of the pioneers in the breed, judges Ch. Karma Kricket Puff Winners Bitch over an entry of 31 bitches at the 1966 International Kennel Club show. Owner Rena Martin handled.

Included in this service is professional advice on when and where to show your dog, grooming, a statement of your wins at each show, and all trophies and ribbons that the dog accumulates. Any cash award is kept by the handler as a sort of "bonus."

When engaging a handler, it is advisable to select one that does not take more dogs to a show than he can properly and comfortably handle. You want your dog to receive his individual attention and not be rushed into the ring at the last moment because the handler has been busy with too many other dogs in other rings. Some handlers require that you deliver the dog to their establishment a few days ahead of the show so they have ample time to groom and train it. Others will accept well-behaved and previously trained and groomed dogs at ringside, if they are familiar with the dog and the owner. This should be determined well in advance of the show date. NEVER expect a handler to accept a dog at ringside that is not groomed to perfection!

There are several sources for locating a professional handler. Dog magazines carry their classified advertising; a note or telephone call to the American Kennel Club will put you in touch with several in your area. Usually, you will be billed after the day of the show.

DO YOU REALLY NEED A HANDLER?

The answer to the above question is sometimes yes! However, the answer most exhibitors give is, "But I can't *afford* a professional handler!" or, "I want to show my dog myself. Does that mean my dog will never do any big winning?"

Do you *really* need a handler to win? If you are mishandling a good dog that should be winning and isn't, because it is made to look

On the right, Ch. Kyi Chu Kaliph Nor winning Best of Breed; on the left is his daughter, Ch. Karma Kricket Puff, winning Best of Opposite Sex under the late judge Neal Coleman. Owner Rena Martin handles Nor and her daughter handles Nor's daughter.

simply terrible in the ring by its owner, the answer is yes. If you don't know how to handle a dog properly, why make your dog look bad when a handler could show it to its best advantage?

Some owners simply cannot handle a dog well and still wonder why their dogs aren't winning in the ring, no matter how hard they try. Others are nervous and this nervousness travels down the leash to the dog and the dog behaves accordingly. Some people are extroverts by nature, and these are the people who usually make excellent handlers. Of course, the biggest winning dogs at the shows usually have a lot of "show off" in their nature, too, and this helps a great deal.

Ch. Miradel's Hsien Seng Chili pictured winning at the 1961 Devon Kennel Club show. Chili was Winners Dog, Best of Winners and Best of Breed for a three-point major. Owned by the Miradel Kennels, Campbell, California.

THE COST OF CAMPAIGNING A DOG WITH A HANDLER

At present many champions are shown an average of 25 times before completing a championship. In entry fees at today's prices, that adds up to about $200. This does not include motel bills, traveling expenses or food. There have been dog champions finished in fewer shows, say five to ten shows, but this is the exception rather than the rule. When and where to show should be thought out carefully so that you can perhaps save money on entries. Here is one of the services a

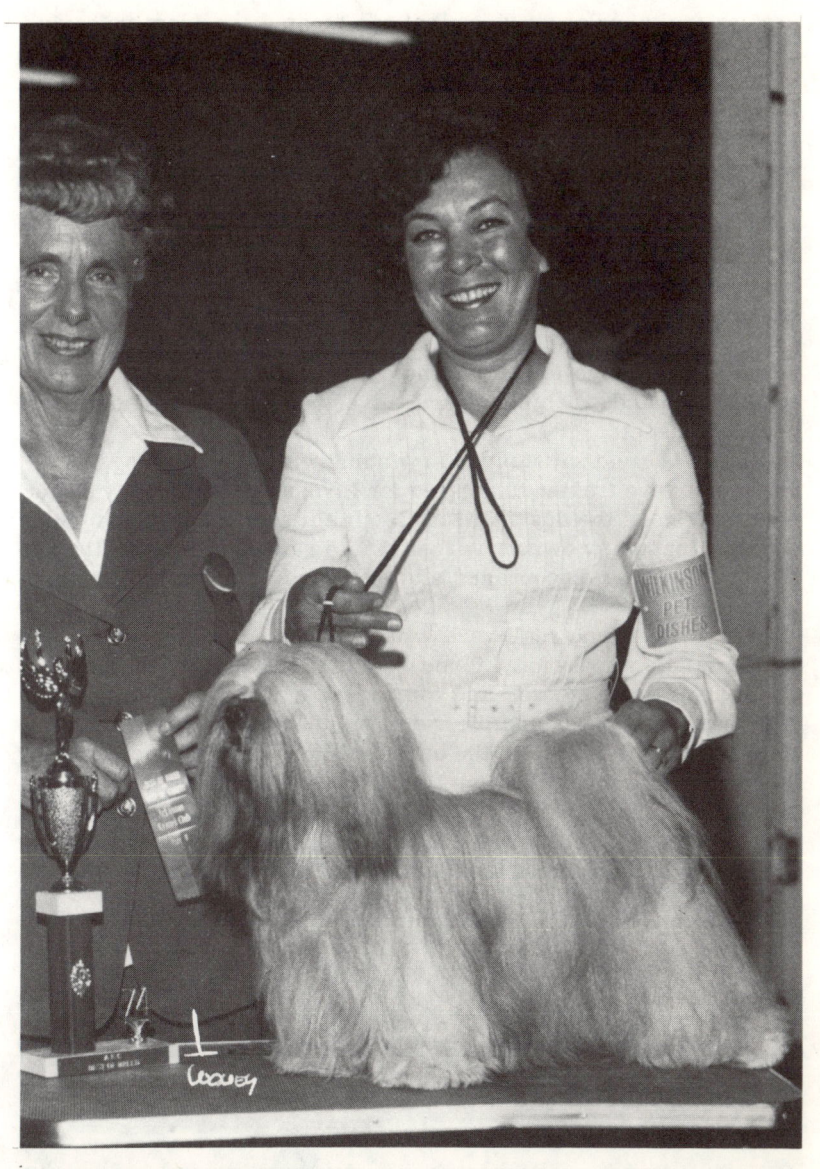

Ch. Mingtree The Wooly Boozer is pictured winning at a 1974 Arkansas Kennel Club Show. The Boozer is owned by Mrs. J. Robert Norman of New Orleans, Louisiana.

professional handler provides that can mean a considerable saving. Hiring a handler can save you money in the long run if you just wish to make a champion. If your dog has been winning reserves and not taking the points and a handler can finish him in five to ten shows, you would be ahead financially. If your dog is not really top quality, the length of time it takes even a handler to finish it (depending upon competition in the area) could add up to a large amount of money.

Campaigning a show specimen that not only captures the wins in his breed but wins Group and Best in Show awards gets up into the big money. To cover the nation's major shows and rack up a record as one of the top dogs in the nation usually costs an owner between ten and fifteen thousand dollars a year. This includes not only the professional handler's fee for taking the dog into the ring, but the cost of conditioning and grooming, board, advertising in the dog magazines, photographs, etc.

There is great satisfaction in winning with your own dog, especially if you have trained and cared for it yourself. With today's enormous entries at the dog shows and so many worthy dogs competing for top wins, many owners who said "I'd rather do it myself!" and meant it became discouraged and eventually hired a handler anyway.

However, if you really are in it just for the sport, you can and should handle your own dog if you want to. You can learn the tricks by attending training classes, and you can learn a lot by carefully observing the more successful professional handlers as they perform in the ring. Model yourself after the ones that command respect as being the leaders in their profession. But, if you find you'd really rather be at ringside looking on, then do get a handler so that your worthy dog gets his deserved recognition in the ring. To own a good dog and win with it is a thrill, so good luck, no matter how you do it.

14. GENERAL CARE AND MANAGEMENT

TATTOOING

Ninety per cent success has been reported on the return of stolen or lost dogs that have been tattooed. More and more this simple, painless, inexpensive method of positive identification for dogs is being reported all over the United States. Long popular in Canada, along with nose prints, the idea gained interest in this country when dognapping started to soar as unscrupulous people began stealing dogs for resale to research laboratories. Pet dogs that wander off and lost hunting dogs have always been a problem. The success of tattooing has been significant.

Tattooing can be done by the veterinarian for a minor fee. There are several dog "registries" that will record your dog's number and help you locate it should it be lost or stolen. The number of the dog's American Kennel Club registration is most often used on thoroughbred dogs, or the owner's Social Security number in the case of mixed breeds. The best place for the tattoo is the groin. Some prefer the inside of an ear, and the American Kennel Club has ruled that the judges officiating at A.K.C. dog shows not penalize the dog for the tattoo mark.

The tattoo mark serves not only to identify your dog should it be lost or stolen, but offers positive identification in large kennels where several litters of the same approximate age are on the premises. It is a safety measure against unscrupulous breeders "switching" puppies. Any age is a proper age to tattoo, but for safety's sake, the sooner the better.

The buzz of the needle might cause your dog to be apprehensive, but the pricking of the needle is virtually painless. The risk of infection is negligible when done properly, and the return of your beloved pet may be the reward for taking the time to insure positive identification for your dog. Your local kennel club will know of a dog registry in your area.

OUTDOOR HOUSEBREAKING

If you are particular about your dog's behavior in the house, where you expect him to be clean and respectful of the carpets and

"The windblown Lhasas" at the 1972 Bucks County Kennel Club show are, left to right, American and Canadian Ch. Tal-Hi Kori Ti-Ko, Ch. Kasha's Tsonya of Tal-Hi, and Tal-Hi Pret-Ti Celeste. Ti-Ko is being handled by Beverly Reed; her dam, Tsonya, by Ann Hoffman, and Celeste by her owner Julie Hamlin. Julie handled Celeste to a Best of Breed win at the 1975 Finger Lakes Kennel Club show.

Danish, Belgium and Int. Ch. Shaggy Wonder U'Tou Fou, bred by Mrs. Mewis de Ryck and owned by Ann Dilso, Nordhoj Kennels, Denmark.

American and Canadian Ch. Joi-San's Gol-Den Mocca of Ky, owned by Mr. and Mrs. James C. Lurton of Lexington, Kentucky, and Joyce Stambaugh of New Providence, New Jersey. This lovely gold dog is a multiple Best in Show winner and was sired by Ch. Arborhill's Bhran-Dieh *ex* Chu Shu's Kiri. Joyce Stambaugh was the breeder; Annette Lurton is the handler.

furniture, you should also want him to have proper manners outdoors. Just because the property belongs to you doesn't necessarily mean he should be allowed to empty himself any place he chooses. Before long the entire yard will be fouled and odorous and the dog will be completely irresponsible on other people's property as well. Dogs seldom recognize property lines.

If your dog does not have his own yard fenced in, he should be walked on leash before being allowed to run free and before being penned up in his own yard. He will appreciate his own run being kept clean. You will find that if he has learned his manners outside, his manners inside will be better. Good manners in "toilet training" are especially important with big dogs!

Petite Mouche, a parti-color female from the Banzai Kennel, owned by Asta and Jorgen Hindlev of Hjortebjerg, Denmark.

OTHER IMPORTANT OUTDOOR MANNERS

Excessive barking is perhaps the most objectionable habit a dog indulges in outdoors. It annoys neighbors and makes for a noisy dog in the house as well. A sharp jerk on the leash will stop a dog from excessive barking while walking; trees and shrubs around a dog run will cut down on barking if a dog is in his own run. However, it is unfair to block off his view entirely. Give him some view—preferably of his own home—to keep his interest. Needless to say, do not leave a dog that barks excessively out all night.

You will want your dog to bark at strangers, so allow him this privilege. Then after a few "alerting" barks tell the dog to be quiet (with the same word command each time). If he doesn't get the idea, put him on leash and let him greet callers with you at the door until he does get the idea.

Do not let your dog jump on visitors either. Leash training may be necessary to break this habit as well. As the dog jumps in the air, pull back on the lead so that the dog is returned to the floor abruptly. If he attempts to jump up on you, carefully raise your knee and push him away by leaning against his chest.

Do not let your dog roam free in the neighborhood no matter how well he knows his way home. Especially do not let your dog roam free to empty himself on the neighbors' property or gardens!

A positive invitation to danger is to allow your dog to chase cars or bicycles. Throwing tin cans or chains out of car windows at them has been suggested as a cure, but can also be dangerous if they hit the dog instead of the street. Streams of water from a garden hose or water pistol are the least dangerous, but leash control is still the most scientific and most effective.

If neighbors report that your dog barks or howls or runs from window to window while you are away, crate training or room training for short periods of time may be indicated. If you expect to be away for longer periods of time, put the dog in the basement or a single room where he can do the least damage. The best solution of all is to buy him another dog or cat for companionship. Let them enjoy each other while you are away and have them both welcome you home!

GERIATRICS

If you originally purchased good healthy stock and cared for your dog throughout his life, there is no reason why you cannot expect your dog to live to a ripe old age. With research and the remarkable foods produced for dogs, especially this past decade or so, his chances of longevity have increased considerably. If you have cared for him well, your dog will be a sheer delight in his old age, just as he was while in his prime.

We can assume you have fed him properly if he is not too fat. Have you ever noticed how fat people usually have fat dogs because they indulge their dogs' appetite as they do their own? If there has been no great illness, then you will find that very little additional care and attention are needed to keep him well. Exercise is still essential, as is proper food, booster shots, and tender loving care.

Even if a heart condition develops, there is still no reason to believe your dog cannot live to an old age. A diet may be necessary, along with medication and limited exercise, to keep the condition under control. In the case of deafness, or partial blindness, additional care must be taken to protect the dog, but neither infirmity will in any way shorten his life. Prolonged exposure to temperature variances, overeating, excessive exercise, lack of sleep, or being housed with younger, more active dogs may take an unnecessary toll on the dog's energies and introduce serious trouble. Good judgment, periodic veterinary checkups and individual attention will keep your dog with you for many added years.

When discussing geriatrics, the question of when a dog becomes old or aged usually is asked. We have all heard the old saying that one year of a dog's life is equal to seven years in a human. This theory is strictly a matter of opinion, and must remain so, since so many outside factors enter into how quickly each individual dog "ages." Recently, a new chart was devised which is more realistically equivalent:

DOG	MAN
6 months	10 years
1 year	15 years
2 years	24 years
3 years	28 years
4 years	32 years
5 years	36 years
6 years	40 years
7 years	44 years
8 years	48 years
9 years	52 years
10 years	56 years
15 years	76 years
21 years	100 years

It must be remembered that such things as serious illnesses, poor food and housing, general neglect and poor beginnings as puppies will take their toll on a dog's general health and age him more quickly than a dog that has led a normal, healthy life. Let your veterinarian help you determine an age bracket for your dog in his later years.

While good care should prolong your dog's life, there are several "old age" disorders to be on the lookout for no matter how well he may be doing. The tendency toward obesity is the most common, but constipation is another. Aging teeth and a slowing down of the digestive processes may hinder digestion and cause constipation, just as any major change in diet can bring on diarrhea. There is also the possibility of loss or impairment of hearing or eyesight which will also tend to make the dog wary and distrustful. Other behavioral changes may result as well, such as crankiness, loss of patience and lack of interest; these are the most obvious changes. Other ailments may manifest themselves in the form of rheumatism, arthritis, tumors and warts, heart disease, kidney infections, male prostatism and female disorders. Of course, all of these require a veterinarian's checking the degree of seriousness and proper treatment.

Take care to avoid infectious diseases. When these hit the older dog, they can debilitate him to an alarming degree, leaving him open to more serious complications and a shorter life.

DOG INSURANCE

Much has been said for and against canine insurance, and much more will be said before this kind of protection for a dog becomes universal and/or practical. There has been talk of establishing a Blue Cross-type plan similar to that now existing for humans. However, the best insurance for your dog is *you!* Nothing compensates for tender, loving care. Like the insurance policies for humans, there will be a lot of fine print in the contracts revealing that the dog is not covered after all. These limited conditions usually make the acquisition of dog insurance expensive and virtually worthless.

Blanket coverage policies for kennels or establishments which board or groom dogs can be an advantage, especially in transporting dogs to and from their premises. For the one-dog owner, however, whose dog is a constant companion, the cost for limited coverage is not necessary.

THE HIGH COST OF BURIAL

Pet cemeteries are mushrooming across the nation. Here, as with humans, the sky can be the limit for those who wish to bury their pets ceremoniously. The costs of satin-lined caskets, grave stones, flowers, etc. run the gamut of prices to match the emotions and means of the owner. This is strictly a matter of what the bereaved owner wishes to do.

IN THE EVENT OF YOUR DEATH. . .

This is a morbid thought perhaps, but ask yourself the question, "If death were to strike at this moment, what would become of my beloved dogs?"

Perhaps you are fortunate enough to have a relative, friend or spouse who could take over immediately, if only on a temporary basis. Perhaps you have already left instructions in your last will and testament for your pet's dispensation, as well as a stipend for their perpetual care.

Provide definite instructions before a disaster occurs and your dogs are carted off to the pound, or stolen by commercially minded neighbors with "resale" in mind. It is a simple thing to instruct your lawyer about your wishes in the event of sickness or death. Leave instructions as to feeding, etc., posted on your kennel room or kitchen bulletin board, or wherever your kennel records are kept. Also, tell several people what you are doing and why. If you prefer to keep such instructions private, merely place them in sealed envelopes in a known place with directions that they are to be opened only in the event of your demise. Eliminate the danger of your animals suffering in the event of an emergency that prevents your personal care of them.

Witneylea Golden Glint (whelped in August, 1974), a red-gold with black fringes, photographed at 14 months at her owners' Witneylea Kennels in Oxon, England. Her sire is Ramblersholt Prin-ne-La *ex* Georgina of Witneylea.

KEEPING RECORDS

Whether or not you have one dog, or a kennel full of them, it is wise to keep written records. It takes only a few moments to record dates of inoculations, trips to the vet, tests for worms, etc. It can avoid confusion or mistakes, or having your dog not covered with immunization if too much time elapses between shots because you have to guess at the time the last shot was given.

Make the effort to keep all dates in writing rather than trying to commit them to memory. A rabies injection date can be a problem if you have to recall that "Fido had the shot the day Aunt Mary got back from her trip abroad, and, let's see, I guess that was around the end of June."

In an emergency, these records may prove their value if your veterinarian cannot be reached and you have to use another, or if you move and have no case history on your dog for the new veterinarian. In emergencies, you do not always think clearly or accurately, and if dates, and types of serums used, etc., are a matter of record, the veterinarian can act more quickly and with more confidence.

15. YOUR DOG, YOUR VETERINARIAN AND YOU

The purpose of this chapter is to explain why you should never attempt to be your own veterinarian. Quite the contrary, we urge emphatically that you establish a good liaison with a reputable veterinarian who will help you maintain happy, healthy dogs. Our purpose is to bring you up to date on the discoveries made in modern canine medicine and to help you work with your veterinarian by applying these new developments to your own animals.

We have provided here "thumbnail" histories of many of the most common types of diseases your dog is apt to come in contact with during his lifetime. We feel that if you know a little something about the diseases and how to recognize their symptoms, your chances of catching them in the preliminary stages will help you and your veterinarian effect a cure before a serious condition develops.

Today's dog owner is a realistic, intelligent person who learns more and more about his dog—inside and out—so that he can care for and enjoy the animal to the fullest. He uses technical terms for parts of the anatomy, has a fleeting knowledge of the miracles of surgery and is fully prepared to administer clinical care for his animals at home. This chapter is designed for study and/or reference and we hope you will use it to full advantage.

We repeat, we do *not* advocate your playing "doctor." This includes administering medication without veterinary supervision, or even doing your own inoculations. General knowledge of diseases, their symptoms and side effects will assist you in diagnosing diseases for your veterinarian. He does not expect you to be an expert, but will appreciate your efforts in getting a sick dog to him before it is too late and he cannot save its life.

ASPIRIN: A DANGER

There is a common joke about doctors telling their patients when they telephone with a complaint, to take an aspirin, go to bed and let him know how things are in the morning! Unfortunately, that is exactly the way it turns out with a lot of dog owners who think aspirins are cure-alls and give them to their dogs indiscriminately. Then they call the veterinarian when the dog has an unfavorable reaction.

Aspirins are not panaceas for everything—certainly not for every dog. In an experiment, fatalities in cats treated with aspirin in one laboratory alone numbered ten out of thirteen within a two-week period. Dogs' tolerance was somewhat better, as far as actual fatalities, but there was considerable evidence of ulceration in varying degrees on the stomach linings when necropsy was performed.

Aspirin has been held in the past to be almost as effective for dogs as for people when given for many of the everyday aches and pains. The fact remains, however, that medication of any kind should be administered only after veterinary consultation and a specific dosage suitable to the condition is recommended.

While aspirin is chiefly effective in reducing fever, relieving minor pains and cutting down on inflammation, the acid has been proven harmful to the stomach when given in strong doses. Only your veterinarian is qualified to determine what the dosage is, or whether it should be administered to your particular dog at all.

WHAT THE THERMOMETER CAN TELL YOU

You will notice in reading this chapter dealing with the diseases of dogs that practically everything a dog might contract in the way of sickness has basically the same set of symptoms. Loss of appetite, diarrhea, dull eyes, dull coat, warm and/or runny nose, and FEVER!

Therefore, it is most advisable to have a thermometer on hand for checking temperature. There are several inexpensive metal rectal-type thermometers that are accurate and safer than the glass variety which can be broken. This may happen either by dropping, or perhaps even breaking off in the dog because of improper insertion or an aggravated condition with the dog that makes him violently resist the injection of the thermometer. Either kind should be lubricated with Vaseline to make the insertion as easy as possible, after it has been sterilized with alcohol.

The normal temperature for a dog is 101.5° Fahrenheit, as compared to the human 98.6° F. Excitement as well as illness can cause

Opposite:
Ch. Ja-Ma's Me-Tu 'O Kai-Bi, pictured winning on the way to her championship with handler Allan Leiberman. This stylish little bitch was whelped in April, 1975 and was sired by Ch. Martin's King Kong Puff out of Ch. Lifelong's Stolen Hours. Bred by Janet and Marvin Whitman, she is co-owned by Janet Whitman and Kay Oppenheimer.

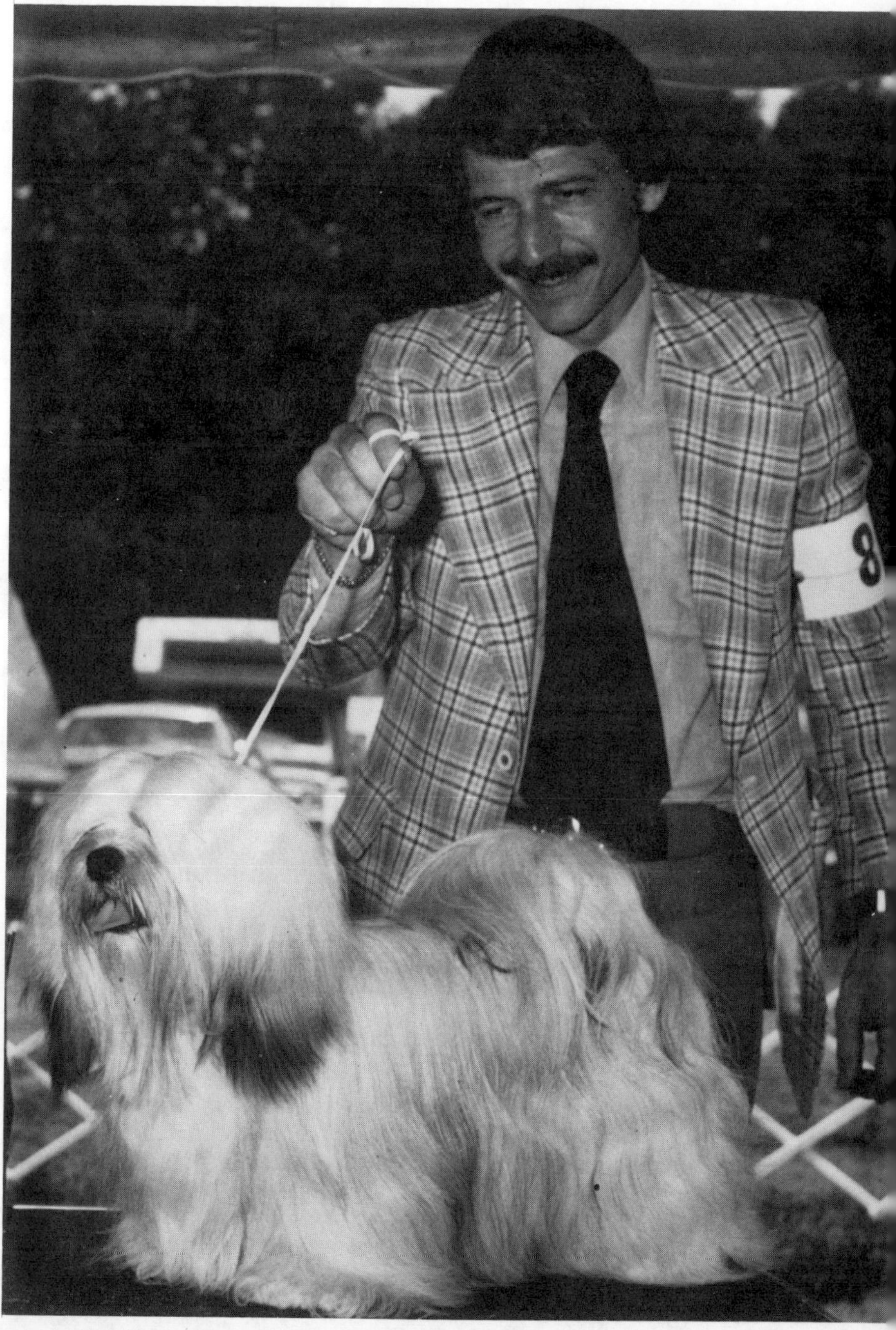

this to vary a degree or two, but any sudden or extensive rise in body temperature must be considered as cause for alarm. Your first indication will be that your dog feels unduly "warm" and this is the time to take the temperature, not when the dog becomes very ill or manifests additional serious symptoms. With a thermometer on hand, you can check temperatures quickly and perhaps prevent some illness from becoming serious.

COPROPHAGY

Perhaps the most unpleasant of all phases of dog breeding is to come up with a dog that takes to eating stool. This practice, which is referred to politely as coprophagy, is one of the unsolved mysteries in the dog world. There simply is no explanation to why some dogs do it.

However, there are several logical theories, all or any of which may be the cause. Some say nutritional deficiencies; others say that dogs inclined to gulp their food (which passes through them not entirely digested) find it still partially palatable. There is another theory that the preservatives used in some meat are responsible for an appealing odor that remains through the digestive process. Then again poor quality meat can be so tough and unchewable that dogs swallow it whole and it passes through them in large undigested chunks.

There are others who believe the habit is strictly psychological, the result of a nervous condition or insecurity. Others believe the dog cleans up after itself because it is afraid of being punished as it was when it made a mistake on the carpet as a puppy. Others claim boredom is the reason, or even spite. Others will tell you a dog does not want its personal odor on the premises for fear of attracting other hostile animals to itself or its home.

The most logical of all explanations and the one most veterinarians are inclined to accept is that it is a deficiency of dietary enzymes. Too much dry food can be bad and many veterinarians suggest trying meat tenderizers, monosodium glutamate, or garlic powder which gives the stool a bad odor and discourages the dog. Yeast or certain vitamins or a complete change of diet are even more often suggested. By the time you try each of the above you will probably discover that the dog has outgrown the habit anyway. However, the condition cannot be ignored if you are to enjoy your dog to the fullest.

There is no set length of time that the problem persists, and the only real cure is to walk the dog on leash, morning and night and after every meal. In other words, set up a definite eating and exercising schedule before coprophagy is an established pattern.

MASTURBATION

A source of embarrassment to many dog owners, masturbation can be eliminated with a minimum of training.

Jerec's Ski-tse Drax, a golden female, winning a major under judge Mrs. Ramona Van Court at the 1971 Palm Beach Kennel Club show with Marjorie Lewis handling. Bred by the Drax Kennels in Hialeah, Florida. Earl Graham photograph.

The dog which is constantly breeding anything and everything, including the leg of the piano or perhaps the leg of your favorite guest, can be broken of the habit by stopping its cause.

The over-sexed dog—if truly that is what he is—which will never be used for breeding can be castrated. The kennel stud dog can be broken of the habit by removing any furniture from his quarters or keeping him on leash and on verbal command when he is around people, or in the house where he might be tempted to breed pillows, people, etc.

Hormone inbalance may be another cause and your veterinarian may advise injections. Exercise can be of tremendous help. Keeping the dog's mind occupied by physical play when he is around people will also help relieve the situation.

Samtem of Ro Nang, a white and gold, photographed in 1970 by D.G.B. Partridge for owner Mrs. U.M. Collins of Fife, Scotland. Samtem is a first-prize winner at championship shows.

American and Canadian Champion Kyi Chu Shara, Best in Show winner, pictured here winning the Non-Sporting Group under judge Frank Foster Davis at the 1966 Langley Kennel Club Show with handler Jane Kay. Mrs. Joseph Denmark, Show Chairman, completes the picture. Shara is owned by Mrs. Keke Blumberg of the Potala Lhasa Apso, Rydal, Pennsylvania. Shara is a Register of Merit dog.

Females might indulge in sexual abnormalities like masturbation during their heat cycle, or again, because of a hormone imbalance. But if they behave this way because of a more serious problem, a hysterectomy may be indicated.

A sharp "no!" command when you can anticipate the act, or a sharp "no!" when caught in the act will deter most dogs if you are consistent in your correction. Hitting or other physical abuse will only confuse a dog.

RABIES

The greatest fear in the dog fancy today is still the great fear it has always been—rabies!

What has always held true about this dreadful disease still holds true today. The only way rabies can be contracted is through the saliva of a rabid dog entering the bloodstream of another animal or person. There is, of course, the Pasteur treatment of rabies which is very effective. There was of late the incident of a little boy bitten by a rabid bat having survived the disease. However, the Pasteur treatment is administered immediately if there is any question of exposure. Even more than dogs being found to be rabid, we now know that the biggest carriers are bats, skunks, foxes, rabbits and other warm-blooded animals, which pass it from one to another, since they do not have the benefit of inoculation. Dogs that run free should be inoculated for protection against these animals. For city or house dogs that never leave their owners side, it may not be as necessary.

For many years, Great Britain, because it is an island and because of the country's strictly enforced six-month quarantine, was

Yogi and Pasha photographed at the Mio Lhasa Apso kennels of Joan Pettit in Woodmere, Long Island, New York, when they were 7½ months of age.

Winner at Westminster in 1961 was Licos Shor Shan La, owned by Mrs. David W. Bryant. Maxine Beam handled for Mrs. Bryant; judge William Kendrick awarded this Best of Breed win.

entirely free of rabies. But in 1969, a British officer brought back his dog from foreign duty and the dog was found to have the disease soon after being released from quarantine. There was a great uproar about it, with Britain killing off wild and domestic animals in a great scare campaign, but the quarantine is once again down to six months and things seem to have returned to a normal, sensible attitude.

Health departments in rural towns usually provide rabies inoculations free of charge. If your dog is outdoors a great deal, or exposed to other animals that are, you might wish to call the town hall and get information on the program in your area. One cannot be too cautious about this dread disease. While the number of cases diminishes each year, there are still thousands being reported and there is still the constant threat of an outbreak where animals roam free. And never forget, there is no cure.

Rabies is caused by a neurotropic virus which can be found in the saliva, brain and sometimes the blood of the warm-blooded animal afflicted. The incubation period is usually two weeks or as long as six months, which means you can be exposed to it without any visible symptoms. As we have said, while there is still no known cure, it can be controlled. It is up to every individual to help effect this control by reporting animal bites, educating the public to the dangers and symptoms and prevention of it, so that we may reduce the fatalities.

There are two kinds of rabies; one form is called "furious" and the other is referred to as "dumb." The mad dog goes through several stages of the disease. His disposition and behavior change radically and suddenly; he becomes irritable and vicious; the eating habits alter, and he rejects food for things like stones and sticks; he becomes exhausted and drools saliva out of his mouth almost constantly. He may hide in corners, look glassy eyed and suspicious, bite at the air as he races around snarling and attacking with his tongue hanging out. At this point paralysis sets in, starting at the throat so that he can no longer drink water though he desires it desperately; hence, the term hydrophobia is given. He begins to stagger and eventually convulse and death is imminent.

In "dumb" rabies paralysis is swift; the dog seeks dark, sheltered places and is abnormally quiet. Paralysis starts with the jaws, spreads down the body and death is quick. Contact by humans or other animals with the drool from either of these types of rabies on open skin can produce the fatal disease, so extreme haste and proper diagnosis is essential. In other words, you do not have to be bitten by a rabid dog to have the virus enter your system. An open wound or cut that comes in touch with the saliva is all that is needed.

The incubation and degree of infection can vary. You usually contract the disease faster if the wound is near the head, since the virus travels to the brain through the spinal cord. The deeper the wound, the more saliva is injected into the body, the more serious the infec-

Ch. Hall's Prince Li Chin, pictured winning the Non-Sporting Group at the 1975 Texarkana Kennel Club show under judge Edd Biven. Both the Breed and Group wins were won with owner-handler Celia Hall, who co-owns him with Mr. Scott R. Hall, Chin-Ti Lhasas, Memphis, Tennessee.

tion. So, if bitten by a dog under any circumstances—or any warm-blooded animal for that matter—immediately wash out the wound with soap and water, bleed it profusely, and see your doctor as soon as possible.

Also, be sure to keep track of the animal that bit, if at all possible. When rabies is suspected the public health officer will need to send the animal's head away to be analyzed. If it is found to be rabies free, you will not need to undergo treatment. Otherwise, your doctor may advise that you have the Pasteur treatment, which is extremely painful. It is rather simple, however, to have the veterinarian examine a dog for rabies without having the dog sent away for positive diagnosis of the disease. A ten-day quarantine is usually all that is necessary for everyone's peace of mind.

This darling 12-week-old puppy is Kyi-Chu of Eversley, bred by Mrs. B.J. Collins of Eversley Kennels in Scotland. This picture was taken in 1969.

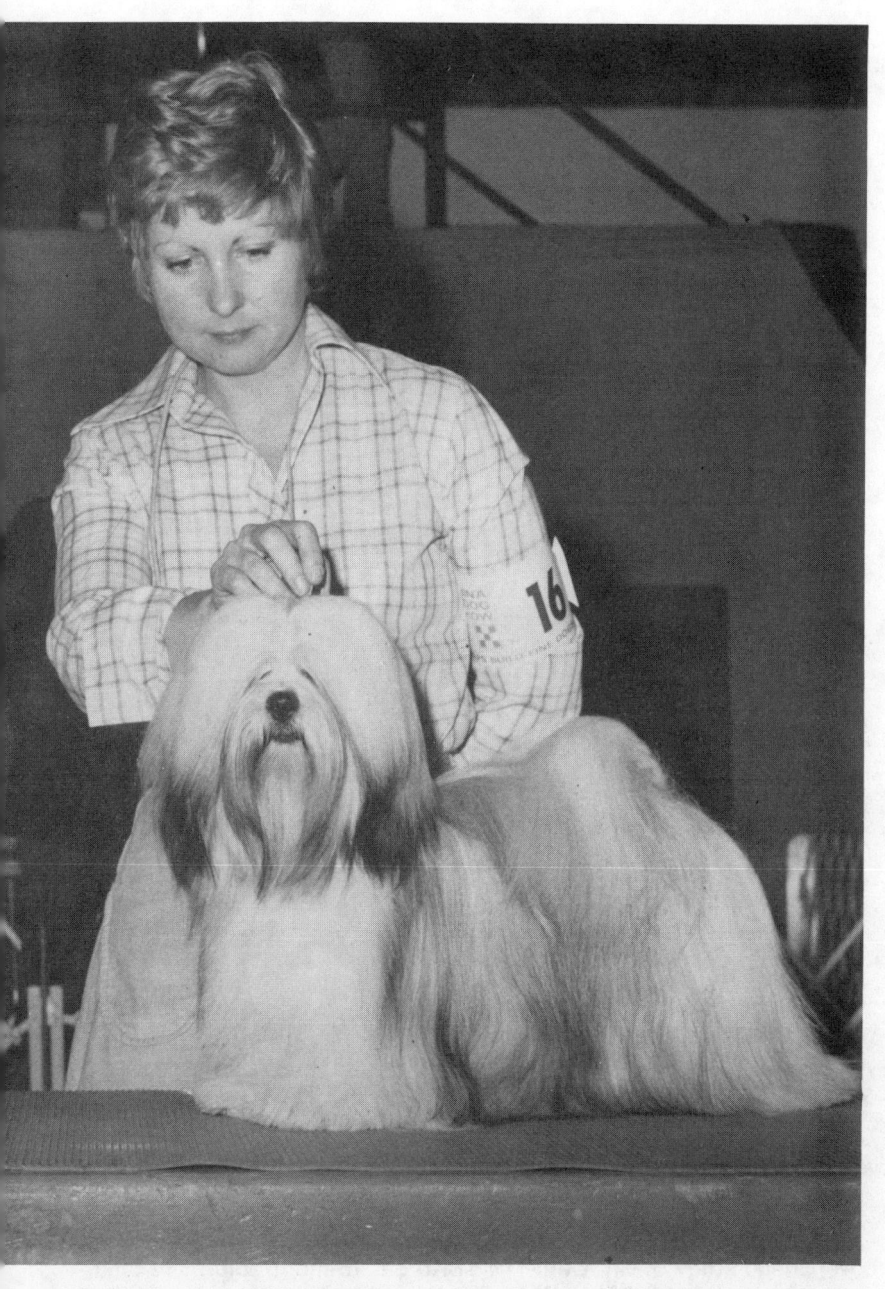

Ch. Arborhills Mehl-O-Dieh of Ja-Ma, owned by Maxine Felberg of Spring Valley, New York. The sire was Ch. Zijuh Morbu *ex* Ch. Arborhills Lee-Sah.

Lovely head study of Ch. Chin-Ti's Ti Ko La, 16-month-old male bred and owned by Mr. and Mrs. Scott R. Hall, Chin-Ti Lhasas, Memphis, Tennessee. Ti Ko finished with a total of 17 points including 12 points in major wins. He was sired by Group-winning Ch. Hall's Prince Li Chin. Photo by Celia Hall.

Rabies is no respecter of age, sex or geographical location. It is found all over the world from North Pole to South Pole, and has nothing to do with the old wives' tale of dogs going mad in the hot summer months. True, there is an increase in reported cases during summer, but only because that is the time of the year for animals to roam free in good weather and during the mating season when the battle of the sexes is taking place. Inoculation and a keen eye for symptoms and bites on our dogs and other pets will help control the disease until a cure is found.

VACCINATIONS

If you are to raise a puppy, or a litter of puppies, successfully, you must adhere to a realistic and strict schedule of vaccination. Many puppyhood diseases can be fatal—all of them are debilitating. According to the latest statistics, 98 per cent of all puppies are being inoculated after 12 weeks of age against the dread distemper, hepatitis and leptospirosis and manage to escape these horrible infections. Orphaned puppies should be vaccinated every two weeks until the age of 12 weeks. Distemper and hepatitis live-virus vaccine should be used, since they are not protected with the colostrum normally supplied to them through the mother's milk. Puppies weaned at six to seven weeks should also be inoculated repeatedly because they will no longer be receiving mother's milk. While not all will receive protection from the serum at this early age, it should be given and they should be vaccinated once again at both nine and twelve weeks of age.

Leptospirosis vaccination should be given at four months of age with thought given to booster shots if the disease is known in the area, or in the case of show dogs which are exposed on a regular basis to many dogs from far and wide. While annual boosters are in order for distemper and hepatitis, every two or three years is sufficient for leptospirosis, unless there is an outbreak in your immediate area. The one exception should be the pregnant bitch since there is reason to believe that inoculation might cause damage to the fetus.

Strict observance of such a vaccination schedule will not only keep your dog free of these debilitating diseases, but will prevent an epidemic in your kennel, or in your locality, or to the dogs which are competing at the shows.

SNAKEBITE

As field trials and hunts and the like become more and more popular with dog enthusiasts, the incident of snakebite becomes more of a likelihood. Dogs that are kept outdoors in runs or dogs that work the fields and roam on large estates are also likely victims.

Most veterinarians carry snakebite serum, and snakebite kits are sold to dog owners for just such purpose. To catch a snakebite in

Ch. Treepine Singapore Sling pictured winning Best of Opposite Sex at the 1975 Lhasa Apso Club of Quebec Specialty show under judge Robert Braithwaite. Bred by Mr. and Mrs. E.G. Carpenter of Ontario, Singapore is owned by Dr. Ellen Brown, the "matriarch" of the breed in Canada. The sire of Singapore Sling was Ch. Balrene Simon Says *ex* Ch. Balrene Talli.

time might mean the difference between life and death, and whether your area is populated with snakes or not, it behooves you to know what to do in case it happens to you or your dog.

Your primary concern should be to get to a doctor or veterinarian immediately. The victim should be kept as quiet as possible (excitement or activity spreads the venom through the body more quickly) and if possible the wound should be bled enough to clean it out before applying a tourniquet, if the bite is severe.

First of all, it must be determined if the bite is from a poisonous or non-poisonous snake. If the bite carries two horseshoe shaped pinpoints of a double row of teeth, the bite can be assumed to be non-poisonous. If the bite leaves two punctures or holes—the result of the two fangs carrying venom—the bite is very definitely poisonous and time is of the essence.

Recently, physicians have come up with an added help in the case of snakebite. A first aid treatment referred to as hypothermia, which is the application of ice to the wound to lower body temperatures to a point where the venom spreads less quickly, minimizes swelling, helps prevent infection and has some influence on numbing the pain. If ice is not readily available, the bite may be soaked in ice-cold water. But even more urgent is the need to get the victim to a hospital or a veterinarian for additional treatment.

American and Canadian Ch. Kimrick's Jeh Sah Cah pictured winning Best of Winners at the 1969 Westminster Kennel Club show under judge Joseph Faigel. Owned by Mr. and Mrs. Wilson J. Browning, Jr., Taglha Lhasas, Norfolk, Virginia.

EMERGENCIES

No matter how well you run your kennel or keep an eye on an individual dog, there will almost invariably be some emergency at some time that will require quick treatment until you get the animal to the veterinarian. The first and most important thing to remember is to keep calm! You will think more clearly and your animal will need to know he can depend on you to take care of him. However, he will be frightened and you must beware of fear biting. Therefore, do not shower him with kisses and endearments at this time, no matter how sympathetic you feel. Comfort him reassuringly, but keep your wits about you. Before getting him to the veterinarian try to alleviate the pain and shock.

If you can take even a minor step in this direction it will be a help toward the final cure. Listed here are a few of the emergencies which might occur and what you can do AFTER you have called the vet and told him you are coming.

BURNS

If you have been so foolish as not to turn your pot handles toward the back of the stove—for your children's sake as well as your dog's—and the dog is burned, apply ice or ice cold water and treat for shock. Electrical or chemical burns are treated the same; but with an acid or alkali burn, use, respectively, a bicarbonate of soda or vinegar solution. Check the advisability of covering the burn when you call the veterinarian.

DROWNING

Most animals love the water, but sometimes get in "over their heads." Should your dog take in too much water, hold him upside down and open his mouth so that water can empty from the lungs, then apply artificial respiration, or mouth-to-mouth resuscitation. Then treat for shock by covering him with a blanket, administering a stimulant such as coffee with sugar and soothing him with voice and hand.

FITS AND CONVULSIONS

Prevent the dog from thrashing about and injuring himself, cover with a blanket and hold down until you can get him to the veterinarian.

FROSTBITE

There is no excuse for an animal getting frostbite if you are on your toes and care for the animal. However, should frostbite set in, thaw out the affected area slowly with a circulatory motion and stimulation. Use vaseline to help keep the skin from peeling off and/or drying out.

Ch. Jerec's Gres Ma Drax, silver grizzle female pictured winning her third and final five-point major win under judge Hollis Wilson. Gres was owner-handled by Joan Ernst. Olson Studio photograph.

HEART ATTACK

Be sure the animal keeps breathing by applying artificial respiration. A mild stimulant may be used and give him plenty of air. Treat for shock as well, and get to the veterinarian quickly.

SUFFOCATION

Artificial respiration and treat for shock with plenty of air.

Hamilton Achok, pictured winning Best of Breed at a 1959 San Mateo Kennel Club Show under judge Colonel E.E. Ferguson. Owner is Marilyn Sorci, Shangri-La Kennels.

SUN STROKE

Cooling the dog off immediately is essential. Ice packs, submersion in ice water, and plenty of cool air are needed.

WOUNDS

Open wounds or cuts which produce bleeding must be treated with hydrogen peroxide and tourniquets should be used if bleeding is excessive. Also, shock treatment must be given and the animal must be kept warm.

Ch. Sah Si Tsu, pictured winning at the 1972 Bronx Kennel Club Show in New York for a 5-point major. Sah Si was Best of Winners and Best Opposite Sex at the 1972 Westminster Kennel Club Show also. Owned by John and Mary Mahan, Majoma's Lhasas, Westwood, Massachusetts.

THE FIRST AID KIT

It would be sheer folly to try to operate a kennel or to keep a dog without providing for certain emergencies that are bound to crop up when there are active dogs around. Just as you would provide a first aid kit for people, you should also provide a first aid kit for the animals on the premises.

The first aid kit should contain the following items:

BFI or other medicated powder
jar of vaseline
Q-tips
bandage—1 inch gauze
adhesive tape
Band-Aids
cotton
boric acid powder

A trip to your veterinarian is always safest, but there are certain preliminaries for cuts and bruises of a minor nature that you can care for yourself.

Cuts, for instance, should be washed out and medicated powder or vaseline applied with a bandage. The lighter the bandage the better, so that the most air possible can reach the wound. Q-tips can be used for removing debris from the eyes after which a mild solution of boric acid wash can be applied. As for sores, use dry powder on wet sores, and vaseline on dry sores. Use cotton for washing out wounds and drying them.

A particular caution must be given here on bandaging. Make sure that the bandage is not too tight to hamper the dog's circulation. Also, make sure the bandage is made correctly so that the dog does not bite at it trying to get it off. A great deal of damage can be done to a wound by a dog tearing at a bandage to get it off. If you notice the dog is starting to bite at it, do it over or put something on the bandage that smells and tastes bad to him. Make sure, however, that the solution does not soak through the bandage and enter the wound. Sometimes, if it is a leg wound, a sock or stocking slipped on the dog's leg will cover the bandage edges and will also keep it clean.

HOW NOT TO POISON YOUR DOG

Ever since the appearance of Rachel Carson's book *Silent Spring*, people have been asking, "Just how dangerous are chemicals?" In the animal world where disinfectants, room deodorants, parasitic sprays, solutions and aerosols are so widely used, the question has taken on even more meaning. Veterinarians are beginning to ask, "What kind of disinfectant do you use?" or "Have you any fruit trees that have been sprayed recently?" When animals are brought in to

American and Canadian Champion Potala Keke's Yum Yum wins Best in Show at the 1975 Muskogee Oklahoma Kennel Club show under judge Florence Gamburg. Yum Yum was the Top Winning Lhasa Bitch for 1974 and 1975, and she is the dam of six champions including Ch. Potala Keke's Tomba Tu. Her handler here is Carolyn Herbel. Her breeder and owner is Keke Blumberg, Potala Lhasa Apsos, Rydal, Pennsylvania.

their offices in a toxic condition, or for unexplained death, or when entire litters of puppies die mysteriously, there is good reason to ask such questions.

The popular practice of protecting animals against parasites has given way to their being exposed to an alarming number of commercial products, some of which are dangerous to their very lives. Even flea collars can be dangerous, especially if they get wet or somehow touch the genital regions or eyes. While some products are a great deal more poisonous than others, great care must be taken that they be applied in proportion to the size of the dog and the area to be covered. Many a dog has been taken to the vet with an unusual skin problem that was a direct result of having been bathed with a deter-

Three-month-old Milaripa Dharma, whelped in 1971, seems to be contemplating bringing the master his shoe. The sire was Ch. Dixie Beau of Everglo *ex* Licos Kargan La. Owner is Mary S. Carter.

gent rather than a proper shampoo. Certain products that are safe for dogs can be fatal for cats. Extreme care must be taken to read all ingredients and instructions carefully before use on any animal.

The same caution must be given to outdoor chemicals. Dog owners must question the use of fertilizers on their lawns. Lime, for instance, can be harmful to a dog's feet. The unleashed dog that covers the neighborhood on his daily rounds is open to all sorts of tree and lawn sprays and insecticides that may prove harmful to him, if not as a poison, as a producer of an allergy. Many puppy fatalities are reported when they consume mothballs.

There are various products found around the house which can be lethal, such as rat poison, boric acid, hand soap, detergents and insecticides. The garage, too, may provide dangers: antifreeze for the car, lawn, garden and tree sprays, paints, etc., are all available for tipping over and consuming. All poisons should be placed on high shelves for the sake of your children as well as your animals.

Perhaps the most readily available of all household poisons are plants. Household plants are almost all poisonous, even if taken in small quantities. Some of the most dangerous are the elephant ear, the narcissus bulb, any kind of ivy leaves, burning bush leaves, jimson weed, dumb cane weed, mock orange fruit, castor beans, Scotch broom seeds, the root or seed of the plant called four o'clock, cyclamen, pimpernel, lily of the valley, the stem of the sweet pea, rhododendrons of any kind, spider lily bulbs, bayonet root, foxglove leaves, tulip bulbs, monkshood roots, azalea, wisteria, poinsettia leaves, mistletoe, hemlock, locoweed and arrowglove. In all, there are over 500 poisonous plants in the United States. Peach, elderberry and cherry trees can cause cyanide poisoning if the bark is consumed. Rhubarb leaves, either raw or cooked, can cause death or violent convulsions. Check out your closets, fields and grounds around your home to see what might be of danger to your pets.

SYMPTOMS OF POISONING

Be on the lookout for vomiting, hard or labored breathing, whimpering, stomach cramps and trembling as a prelude to the convulsions. Any delay in a visit to your veterinarian can mean death. Take along the bottle or package or a sample of the plant you suspect to be the cause to help the veterinarian determine the correct antidote.

The most common type of poisoning, which accounts for nearly one-fourth of all animal victims, is staphylococcic-infected food. Salmonella ranks third. These can be avoided by serving fresh food and not letting it lie around in hot weather.

There are also many insect poisonings caused by animals eating cockroaches, spiders, flies, butterflies, etc. Toads and some frogs give off a fluid which can make a dog foam at the mouth—and even kill him—if he bites just a little too hard!

One of Alfred Stillman's puppies photographed by famous dog photographer Joan Ludwig.

Some misguided dog owners think it is "cute" to let their dogs enjoy a cocktail with them before dinner. There can be serious effects resulting from encouraging a dog to drink—sneezing fits, injuries as a result of intoxication and heart stoppage are just a few. Whiskey for medicinal purposes or beer for brood bitches should be administered only on the advice of your veterinarian.

There have been cases of severe damage and death when dogs emptied ash trays and consumed cigarettes, resulting in nicotine poisoning. Leaving a dog alone all day in a house where there are cigarettes available on a coffee table is asking for trouble. Needless to say, the same applies to marijuana. The narcotic addict who takes his dog along with him on "a trip" does not deserve to have a dog. All the ghastly side effects are as possible for the dog as for the addict, and for a person to submit an animal to this indignity is indeed despicable. Don't think it doesn't happen. Ask the veterinarians that practice near some of your major hippie havens! Unfortunately, in all our major cities the practice is becoming more and more of a problem for the veterinarian.

Be on the alert and remember that in the case of any type of poisoning, the best treatment is prevention.

Troubadour de Gandamak sitting on a 17th Century Chinese prayer table. The prayer table, carved over 300 years ago, shows a Lhasa Apso carved into the magnificent wood; this can be seen on the front lower right of the picture silhoutted against the dog's body coat.

THE CURSE OF ALLERGY

The heartbreak of a child being forced to give up a beloved pet because he is suddenly found to be allergic to it is a sad but true story. Many families claim to be unable to have dogs at all; others seem to be able only to enjoy them on a restricted basis. Many children know animals only through occasional visits to a friend's house or the zoo.

While modern veterinary science has produced some brilliant allergists, such as Dr. Edward Baker of New Jersey, the field is still working on a solution for those who suffer from exposure to their pets. There is no permanent cure as yet.

Over the last quarter of a century there have been many attempts at a permanent cure, but none has proven successful be-

Annapurna Ratzine, bred and owned by Miss V. Dupont of France. Sired by Ch. Oracles du Chomolari *ex* Annapurna Gautama.

cause the treatment was needed too frequently or was too expensive to maintain over extended periods of time.

However, we find that most people who are allergic to their animals are also allergic to a variety of other things as well. By eliminating the other irritants, and by taking medication given for the control of allergies in general, many are able to keep pets on a restricted basis. This may necessitate the dog's living outside the house, being groomed at a professional grooming parlor instead of by the owner or merely being kept out of the bedroom at night. A discussion of this "balance" factor with your medical and veterinary doctors may give new hope to those willing to try.

A paper presented by Mathilde M. Gould, M.D., a New York allergist, before the American Academy of Allergists in the 1960's, and reported in the September-October 1964 issue of the *National Humane Review* magazine, offered new hope to those who are allergic by a method referred to as hyposensitization. You may wish to write to the magazine and request the article for discussion with your medical and veterinary doctors on your individual problem.

DO ALL DOGS CHEW?

All young dogs chew! Chewing is the best possible method of cutting teeth and exercising gums. Every puppy goes through this teething process. True, it can be destructive if not watched carefully, and it is really the responsibility of every owner to prevent the damage before it occurs.

When you see a puppy pick up an object to chew, immediately remove it from his mouth with a sharp "no!" and replace the object with a Nylon or rawhide bone which should be provided for him to do his serious chewing. Puppies take anything and everything into their mouths so they should be provided with proper toys which they cannot chew up and swallow.

BONES

There are many opinions on the kind of bones a dog should have. Anyone who has lost a puppy or dog because of a bone chip puncturing the stomach or intestinal wall will say "no bones" except for the Nylon or rawhide kind you buy in pet shops. There are those who say shank or knuckle bones are permissible. Use your own judgment, but when there are adequate processed bones which you know to be safe, why risk a valuable animal? Cooked bones, soft enough to be pulverized and put in the food can be fed if they are reduced almost to a powder. If you have the patience for this sort of thing, okay. Otherwise, stick to the commercial products.

As for dogs and puppies chewing furniture, shoes, etc., replace the object with something allowable and safe and put yourself on record as remembering to close closet doors. Keep the puppy in the same room with you so you can stand guard over the furniture.

Electrical cords and sockets, or wires of any kind, present a dangerous threat to chewers. Glass dishes which can be broken are hazardous if not picked up right after feeding.

Chewing can also be a form of frustration or nervousness. Dogs sometimes chew for spite, if owners leave them alone too long or too often. Bitches will sometimes chew if their puppies are taken away from them too soon; insecure puppies often chew thinking they're nursing. Puppies which chew wool or blankets or carpet corners or certain types of materials may have a nutritional deficiency or something lacking in their diet, such as craving the starch that might be left in material after washing. Perhaps the articles have been near something that tastes good and they retain the odor.

The act of chewing has no connection with particular breeds or ages, any more than there is a logical reason for dogs to dig holes outdoors or dig on wooden floors indoors.

So we repeat, it is up to you to be on guard at all times until the need—or habit—passes.

NYLABONE® is a necessity that is available at your local petshop (not in supermarkets). The puppy or grown dog chews the hambone flavored nylon into a frilly dog toothbrush, massaging his gums and cleaning his teeth as he plays. Veterinarians highly recommend this product. . . but beware of cheap imitations which might splinter or break.

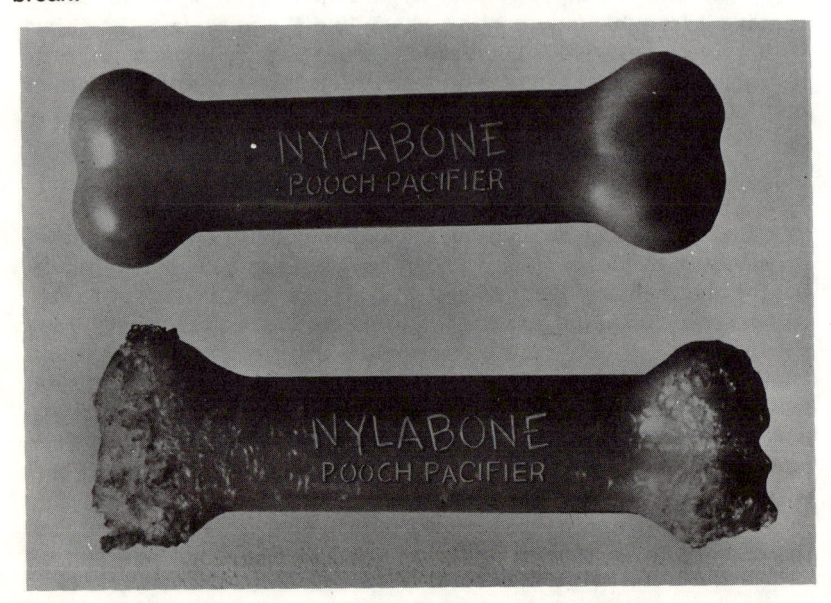

Ch. Martin's Kiwi Puff, photographed winning the Non-Sporting Group under the late judge O. Harriman at the Heart of America Kennel Club show in 1968. Owner-handled by Rena Martin of Highland Park, Illinois. The sire was Ch. Kyi Chu Kaliph Nor *ex* Ch. Karma Kricket Puff.

291

HIP DYSPLASIA

Hip dysplasia, or HD, is one of the most widely discussed of all animal afflictions, since it has appeared in varying degrees in just about every breed of dog. True, the larger breeds seem most susceptible, but it has hit the small breeds and is beginning to be recognized in cats as well.

While HD in man has been recorded as far back as 370 B.C., HD in dogs was more than likely referred to as rheumatism until veterinary research came into the picture. In 1935, Dr. Otto Schales, at Angell Memorial Hospital in Boston, wrote a paper on hip dysplasia and classified the four degrees of dysplasia of the hip joint as follows:

Grade 1 — slight (poor fit between ball and socket).
Grade 2—moderate (moderate but obvious shallowness of the socket).
Grade 3—severe (socket quite flat).
Grade 4—very severe (complete displacement of head of femur at early age).

HD is an incurable, hereditary, though not congenital disease of the hip sockets. It is transmitted as a dominant trait with irregular manifestations. Puppies appear normal at birth but the constant wearing away of the socket means the animal moves more and more on muscle, thereby presenting a lameness, a difficulty in getting up and severe pain in advanced cases.

The degree of severity can be determined around six months of age, but its presence can be noticed from two months of age. The problem is determined by x-ray, and if pain is present it can be relieved temporarily by medication. Exercise should be avoided since motion encourages the wearing away of the bone surfaces.

Dogs with HD should not be shown or bred if quality in the breed is to be maintained. It is essential to check a pedigree for dogs known to be dysplastic before breeding, since this disease can be dormant for many generations.

ELBOW DYSPLASIA

The same condition can also affect the elbow joints and is known as elbow dysplasia. This also causes lameness, and dogs so affected should not be used for breeding.

THE UNITED STATES REGISTRY

In the United States we have a central Hip Dysplasia Foundation, known as the OFA (Orthopedic Foundation for Animals). This HD control registry was formed in 1966. X-rays are sent for expert evaluation by qualified radiologists.

24. THE BLIGHT OF PARASITES

Anyone who has ever spent countless hours peering down intently at his dog's warm, pink stomach waiting for a flea to appear will readily understand why we call this chapter "the blight of parasites." For it is that dreaded onslaught of the pesky flea that heralds the subsequent arrival of worms.

If you have seen even one flea scoot across that vulnerable expanse of skin you can be sure there are more fleas lurking on other favorite areas of your dog. They seldom travel alone. So it is now an established fact that *la puce,* as the French would say when referring to the flea, has set up housekeeping on your dog and it is going to demand a great deal of your time before you manage to evict them completely, and probably just temporarily, no matter which species your dog is harboring.

Fleas are not always choosy about their host, but chances are your dog has what is commonly known as *Ctenocephalides canis*, the dog flea. If you are a lover of cats also, your dog might even be playing host to a few *Ctenocephalides felis,* the cat flea, or vice versa! The only thing you can be really sure of is that your dog is supporting an entire community of them, all hungry and all sexually oriented, and you are going to have to be persistent in your campaign to get rid of them.

One of the chief reasons they are so difficult to catch is that what they lack in beauty and eyesight (they are blind at birth, throughout infancy and see very poorly or are blind during adulthood), they make up for in their fantastic ability to jump and scurry about.

While this remarkable ability to jump—some say 150 times the length of their bodies—stands them in good stead with circus entrepeneurs and has given them claim to fame as chariot pullers and acrobats in side show attractions, the dog owner can be reduced to tears at the very thought of the onset of fleas.

Modern research has provided a remedy in the form of flea sprays, dips, collars and tags which can be successful in varying degrees. But there are those who swear by the good old-fashioned

Ch. Karma Rus-Tikuli, pictured winning at the 1972 Saw Mill River Kennel Club show with his handler Allan Lieberman. Another Rus-Ti son, with two champion litter sisters bred by Dorothy Cohen of Las Vegas, Nevada.

method of removing them by hand, which can be a challenge to your sanity as well as your dexterity.

Since the fleas' conformation (they are built like envelopes, long and flat) with their spiny skeletal system on the outside of their bodies is specifically provided for slithering through hair forests, they are given a distinct advantage to start with. Two antennae on the head select the best spot for digging and then two mandibles penetrate the skin and hit a blood vessel. It is also at this moment that the flea brings into play his spiny contours to prop himself against a few surrounding hairs which prevent him from being scratched off as he puts the bite on your dog. A small tubular tongue is then lowered into the hole to draw out blood and another tube is injected into the hole to pump the saliva of the flea into the wound which prevents the blood from clotting. This allows the flea to drink freely. Simultaneously your dog jumps into the air and gets one of those back legs into action scratching endlessly and in vain.

Now while you may catch an itinerant flea as he mistakenly shortcuts across your dog's stomach, the best hunting grounds are usually in the deep fur down along the dog's back from the neck to the base of the tail. However, the flea like every other creature on earth must have water, so several times during its residency it will make its way to the moister areas of your dog, such as the corners of the mouth, the eyes or the genital areas. This is when the flea collars and tags are useful. The fumes from them prevent the fleas from passing the neck to get to the head of your dog.

Your dog can usually support several generations of fleas if he doesn't scratch himself to death or go out of his mind with the itching in the interim. The population of the flea is insured by the strong mating instinct and the wise personal decision of the female flea as to the best time to deposit her eggs. She has the useful capacity to store semen until the time is right to lay the eggs after some previous brief encounter with a passing member of the opposite sex.

When the time comes for her to lay the eggs, she does so without so much as a backward glance and moves on. The dog, during a normal day's wandering, shakes the eggs off along his way, and there the eggs remain until hatched and the baby fleas are ready to jump back on a dog. If any of the eggs remain on the dog, chances are your dog will help them emerge from their shells with his scratching when some adult flea passes in the vicinity.

Larval fleas look like very small and slender maggots; they begin their lives feasting off their own egg shells until your dog comes along and offers the return to the world of adult fleas, whose excrement provides the predigested blood pellets they must have to thrive. They cannot survive on fresh blood, nor are they capable at this tender age of digging for it themselves. We are certain that the expression "two can eat as cheaply as one" originated after some curious scientist made a detailed study of the life cycle of the flea.

After a couple of weeks of this free loading, the baby flea makes his own cocoon and becomes a pupa. This stage lasts long enough for the larval flea to grow legs, mandibles, and sharp spines and to flatten out and in general get to be identifiable as the commonly known and obnoxious *Ctenocephalides canis*. The process can take several weeks or several months, depending on weather conditions, heat, moisture, etc., but generally three weeks is all that is required to enable it to start chomping on your dog in its own right.

And so the life of the flea is renewed and begun again, and if you don't have plans to stem the tide, you will certainly see a population explosion that will make the human one resemble an endangered species. Getting rid of fleas can be accomplished by the aforementioned spraying of the dog, or the flea collars and tags, but air, sunshine and a good shaking out of beds, bedding, carpets, cushions, etc., certainly must be undertaken to get rid of the eggs or larvae lying around the premises.

However, if you love the thrill of the chase, and have the stomach for it, you can still try to catch them on safari across your dog's stomach. Your dog will love the attention, that is, if you don't keep pinching a bit of skin instead of that little blackish critter. Chances are great you will come up with skin rather than the flea and your dog will lose interest and patience.

Should you be lucky enough to get hold of one, you must either squeeze it to death (which isn't likely) or break it in two with a sharp, strong fingernail (which also isn't likely) or you must release it *underwater* in the toilet bowl and flush immediately. This prospect is only slightly more likely. We strongly suggest that you shape up, clean up, shake out and spray—on a regular basis.

There are those people, however, who are much more philosophical about the flea, since, like the cockroach, it has been around since the beginning of the world. For instance, that old-time philosopher, David Harum, who has been much quoted with his remark, "A reasonable amount of fleas is good for a dog. They keep him from broodin' on bein' a dog." We would rather agree with John Donne who in his *Devotions* reveals that, "The flea, though he kill none, he does all the harm he can." This is especially true if your dog is a show dog! If the scratching doesn't ruin the coat, the inevitable infestations of the parasites the fleas will leave with your dog will!

So we readily see that dogs can be afflicted by both internal and external parasites. The external parasites are known as the aforementioned fleas, plus ticks and lice; while all of these are bothersome, they can be treated. However, the internal parasites, or worms of various kinds, are usually well-infested before discovery and require more substantial means of ridding the dog of them completely.

INTERNAL PARASITES

The most common worms are the round worms. These, like many other worms, are carried and spread by the flea and go through a cycle within the dog host. They are excreted in egg or larval form and passed on to other dogs in this manner.

Worm medicine should be prescribed by a veterinarian, and dogs should be checked for worms at least twice a year, or every three months if there is a known epidemic in your area, and during the summer months when fleas are plentiful.

Major types of worms are hookworms, whipworms, tapeworms (the only non-round worm in this list), ascarids (the "typical" round worms), heartworms, kidney and lung worms. Each can be peculiar

Ch. Kyi-Chu Kaliph Nor, photographed in this lovely headstudy, is the sire of seven champions. He is owned by Rena Martin of Highland Park, Illinois.

Baijais Phu Tuu, pictured winning Best of Breed from the classes at the 1969 Framingham Kennel Club show under judge L.E. Piper. Phu Tuu was owned and shown by the late Sylvia Hee.

to a part of the country or may be carried by a dog from one area to another. Kidney and lung worms are quite rare, fortunately. The others are not. Symptoms for worms might be vomiting intermittently, eating grass, lack of pep, bloated stomach, rubbing their tail along the ground, loss of weight, dull coat, anemia and pale gums, eye discharge, or unexplained nervousness and irritability. A dog with worms will usually eat twice as much as he normally would also.

Never worm a sick dog, or a pregnant bitch after the first two weeks she has been bred, and never worm a constipated dog. . . it will retain the strong medicine within the body for too long a time. The best, safest way to determine the presence of worms is to test for them before they do excessive damage.

HOW TO TEST FOR WORMS

Worms can kill your dog if the infestation is severe enough. Even light infestations of worms can debilitate a dog to the point where he is more susceptible to other serious diseases that can kill, if the worms do not.

Today's medication for worming is relatively safe and mild, and worming is no longer the traumatic experience for either dog or owner that it used to be. Great care must be given, however, to the proper administration of the drugs. Correct dosage is a "must" and clean quarters are essential to rid your kennel of these parasites. It is almost impossible to find an animal that is completely free of parasites, so we must consider worming as a necessary evil.

However mild today's medicines may be, it is inadvisable to worm a dog unnecessarily. There are simple tests to determine the presence of worms and this chapter is designed to help you learn how to make these tests yourself. Veterinarians charge a nominal fee for this service, if it is not part of their regular office visit examination. It is a simple matter to prepare fecal slides that you can read yourself on a periodic basis. Over the years it will save you much time and money, especially if you have more than one dog or a large kennel.

All that is needed by way of equipment is a microscope with 100x power. These can be purchased in the toy department in a department or regular toy store for a few dollars, depending on what else you want to get with it, but the basic, least expensive sets come with the necessary glass slides and attachments.

After the dog has defecated, take an applicator stick, or a toothpick with a flat end, or even an old-fashioned wooden matchstick, and gouge off a piece of the stool about the size of a small pea. Have one of the glass slides ready with a large drop of water on it. Mix the two together until you have a cloudy film over a large area of the slide. This smear should be covered with another slide, or a cover slip—though it is possible to obtain readings with just the one open slide. Place your slide under the microscope and prepare to focus in on it.

English Ch. Tungwei of Coburg, dam and granddam of champions and the first of many Lhasas at Mrs. A. Matthews' Hardacre Kennels in Sussex, England.

To read the slide you will find that your eye should follow a certain pattern. Start at the top and read from left to right, then right back to the left side and then left over to the right side once again until you have looked at every portion of the slide from the top left to the bottom right side, as illustrated here:

Make sure that your smear is not too thick or watery or the reading will be too dark and confused to make proper identification.

After the dog has defecated, a portion of the stool, say a square inch from different sections of it, should be placed in a glass jar or plastic container, and labeled with the dog's name and address of the owner. If the sample cannot be examined within three to four hours after passage, it should be refrigerated. Your opinion as to what variety of worms you suspect is sometimes helpful to the veterinarian and may be noted on the label of the jar you submit to him for the examination.

Checking for worms on a regular basis is advisable not only for the welfare of the dog but for the protection of your family, since most worms are transmissible, under certain circumstances, to humans.

17. FEEDING AND NUTRITION

FEEDING PUPPIES

Two meat and two milk meals serve best and should be served alternately, of course. Assuming the 6 A.M. feeding is a milk meal, the contents should be as follows: Goat's milk is the very best milk to feed puppies but is expensive and usually available only at drug stores, unless you live in farm country where it could be readily available fresh and still less expensive. If goat's milk is not available, use evaporated milk (which can be changed to powdered milk later on) diluted two parts evaporated milk and one part water, along with raw egg yolk, honey or Karo syrup, sprinkled with high-protein baby cereal and some wheat germ. As the puppies mature, cottage cheese may be added or, at one of the two milk meals, it can be substituted for the cereal.

NOONTIME

There are many diets today for young puppies, including all sorts of products on the market for feeding the newborn, for supplementing the feeding of the young and for adding this or that to diets, depending on what is lacking in the way of a complete diet.

When weaning puppies, it is necessary to put them on four meals a day, even while you are tapering off with the mother's milk. Feeding at six in the morning, noontime, six in the evening and midnight is about the best schedule, since it fits in with most human eating plans. Meals for the puppies can be prepared immediately before or after your own meals, without too much of a change in your own schedule.

6 A.M.

A puppy chow which has been soaked in warm water or beef broth according to the time specified on the wrapper should be mixed with raw or simmered chopped meat in equal proportions with vitamin powder added.

6 P.M.

Repeat the milk meal—perhaps varying the type of cereal from wheat to oats, or corn or rice.

MIDNIGHT

Repeat the meat meal. If raw meat was fed at noon, the evening meal might be simmered.

Please note that specific proportions on this suggested diet are not given. However, it's safe to say that the most important ingredients are the milk and cereal, and the meat and puppy chow which forms the basis of the diet. Your veterinarian can advise on the portion sizes if there is any doubt in your mind as to how much to use.

If you notice that the puppies are cleaning their plates you are perhaps not feeding enough to keep up with their rate of growth. Increase the amount at the next feeding. Observe them closely; puppies should each "have their fill," because growth is very rapid at this age. If they have not satisfied themselves, increase the amount so that they do not have to fight for the last morsel. They will not overeat if they know there is enough food available. Instinct will usually let them eat to suit their normal capacity.

English Ch. Shelaurie Piperman of Hardacre, Best in Show winning Lhasa at the age of two at the 1975 Lhasa Apso Club championship show. The sire was Hardacre Pied Piper ex Belazeith Sa-Tru, a daughter of the famous Ch. Hitchcock. Owned by Mrs. A. Matthews, Hardacre Kennels, Sussex, England.

Puppies at play in the nursery at Dorothy Cohen's Karma Kennels in Las Vegas, Nevada. Notice full size doors in the rear of each kennel so that people can go out into the runs with the dogs to play.

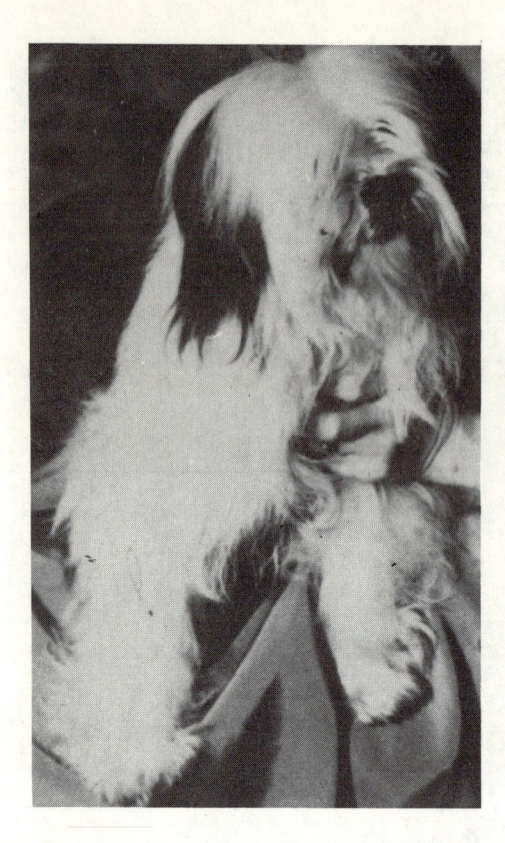

Conquistador Kismet, photographed at 18 months of age. Kismet was whelped in June, 1953 and died in 1970. Unfortunately Lhasas did not receive championships in England when this dog was campaigned, but he was Best of Breed at the 1955 Crufts show and was virtually undefeated in the breed. His sire was Tsarong of Furzyhurst ex Trana of Furzyhurst. Bred, owned, and shown by Mrs. Middleton Ferris (now Mrs. Tyrcha). This dog is behind most present-day show stock, other than imports, and his breeding goes back to the early imports direct from Tibet.

If there is any doubt in your mind as to any ingredient you are feeding, ask yourself, "Would I give it to my own baby?" If the answer is no, then don't give it to your puppies. At this age, the comparison between puppies and human babies can be a good guide.

If there is any doubt in your mind, I repeat: ask your veterinarian to be sure.

Many puppies will regurgitate their food, perhaps a couple of times, before they manage to retain it. If they do bring up their food, allow them to eat it again, rather than clean it away. Sometimes additional saliva is necessary for them to digest it, and you do not want them to skip a meal just because it is an unpleasant sight for you to observe.

This same regurgitation process holds true sometimes with the bitch, who will bring up her own food for her puppies every now and then. This is a natural instinct on her part which stems from the days when dogs were giving birth in the wilds. The only food the mother could provide at weaning time was too rough and indigestible for her puppies. Therefore, she took it upon herself to pre-digest the food until it could be taken and retained by her young. Bitches today will sometimes resort to this, especially bitches which love having litters and have a strong maternal instinct. Some dams will help you wean their litters and even give up feeding entirely once they see you are taking over.

Lhasa Apso puppies, photographed at one week of age. Bred and owned by Joan Pettit, Mio Lhasa Apso, Woodmere, Long Island, New York.

WEANING THE PUPPIES

When weaning the puppies, the mother is kept away from the little ones for longer and longer periods of time. This is done over a period of several days. At first she is separated from the puppies for several hours, then all day, leaving her with them only at night for comfort and warmth. This gradual separation aids in helping the mother's milk to dry up gradually, and she suffers less distress after feeding a litter.

If the mother continues to carry a great deal of milk with no signs of its tapering off, consult your veterinarian before she gets too uncomfortable. She may cut the puppies off from her supply of milk too abruptly if she is uncomfortable, before they should be completely on their own.

There are many opinions on the proper age to start weaning puppies. If you plan to start selling them between six and eight weeks, weaning should begin between two and three weeks of age. Here again, each bitch will pose a different situation. The size and weight of the litter should help determine the time, and your veterinarian will have an opinion, as he determines the burden the bitch is carrying by the size of the litter and her general condition. If she is being pulled down by feeding a large litter, he may suggest that you start at two weeks. If she is glorying in her motherhood without any apparent taxing of her strength, he may suggest three to four weeks. You and he will be the best judges. But remember, there is no substitute that is as perfect as mother's milk—and the longer the puppies benefit from it the better. Other food yes, but mother's milk first and foremost for the healthiest puppies!

Ch. Ruffway T'ang Chu, pictured winning the Non-Sporting Group at the 1974 Wheaton Kennel Club show under judge Nelson Radcliffe. Handled by owner Georgia E. Palmer, Addison, Illinois.

Ch. King Kong Puff, handled by Daryl Martin of Highland Park, Illinois. This win at a show in the mid-1970's.

FEEDING THE ADULT DOG

The puppies' schedule of four meals a day should drop to three by six months and then to two by nine months; by the time the dog reaches one year of age, it is eating one meal a day.

The time when you feed the dog each day can be a matter of the dog's preference or your convenience, so long as once in every 24 hours the dog receives a meal that provides him with a complete, balanced diet. In addition, of course, fresh clean water should be available at all times.

There are many brands of dry food, kibbles and biscuits on the market which are all of good quality. There are also many varieties of canned dog food which are of good quality and provide a balanced diet for your dog. But, for those breeders and exhibitors who show their dogs, additional care is given to providing a few "extras" which enhance the good health and good appearance of show dogs.

A good meal or kibble mixed with water or beef broth and raw meat is perhaps the best ration to provide. In cold weather many breeders add suet or corn oil (or even olive or cooking oil) to the mixture and others make use of the bacon fat after breakfast by pouring it over the dog's food.

Salting a dog's food in the summer helps replace the salt he "pants away" in the heat. Many breeders sprinkle the food with garlic powder to sweeten the dog's breath and prevent gas, especially in breeds that gulp or wolf their food and swallow a lot of air. I prefer garlic powder; the salt is too weak and the clove is too strong.

There are those, of course, who cook very elaborately for their dogs, which is not necessary if a good meal and meat mixture is provided. Many prefer to add vegetables, rice, tomatoes, etc., in with everything else they feed. As long as the extras do not throw the nutritional balance off, there is little harm, but no one thing should be fed to excess. Occasionally liver is given as a treat at home. Fish, which most veterinarians no longer recommend even for cats, is fed to puppies, but should not be given in excess of once a week. Always remember that no one thing should be given as a total diet. Balance is most important; a 100 per cent meat diet can kill a dog.

THE ALL-MEAT DIET CONTROVERSY

In March of 1971, the National Research Council investigated a great stir in the dog fancy about the all-meat dog-feeding controversy. It was established that meat and meat by-products constitute a complete balanced diet for dogs only when it is further fortified with vitamins and minerals.

Therefore, a good dog chow or meal mixed with meat provides the perfect combination for a dog's diet. While the dry food is a complete diet in itself, the fresh meat additionally satisfies the dog's anatomically and physiologically meat-oriented appetite. While dogs are actually carnivores, it must be remembered that when they were feeding themselves in the wild they ate almost the entire animal they captured, including its stomach contents. This provided some of the vitamins and minerals we must now add to the diet.

In the United States, the standard for diets which claims to be "complete and balanced" is set by the Subcommittee on Canine Nutrition of the National Research Council (NRC) of the National Academy of Sciences. This is the official agency for establishing the nutritional requirements of dog foods. Most foods sold for dogs and cats meet these requirements, and manufactuers are proud to say so on their labels, so look for this when you buy. Pet food labels must be approved by the Association of American Feed Control Officials, Pet Foods Committee. Both the Food and Drug Administration and the Federal Trade Commission of the AAFCO define the word "balanced" when referring to dog food as:

"Balanced is a term which may be applied to pet food having all known required nutrients in a proper amount and proportion based upon the recommendations of a recognized authority (The National

One of Dorothy Cohen's Lhasas, Ch. Hamilton Tatsienlu.

Ch. Americal's Torma Lu, pictured here with handler Frank Sabella. Torma Lu was owned by Marie Stillman.

Research Council is one) in the field of animal nutrition, for a given set of physiological animal requirements."

With this much care given to your dog's diet, there can be little reason for not having happy well-fed dogs in proper weight and proportions for the show ring.

OBESITY

As we mentioned before, there are many "perfect" diets for your dogs on the market today. When fed in proper proportions, they should keep your dogs in "full bloom." However, there are those owners who, more often than not, indulge their own appetites and are inclined to overfeed their dogs as well. A study in Great Britain in the early 1970's found that a major percentage of obese people also had

Ch. Kyi-Chu Mi-Tu, pictured winning Best of Winners at the Chanango Valley Kennel Club Show for a 3-point major. Owned by John and Mary Mahan, Majowa's Lhasas, Westwood, Massachusetts.

obese dogs. The entire family was overfed and all suffered from the same condition.

Obesity in dogs is a direct result of the animal's being fed more food that he can properly "burn up" over a period of time, so it is stored as fat or fatty tissue in the body. Pet dogs are more inclined to become obese than show dogs or working dogs, but obesity also is a factor to be considered with the older dog, since his exercise is curtailed.

A lack of "tuck up" on a dog, or not being able to feel the ribs, or great folds of fat which hang from the underside of the dog can all be considered as obesity. Genetic factors may enter into the picture, but usually the owner is at fault.

The life span of the obese dog is decreased on several counts. Excess weight puts undue stress on the heart as well as the joints. The dog becomes a poor anesthetic risk and has less resistance to viral or bacterial infections. Treatment is seldom easy or completely effective, so emphasis should be placed on not letting your dog get FAT in the first place!

ORPHANED PUPPIES

The ideal solution to feeding orphaned puppies is to be able to put them with another nursing dam who will take them on as her own. If this is not possible within your own kennel, or a kennel that you know of, it is up to you to care for and feed the puppies. Survival is possible but requires a great deal of time and effort on your part.

Your substitute formula must be precisely prepared, always served heated to body temperature and refrigerated when not being fed. Esbilac, a vacuum-packed powder, with complete feeding instructions on the can, is excellent and about as close to mother's milk as you can get. If you can't get Esbilac, or until you do get Esbilac, there are two alternative formulas that you might use.

Mix one part boiled water with five parts of evaporated milk and add one teaspoonful of di-calcium phosphate per quart of formula. Di-calcium phosphate can be secured at any drug store. If they have it in tablet form only, you can powder the tablets with the back part of a tablespoon. The other formula for newborn puppies is a combination of eight ounces of homogenized milk mixed well with two egg yolks.

You will need baby bottles with three-hole nipples. Sometimes doll bottles can be used for the newborn puppies, which should be fed at six-hour intervals. If they are consuming sufficient amounts, their stomachs should look full, or slightly enlarged, though never distended. The amount of formula to be fed is proportionate to the size, age, growth and weight of the puppy, and is indicated on the can of Esbilac or on the advice of your veterinarian. Many breeders like to keep a baby scale nearby to check the weight of the puppies to be sure they are thriving on the formula.

The show ring winner Chig Jo-Mo, pictured at five months of age winning Best Puppy at the Kennel Club of Northern New Jersey Match show in 1968. Jo-Mo not only went on to a championship but won many friends for the breed with her showmanship and lovely coloring. A William Bushman photo.

At two to three weeks you can start adding Pablum or some other high protein baby cereal to the formula. Also, baby beef can be licked from your fingers at this age, or added to the formula. At four weeks the surviving puppies should be taken off the diet of Esbilac and put on a more substantial diet, such as wet puppy meal or chopped beef. However, Esbilac powder can still be mixed in with the food for additional nutrition. The jarred baby foods of pureed meats make for a smooth changeover also, and can be blended into the diet.

Ch. Hamilton Chang Tang, pictured winning at a show several years ago. Tang's owner is Marie Stillman.

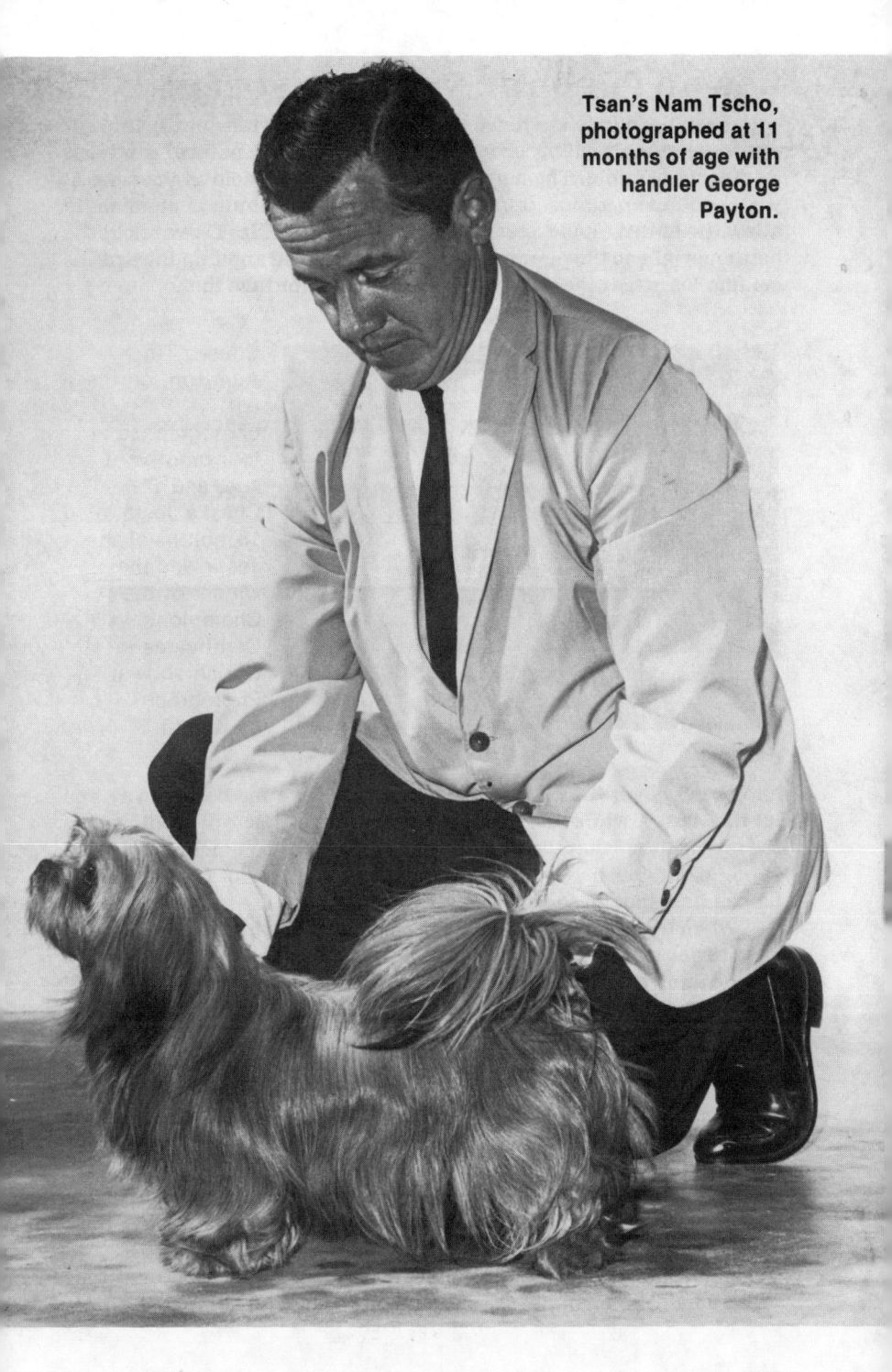

Tsan's Nam Tscho, photographed at 11 months of age with handler George Payton.

HOW TO FEED THE NEWBORN PUPPIES

When the puppy is a newborn, remember that it is vitally important to keep the feeding procedure as close to the natural mother's routine as possible. The newborn puppy should be held in your lap in your hand in an almost upright position with the bottle at an angle to allow the entire nipple area to be full of the formula. Do not hold the bottle upright so the puppy's head has to reach straight up toward the ceiling. Do not let the puppy nurse too quickly or take in too much air

Cheska Ting Agneson, on the left, photographed at four months of age, and Ch. Cheska Jesta, at 18 months of age. Jesta was the winner of ten Championship Certificates in British shows. Photograph by Knight.

and possibly get the colic. Once in a while, take the bottle away and let him rest a while and swallow several times. Before feeding, test the nipple to see that the fluid does not come out too quickly, or by the same token, too slowly so that the puppy gets tired of feeding before he has had enough to eat.

When the puppy is a little older, you can place him on his stomach on a towel to eat, and even allow him to hold on to the bottle or to "come and get it" on his own. Most puppies enjoy eating and this will be a good indication of how strong an appetite he has and his ability to consume the contents of the bottle.

It will be necessary to "burp" the puppy. Place a towel on your shoulder and hold the puppy on your shoulder as if it were a human baby, patting and rubbing it gently. This will also encourage the puppy to defecate. At this time, you should observe for diarrhea or other intestinal disorders. The puppy should eliminate after each feeding with occasional eliminations between times as well. If the puppies do not eliminate on their own after each meal, massage their stomachs and under their tails gently until they do.

You must keep the puppies clean. If there is diarrhea or if they bring up a little formula, they should be washed and dried off. Under no circumstances should fecal matter be allowed to collect on their skin or fur.

All this—plus your determination and perseverance—might save an entire litter of puppies that would otherwise have died without their real mother.

GASTRIC TORSION

Gastric torsion, or bloat, sometimes referred to simply as "twisted stomach," has become more and more prevalent. Many dogs that in the past had been thought to die of blockage of the stomach or intestines because they had swallowed toys or other foreign objects are now suspected of having been the victims of gastric torsion and the bloat that followed.

Though life can be saved by immediate surgery to untwist the organ, the rate of fatality is high. Symptoms of gastric torsion are unusual restlessness, excessive salivation, attempts to vomit, rapid respiration, pain and the eventual bloating of the abdominal region.

The cause of gastric torsion can be attributed to overeating, excess gas formation in the stomach, poor function of the stomach or intestine, or general lack of exercise. As the food ferments in the stomach, gases form which may twist the stomach in a clockwise direction so that the gas is unable to escape. Surgery, where the stomach is untwisted counter-clockwise, is the safest and most successful way to correct the situation.

To avoid the threat of gastric torsion, it is wise to keep your dog well exercised to be sure the body is functioning normally Make sure that food and water are available for the dog at all times, thereby reducing the tendency to overeat. With self-service dry feeding, where the dog is able to eat intermittently during the day, there is not the urge to "stuff" at one time.

If you notice any of the symptoms of the gastric torsion, call your veterinarian immediately! Death can result within a matter of hours!

Subject Index

A

Adult stock, buying, 190
Alerting the veterinarian, 203
Allergies, treatment for, 288-289
All-meat diet controversy, 308-311
Americal, 28-29
American Kennel Gazette, 10
American-Bred class, 240
American Lhasa Apso Club, 127-134
American Lhasa Apso Club Specialty, 1970, 45
Anbara Kennel, 135-136
Appearance, Indian Standard for, 110
Apso, defined, 10
Artificial insemination, 198
Aspirin and the dog, 26
Australian Lhasa Apsos, 67-75

B

Bailey, Col. and Mrs. F.M., 49-54
Balrene Kennels, 77-78
Barcon Kennels, 136-138
Bark Sentinel Lion Dog, 11
Bathing, 172
Berano's Nah-Ni-Soo, 41
Best of Breed or Best of Variety, 240-241
Best of Opposite Sex, 241
Best of Winners, 241
Birth of puppies, 206
Bloat, 316
Body, American Standard for, 102
    English Standard for, 110
    Indian Standard for, 103
Bones, 289-290
Brackenbury Kennels, 57
Bred-by-exhibitor class, 246
Breech birth, 207
British champions, 62-66
Brownrigg, Mrs. W.D.S., 52
Burns, treatment for, 278
Buying a puppy, 175-180

C

Caesarean section, 210-214
Campaigning, cost of, 250-252

Canadian Lhasa Apsos, 77-81
Castrating, 219-222
Champion status in England, 55-56
Character, American Standard for, 102
    English Standard for, 103
Characteristics of the breed, 111-126
Cheltenham-Gloucestershire Championship Show, 49
Chen Kennels, 138
Chewing, 289
Coat, American Standard for, 102
    English Standard for, 103
    General description of, 114
    Indian Standard for, 103
Cohen, Dorothy and Sammy, 30-38
Color, American Standard for, 102
    English Standard for, 103
    General description of, 114
    Indian Standard for, 110
Companion Dog Excellent degree, 234
Coprophagy, 264
Crowhaven Kennels, 138, 118-124
Cutting, Mr. and Mrs. C. Suydam, 15
Ctenocephalides canis, 293-295
Ctenocephalides felis, 293

D

Dalai Lamas, 7-14, 15-20, 24
Dirty ends, avoiding, 172
"Down" command, 229
Drowning, treatment for, 278
Dry births, 210
Dudman, Mrs. F., 60-61

E

Ear care, 172-173
Ears, American Standard for, 102
    English Standard for, 103
Elbow dysplasia, 292
Episiotomy, 214
Evaluating the litter, 219
Eyes, American Standard for, 102
    English Standard for, 103

F

False pregnancy, 210

318

Feeding puppies, 301-305
   Midnight meal, 302
   Noontime meal, 301
   Six a.m. meal, 301
   Six p.m. meal, 302
Feeding the adult dog, 307
Feet, American Standard for, 102
   English Standard for, 103
   Indian Standard for, 110
Fever, 262-264
First aid kit, supplies for, 282
Fits and convulsions, treatment for, 278
Fleas, 293-296
Forequarters, English Standard for, 103
Frostbite, treatment for, 278

G
Gastric torsion, 316
Geriatrics, 257
German show classes, 89
Gestation period, 199-202
Griffing, Robert B., 39-40, 48
Grooming, tips for, 168-173

H
Hamilton Farm Kennel, 18-20, 25
Hamilton Torma, Ch., 28, 32
Handlers, professional, 247-252
Hardacre Kennels, 58
Hayes, Margaret, 10-11
Head, American Standard for, 102
   English Standard for, 103
   Indian Standard for, 110
Health of the breeding stock, 191-192
Health records, keeping, 260
Heart attack, treatment for, 279
Hesketh-Williams, Mrs. D.M., 58-60
Hip Dysplasia, HD, 290-292
Housebreaking, 253-255

J
Joi-San Kennels, 143

K
Karma Kennel Champions, 33-34

Karma Lhasa Apso Kennels, 30-38

L
Labor, 206
Legs, American Standard for, 102
Lhasa Apso Reporter, The, 132
Lhasa Tales, 132
Lloyd, Frank T., Jr., 25
Longevity, 118

M
Magestic Kennels, 143
Masturbation, 264-267
Match shows, 235
Mating, 192-198
Ming Kennels, 25
Miscellaneous class, 242
Morris and Essex Show, 38
Mouth, American Standard for, 102
   English Standard for, 103
Movement, 114
Muggs, 118
Muzzle, American Standard for, 102
Muzzle, how to, 194

N
Neck, English Standard for, 103
Newborn puppies, how to feed, 316-317
Nhamrhet, 144-145
Nicholas, Anna Katherine, 46
Norbulinka Kennels, 146
Novice class, 240

O
Obedience trial standards, 232
Obedience trials, 245
Obesity, 311-312
Open class, 240
Origin of the breed, 7-14
Orlane Kennels, 146
Orphaned puppies, caring for, 312-314

P
Pekingese, 11
Phillips System, 39
Planned parenthood, 183-186

Point show classes, 240-242
Point shows, 236-239
Poison, how not to, 282-285
Poisoning, symptoms of, 285-287
Potala Kennels, 153-154
Practical Dog Book, The, 51
Probing for puppies, 203
Publications, 132
Puppies and worms, 186, 296-300
Puppy class, 240

R

Rabies, 67-69, 268-272
Ramblersholt, 60
Reserve winners, 240
Reward method of training, 223
Rimar Kennels, 157
Rimmon Kennels, 157
Roosevelt, Theodore and Kermit, 15
Roundworms, 296

S

Sacred dogs, 95
Sengti, the Lion Throne, 12
Shedding, 169
Sheng-La Kennels, 157
Shih Tzu/Lhasa controversy, 22-24
Show-quality puppy, buying a, 189-190
Size, American Standard for, 102
   English Standard for, 103
   General description of, 115
Snakebite, treatment for, 275-277
Socializing the puppy, 214-218
Spaying, 219-222
Specialty clubs, 127-128
Stand for examination, 230
Standard, American, 23, 102
Standard, English, 103
Standard, European, 107
Standard, Indian, 110
"Stay" command, 229
Sterilization, for health, 222
Stillman, Marie, 28-29
Suffocation, treatment for, 279
Sun stroke, treatment for, 280

T

Tabu Kennels, 158

Taglha Kennels, 158-159
Tail, American Standard for, 102
   English Standard for, 103
   Indian Standard for, 110
Tal-Hi Lhasas, 161-162
Tattooing, 253
Temperament, 111-126
Tibetan Apso, 106
Tibetan breeds, 10
Tibetan Dog Show, 98-99
Tibetan Lion Dogs, 52
Titles, European, 90
Top brood bitch, 41
Top knot, 173-174
Tracking Dog degree, 234
Training equipment, 226
Training, formal school, 231
Training, when to start, 223
Tsan Kennels, 162-166

U

United States Registry, 292
Utility Dog degree, 234

V

Vaccinations, 275
Verles, 58-59
Veterinary inspection, 186

W

Weaning puppies, 305-306
West of England Ladies Kennel
   Association Open Dog Show, 52-53
Winners Dog and Bitch, 240
World War I, the Lhasa Apso and, 49-51
World War II, the Lhasa Apso and, 54-55
Worms, how to test for, 299-300
Wounds, treatment for, 280

X

Xanadu Lhasa Apsos, 166

Y

Younghusband Exploratory Expedition, 49